MEDIuMSHIP MASTERY II

Advanced Techniques That Work

STEPHEN A. HERMANN

Atendriya Press
Amherst, Massachusetts

Printed in the United States of America

ISBN Paperback: 978-0-578-31841-7

Cover & Interior Design: Creative Publishing Book Design

*This book is dedicated to my wonderful daughters Sadhana Bhakti,
Radhe Shyam, Nitya Priya and Vedavati Emily.*

Table of Contents

By virtue of the processes of the subtle body, the living entity develops and gives up gross bodies. This is known as the transmigration of the soul. Thus the soul becomes subjected to different types of so-called enjoyment, lamentation, fear, happiness and unhappiness.

The caterpillar transports itself from one leaf to another by capturing one leaf before giving up the other. Similarly, according to his previous work, the living entity must capture another body before giving up the one he has. This is because the mind is the reservoir or all kinds of desires.

As long as we desire to enjoy sense gratification, we create material activities. When the living entity acts in the material field, he enjoys the senses, and while enjoying the senses, he creates another series of material activities. In this way the living entity becomes entrapped as a conditioned soul.

Srimad Bhagavatam
Canto 4, Chapter 29, 75-78.

Introduction

This book presents a holistic approach to the development of mediumship, which requires a transformation in body, mind and soul for the medium. I emphasize in my mediumship training programs the time-tested, traditional path to mediumship unfoldment combined with innovative, progressive approaches to development. Mediumship is my passion. I love teaching mediumship and assisting others in their journey of unfoldment. Mediumship development involves considerably more than learning technique. A student medium's unfoldment is impacted by all aspects of his or her life. My approach to development is multifaceted with success dependent upon the aspirant's internal self-growth rather than a structured process or formula. A medium who possesses a greater awareness of his or her soul path will be a far more efficient instrument for the spirit world than an individual lacking such consciousness.

Interest in mediumship is huge worldwide with individuals from all walks of life wanting to learn how to receive spirit messages for themselves and others. As a teacher of mediumship, I cannot overemphasize the importance for students to intellectually understand the process of mediumship. Study the literature that details the lives of pioneering mediums from the nineteenth and early twentieth centuries.

Learn about how they developed as mediums and their experiences working as instruments for the spirit world. Read about the extensive research conducted on mediums by world-renowned scientists who documented many amazing demonstrations of spirit power. Sit in a development circle run by a qualified medium and learn the mechanics of spirit communication with hands-on experience. An in-person development circle is far superior in value to any online group for mediumistic unfoldment. Study with as many gifted mediumship teachers as possible and learn to discipline your mediumship. There are no shortcuts on the path of mediumship development, which is ongoing and never ending. Do you want to cultivate your mediumistic ability? Get in touch with your innate psychic sensitivity first. Psychic awareness is the foundation for quality mediumship. Mediumship development is natural, but as a process it cannot be rushed. Gradual progression is best.

I was about two-and-a-half years old when my mother's father communicated with me. I could see and hear him as though he was physically present. It was the first of many psychic experiences that I experienced during my childhood. I do not consider mediumship abilities to be a special gift reserved for a select few. Mediumistic ability is a skill like art or music that can be cultivated through proper training facilitated by qualified teachers. I sat in my first meditation group as a child in 1975 and experienced deep levels of altered consciousness.

In the past four decades, I have read a myriad of books on psychic and mediumistic development, metaphysics, parapsychology, and related subjects. My intense study of mediumship led me to formally enroll in a Spiritualist seminary and obtain credentials as an ordained minister, certified medium and teacher with the National Spiritualist Association of Churches, the oldest and largest Spiritualist organization in the United States. I also graduated from an intensive two year professional massage therapy training program and received certification as a clinical hypnotherapist. I taught my first mediumship course in 1989. Since then,

I have taught mediumship and healing to thousands of individuals in numerous countries around the world.

My first mediumship teacher was the Reverend Edward Hamilton (1928-1995) who I met in July 1984 at the National Spiritual Alliance headquarters temple at Lake Pleasant, Massachusetts. The New England Spiritualist Camp Meeting Association, established at Lake Pleasant in the 1870s, was a Spiritualist Mecca with the world's leading mediums serving its summer programs. Edward helped me considerably in understanding how to better connect with the spirit world. Edward was quite open-minded and eclectic in his approach to mediumship combining elements of metaphysical teachings and orthodox Christianity with Spiritualist philosophy. Edward's mediumship was extremely evidential and detailed. Edward explained to me how when he initially got involved in studying mediumship he lived and breathed it daily for five solid years.

Although Edward possessed only a high school education, he read as much literature as possible on mediumship and related subjects. Many individuals study mediumship with little understanding of its history and the science of spirit communication. Edward was highly ethical and spiritually oriented as a medium. He never accepted payment for his work as a medium as he believed his mediumship was a service to God and should be freely given to those in need. Many mediums fail to integrate high ethical standards and spirituality in their mediumship.

Pauline Hathaway (1929-2002), a Spiritualist medium, taught me much in her open mediumship development classes at the Church of Two Worlds in Washington, DC. Pauline embarked upon her journey into Spiritualism in 1948, at the age of 19, in Onset, Massachusetts, a village established as a Spiritualist summer camp in 1877. Pauline was similar to Edward in that she possessed high ethical standards and spirituality in regard to her mediumship. Pauline emphasized the fundamental teachings of traditional Spiritualist philosophy in her mediumship classes-a belief in God, the immortality of the soul, communication between the physical and spiritual worlds, treating others in the manner we would like to be treated, personal responsibility, and the opportunity for progression never being closed. These Spiritualist teachings were derived from direct communications from higher teachers in the spirit world. Advanced spirits convey these basic principles consistently through mediums in the form of personal guidance and inspiration.

Sylvia Giunta (1948-2005) was another mediumship teacher with whom I studied with for many years. Sylvia considered herself a Christian Spiritualist and believed in the teachings of Jesus and his work as a master healer and prophet. Sylvia sat in the home circle of a prominent medium at the Lily Dale Assembly in New York, where she developed her abilities as a clairvoyant and trance medium. Lily Dale is the world's largest Spiritualist community, with thousands visiting its grounds each year. I attended Sylvia's home circle for years and experienced many marvelous displays of spirit power and phenomena. Sylvia understood how to facilitate a good circle and create strong vibrations. Although Sylvia held no formal certification as a medium, she was extremely skilled and supportive as a teacher of mediumship. Novice mediums felt comfortable hearing her positive suggestions and expert advice on how to open up their mediumistic abilities and successfully receive spirit messages.

Edward, Pauline, and Sylvia all contributed to making me the medium I am today. Evidential mediumship was not emphasized by my teachers. Pauline always brought through the spirit communicators, along with practical guidance. She taught me to never ask recipients of spirit messages questions or allow them to feed me information. She was horrified when a husband and wife team of mediums asked recipients of their mediumship a multitude of questions while serving as guest workers at the Church of Two Worlds. The wife and husband delivered spirit messages indirectly to the congregation by throwing out information from the spirit world until it was recognized by the correct recipients. Pauline observed that their approach to mediumship gave the impression that they were fishing for information. Another time a visiting medium conducted a transfiguration séance at the church in which he grossly exaggerated his mediumship abilities. Pauline did not hesitate to state the medium's lack of authenticity to others who viewed his performance favorably.

Sylvia often expressed her view that people should go directly to God instead of merely focusing on deceased loved ones. She held the conviction that only God could help us with our problems and not imperfect spirits. As such the spirit messages she delivered focused more on the higher guidance and love. She also regularly channeled spirit teachers at her circles who lectured on spiritual philosophy to the participants.

As a mediumship teacher, I emphasize to my students the importance of spirituality and service. Many mediums are dogmatic in their approach to mediumship and proclaim that the purpose of mediumship is to provide evidence of life after physical death. Although my mediumship is extremely evidential, I do not ascribe to this belief. Not all spirit messages are meant to be evidential. The higher spirits primarily impart evidential messages to comfort the distraught and convince disbelievers. However, in other cases, the higher spirits will provide valuable guidance to assist individuals in their material lives or with their spiritual growth. They also bring forth spiritual philosophy and the means to implement such teachings on a practical level. In addition, the higher spirits provide spiritual healing to relieve affliction from the mind and body of recipients. The ultimate purpose of mediumship is to spiritually awaken people's hearts to their original eternal nature as children of God.

My first book, *Mediumship Mastery: The Mechanics of Receiving Spirit Communications: The Ultimate Guide* provides readers with the fundamental ingredients necessary for dynamic mediumship. I comprehensively cover both basic and advanced approaches, along with many invaluable techniques and exercises. As a result, my first book is utilized for teaching mediumship by many teachers and circle leaders internationally. I do not repeat this material in this second new book. Instead, I provide readers with additional cutting-edge techniques, practices, and exercises to maximize their proficiency as evidential mediums. I also present additional guidance for the unfoldment of both the mental and physical phases of mediumship. I wrote this book for the benefit of both students and teachers of mediumship. I want to help others unfold as instruments for the higher spirits to work through.

I am enthusiastic about mediumship. I love connecting with the spirit world and sharing my knowledge about the mechanics of spirit communication. What you put into your mediumship unfoldment, you will receive back and more. The time and effort an individual puts into his or her mediumship development are never wasted. The best mediumship occurs as a result of the teamwork between the medium and his or her team of spirit helpers, who are constantly learning to effectively work through their medium.

About the Exercises

The exercises and practices presented in this book are mainly designed for teachers and circle leaders to utilize in mediumship training programs. Many of the exercises are variations of each other for achieving specific objectives in the development of mediumistic ability. The majority of exercises require a partner to work with. However, some are appropriate for individual application. I created most of the exercises with the assistance of my spirit teachers. All of the exercises presented have been effectively applied by my students and me. The exercises are appropriate for both novice and experienced students. Modifications to the exercises can be made as necessary, depending upon the specific needs and circumstances of the particular students or group.

Important Rules to Follow While Doing The Exercises

For those working, do not under any circumstances ask the recipient questions while receiving information from the spirit world. Make statements. Mediums must develop confidence in their abilities and learn to trust the spirit world completely.

Recipients, do not give feedback or information to the medium while he or she is bringing through information from the spirit world. Test the medium and test the spirit world. Never feed the medium. This also helps novice mediums keep their analytical minds out of the way. It is always important for participants to provide honest feedback to those they are working with, but wait until after the completion of the exercise.

CHAPTER 1

The Language of Mediumship

The National Spiritualist Association of Churches (USA) defines a medium as "...one whose organism is sensitive to vibrations from the spirit world and through whose instrumentality, intelligences in that world are able to convey messages and produce the phenomena of Spiritualism."[1] Mental mediumship is subjective in nature as it involves the inner intuitive experience of the medium and is dependent upon the attunement of the medium with the spirit personalities. The intellectual, emotional, and spiritual qualities of the medium affect the nature of the mediumship as the medium's mind is directly involved in the process.

The psychic senses correspond with the five physical senses; seeing, hearing, sensing, tasting, and smelling, with the additional inclusion of knowing. Most phases of mental mediumship involve the spirit messages telepathically impressed upon the medium's receptive mind. The following phases of mental mediumship are commonly developed by novices and utilized the most as a means for communication by the higher spirits.

---

[1] National Spiritualist Association of Churches, *NSAC Spiritualist Manual* (15th Edition), Lily Dale, New York, 1991. p. 35.

Clairaliance: Clear smelling. Psychically smelling.

Clairaudience: Clear hearing. Psychically hearing.

Claircognizance: Clear knowing. Psychically knowing.

Clairgustance: Clear tasting. Psychically tasting.

Clairsentience: Clear sensing. Psychically sensing or feeling.

Clairvoyance: Clear seeing. Psychically seeing.

Six Easy Stages

The stages of learning mediumship are like learning how to write. Mediumship development is progressive and involves the following steps.

Relax the Body

Progressively relax the physical body, starting with the head and working down to the toes. Focus on the breath. Allow physical tension to dissipate.

Calm the Mind

Physical relaxation naturally calms the mind. The breath is the key to mastering physical relaxation and mental calmness. A medium's mind needs to be calm to properly receive spirit messages.

Raise One's Vibrations

Pray and meditate as much as possible. Meet the spirit world halfway. A medium should spiritualize his or her thoughts and actions as much as possible.

Get the Analytical Mind Out of the Way

Detach from the analytical part of the mind. Step aside and pay attention to the inner mind and sensations within the physical body.

Attune to the Spirit World

Feel the presence of the spirits and mentally connect with their minds and energies. Mediums must learn to achieve a strong attunement with the spirit world and sustain it for long periods.

Simultaneously Receive and Express the Flow of Thought

Express the messages received from the spirits quickly and efficiently. A medium uses all of his or her psychic senses to receive mental impressions. Mediums must translate and interpret multi-layers of information and accurately articulate it to the recipient.

The first step for the spirit helpers is to get the medium's mind in a receptive state for telepathic communications. For many mediums, this does not happen overnight. Therefore, regular meditation is essential for mediums at all levels of experience.

Once the medium relaxes his or her body and attunes to the spirit world, the spirit operators are able to impress his or her mind with messages. In the physical world, we utilize sound to communicate with others. The spirits use thought as the means to connect with others in both the physical and spirit worlds.

The spirit team are specialists with the process of communicating between the two dimensions. They also must learn the process and how to effectively work through their medium. A student medium will naturally make mistakes in his or her attempts to receive and deliver accurate spirit messages. The spirit operators learning to work with the student medium make adjustments accordingly.

ABCs

In order to cultivate the ability to write, individuals first must learn the alphabet or ABC's. Mediumship is the same way, using simple clairvoyant images, either symbolic or literal, that have no meaning or are generic in nature. For example, an image of an old shoe may have no meaning symbolically or literally, but is presented merely to see if the medium notices it. An image of a calm ocean scene might symbolically represent a sense of mental peace. Children spend much time in school learning how to properly write the alphabet letters. Such repetitive practice is necessary to build a strong foundation for writing skills. Mediumship development is similar in that it requires a solid foundation and much practice is required in all stages of unfoldment.

In the beginning, a medium gradually learns as part of the meditative process to pay attention to the content within his or her mind. The spirit operators initially send such images with no significant meaning to make sure that the medium properly receives them. Student mediums in a development circle should always share with the group their experiences during the meditation. If a student medium says nothing, the spirit operators will not know if the image was received.

Simple Words

A student medium eventually becomes consistently aware of the simple images impressed in his or her mind. After a child learns his or her alphabet, he or she is taught how to write simple words like *cat* or *dog*. Mediumship is the same way. The spirit operators build upon this foundation by impressing a student medium with symbolic images that can require interpretation.

For example, an American flag might represent patriotism or a glass of orange juice might represent the state of Florida.

Symbols

Mental mediumship is a telepathic process. The mechanics of mediumistic communication require many spirit messages to be transmitted in a roundabout way. Symbolic messages are an efficient and effective means of communication. One picture is worth a thousand words. The spirit specialists who work with mediums spend considerable time attuning their minds and energies with their medium. Mediumship is a cooperative effort between the spirit team and their medium. The spirit team knows their medium intimately and understands his or her mediumistic potential.

The Spirit Team

I refer to the individuals who compose the spirit team as helpers and not guides, because they are specialists in various aspects of spirit communication. Any spirit communicating through a trained medium has to want to come through. They have to be permitted, and they must be ready. The typical deceased grandmother knows nothing about the mechanics of spirit communication. Such a spirit needs to learn the process by receiving instruction from spirit specialists and observing spirits coming through mediums to their loved ones in the physical world.

The spirit team works with the spirit teachers of the recipient in facilitating the content of a mediumship session. The higher spirits set the agenda and regulate who comes through and what information is conveyed.

A medium should trust their own interpretation of the symbols that they receive, instead of the interpretations of others. All clairvoyant images, symbolic or literal, are accompanied by a feeling. Student mediums need to trust their feelings as to the meaning of the images they receive. In this way, their symbolic library will grow along with their accuracy as mediums. Generalized messages are easier to communicate telepathically. Spend time learning the correct interpretation of symbols. Don't worry about making mistakes, as the spirit operators will make adjustments.

Simple Sentences

After learning how to spell simple words, a child learns how to compose simple sentences such as *See Spot run* or *See Jane ride the bike.*

Mediumship works the same way. A novice medium initially may only receive single symbolic images that translate into simple messages for the recipient. For example, the image of a sunflower may indicate the recipient is receiving spiritual healing, or the image of a mailbox could mean the arrival of important correspondence by mail.

The spirit operators will generally present several images together for the medium to translate as a message for the recipient. For example, the medium might see images of a barking dog, a desk, and a bag of money. This may indicate that someone is angry with the recipient in a work situation, which will result in lost income for the recipient. A medium sees an image of a melting snowman, a thumbs up gesture, and a flying jet. This could be interpreted as meaning that in the beginning of spring the recipient will make a favorable decision resulting in relocating to a distant location.

More Sophisticated Sentences

As a child progresses educationally he or she increases his or her vocabulary and ability to compose more complex sentences such as *Mary and Bob went to the cinema Saturday afternoon and ate Hawaiian pizza when they arrived home.*

The messages transmitted by the spirit operators also become increasingly sophisticated with the symbology employed containing multi-layers of meaning. For example, a medium sees an empty wine bottle, a razor with shaving cream, a portable toilet and a green field with blue and yellow flowers. The empty wine bottle represents the alcoholism of the spirit communicator who, after multiple attempts using the same method, passed into the spirit world by slitting his wrists. In discussing his first suicide attempt with the recipient he joked, "It was a close shave." This clearly indicated his sarcastic sense of humor. His name was John Green and at one point resided in a city named Greenfield. Hence the images of the portable toilet and green field. He also frequently joked about his job cleaning portable toilets. The blue and yellow flowers represent the healing that he is presently receiving in the spirit world.

A medium sees images of the late actor John Wayne, the outside of a police car, the comic book superhero Batman and French fries. The spirit communicator has a similar macho disposition like John Wayne. Like the actor, he passed away from stomach cancer, grew up in a county named Wayne, and was a huge Batman fan collecting the comic books and keeping Batman memorabilia all over his house. Bruce Wayne is also the name of Batman's secret identity. French fries were his favorite food and the name of his favorite dog.

Paragraphs

As children progress with their writing ability, they are able to compose their ideas more coherently in longer paragraphs and essays. As mediums gain more experience, they naturally are able to bring information through for longer periods of time in a clear and accurate manner. A longer mediumship session goes deeper than a shorter message in providing evidential information and practical guidance for the recipient. Information should always smoothly flow from the spirit communicators through the medium.

Foreign Languages

Writing or speaking a foreign language is generally easier for children than older learners. A language that is derived linguistically from the same root language as one's native language is always easier to learn.

A medium can also convey foreign languages and not even be aware they are doing it. A medium in a deep trance who is completely unconscious can speak other languages when under strong spirit control. It can also occur when the medium is fully conscious and bringing through communications. At a mediumship training weekend, a student brought through a phrase in Polish, during an exercise from the Polish grandmother of the recipient. The student did not know what he was doing as he did not understand the words he was receiving.

The spirit operators can influence a fully conscious medium when doing a mediumship session to speak a foreign language for native speaking recipients of that language. A medium must have exceptionally strong attunement with the spirit world for this to take place. The medium will know the meaning of the information they saying, but the session's content will be completely spoken in the foreign language.

Student mediums learn to receive messages as the spirit helpers learn to transmit communications to them. What matters most in the messages that novice mediums receive is the general idea that can be expressed in multiple ways using the medium's knowledge and vocabulary. The generalized messages emphasized in the beginning serve as a foundation for later work.

When a small child writes words in a sentence may be misspelled or not correctly capitalized with no periods or commas. What matters is the general idea that the child conveys. Novice mediums need to not worry so much about inaccuracies in their work. What matters is the general idea that is conveyed. The spirit helpers note the errors and make adjustments accordingly in their approach to working with their medium. As novice mediums gain greater proficiency along with their spirit team, more precise, exact messages are transmitted. More is expected from experienced mediums who possess a greater capacity to convey precise communications.

The Worldwide Web of Spirit

I teach many mediumship development courses online using a webcam and microphone for the visual and audio. Although I prefer in-person courses, the internet is great for instruction as all the participants can see and hear each other. The process of mediumship can be compared to the use of a webcam and microphone for communication via the internet. In the same way that an individual in the physical world sees and hears another person at a distance via the internet, a medium sees and hears the spirit communicator. When the internet connection is strong, the images and sounds transmitted are clearly seen and heard. However, a weak connection leads to distortions and interruptions in the visual and audio, resulting in incomplete and faulty messages. Mediumship is similarly affected by insufficient energy and poor conditions.

Spirit communication is a delicate process that requires a great amount of careful planning and orchestration by the spirit operators. Telepathic messages must be transmitted and clearly without distortion or incompleteness. Messages often must be conveyed using symbols or metaphors. Imagine the difficulty of communicating via the webcam with no audio. The individual would have to figure out ways to effectively communicate visually. The lack of audio would make many conversations extremely difficult and like the process of mediumship information would need to be communicated in a roundabout way. Great complications would arise if in addition to no audio, the internet connection also was weak. A medium working with clairvoyant images experiences the same challenges. He or she must receive, translate, and deliver the clairvoyant images to the recipient. mediums understandably commit errors because of many factors beyond their control.

If the webcam did not function and only the audio worked, the conversations would be a bit easier than relying completely on vision. However, some information needs to be seen and cannot adequately be described using words. Again, mediumship functions the same way. A clairaudient medium mentally hears the words of the spirit communicators and relates direct messages from them without having to interpret the information. Unfavorable psychic conditions lead to distortions or interruptions of the messages with the medium hearing distorted words or segments of the message.

Strengths and weaknesses are present in all phases of mediumship. Some mediums are strong in one phase and weak with another. As a mediumship teacher, I often focus my students to work on their weaknesses. If a student's weakness is clairaudience, I will spend much time teaching him or her methods to hear the spirit voices. The medium may never be a great clairaudient medium, but he or she will have a much better ability to work with it along with the other phases of mediumship.

Spirit Linguistics Exercises

EXERCISE 1

Awareness of Street Sign Names

In order to cultivate an awareness of names in daily life, play close attention to the names of streets while driving or walking. Each time you view a street sign, repeat its name several times, and create a mental image of the wording. Spend a few moments seeing and feeling a mental image of the street sign with the name. Regular practice of this exercise successfully opens the unconscious mind for receiving the names of streets through clairvoyance and clairaudience.

EXERCISE 2

Awareness of Street Numbers

In daily life, play close attention to the street numbers of buildings that are encountered. Mentally see the number for a short period. Regular practice of this exercise opens the unconscious mind for receiving addresses and numbers through clairvoyance.

EXERCISE 3

Awareness of Geography

Spend time looking at maps-maps of the world, continents, nations, and regions. Study both topographical and regular maps. Study the location of different continents, countries, and regions, and know geography well. Work in learning geography from basic to greater detail of major and minor cities and towns. Practice seeing the images of geographical locations in the mind. Regular practice of this exercise fills the unconscious mind with a knowledge of geography and makes it easier to receive locations in map form through clairvoyance.

EXERCISE 4

Awareness of City Names

Spend time looking at maps of the world, continents, nations, and regions. Study the names of cities, towns and regions. Say the names aloud and mentally. See the spelling of the names mentally for a short period. Regular practice of this exercise programs the unconscious mind to receive geographical names through clairvoyance and clairaudience.

EXERCISE 5

Art and Clairaudience

Participants pair up, hold each other's hands, and attune to the spirit world. Both sides work at the same time or take turns. Using sketch pad and pastels, draw an outline of each other's form, along with colors of the energy field surrounding it. Utilizing clairaudience only, receive the following information from the spirit world; the name of an individual, the name of a place, a song or music, and a phrase or sentence. The same information is obtained separately for both sides, and written on both sides of the outlined form.

EXERCISE 6

Car Art

Participants pair up, hold each other's hands, and attune to the spirit world. Both sides work at the same time or take turns. Using sketch pad and pastels, draw a car or vehicle associated with a spirit connected to the recipient. Draw the inside and outside of the vehicle. Pay close attention to the evidential details.

EXERCISE 7

Glass Hearing

In my book *Mediumship Mastery: The Mechanics of Receiving Spirit Communications: The Ultimate Guide,* I include an exercise for clairaudient development using a conch shell. In place of a conch shell use a tall drinking glass to cultivate clairaudient abilities. Place the glass to the physical ear and listen to the sound within. Repeat this exercise at regular intervals throughout the day. Regular practice leads to the unfoldment of clairaudience.

EXERCISE 8

Sticky Names

Attune to the spirit world. See a blank sticky post-it note in your mind. Allow the spirits to write the names of spirit communicators on it. Other evidential information can be written on the post-it note as well.

EXERCISE 9

Black Board With Colored Chalk

Participants pair up, hold each other's hands, and attune to the spirit world. See a blackboard in your mind. Allow the spirits to write the names of spirit communicators, places, dates, and personal messages on the slate. See the words clearly within your mind. Allow the information to be written in different colored chalk. Feel the energy and significance of the colors used by the spirits to write the information. Take turns working.

EXERCISE 10

Foreign Languages

Participants pair up, hold each other's hands, and attune to the spirit world. The medium allows a spirit, who spoke a foreign language connected to the recipient, to come through. The language ideally is one unknown to the medium and known by the recipient.

At first, you will hear the spirit's voice as indistinct mumbling. Next, the spirit will turn up the volume and emphasize the words or phrases that are spoken in another language. The medium repeats, as best as possible, the words as they sound in his or her mind. Words not recognized by the recipient can be checked with others for validation. Take turns working.

EXERCISE 11

A Variety of Tongues

Participants pair up, hold each other's hands, and attune to the spirit world. The medium connects with three spirit guides connected to the recipient. Each spirit is from a distinct culture and speaks a different language. The medium observes the garb and features of each spirit, feels their personal attributes, and listens to each spirit individually speak their language.

At first, you will hear each spirit's voice as indistinct mumbling. Next, each spirit will turn up the volume and emphasize words or phrases that are spoken in another language. The medium repeats, as best as possible, the words as they sound in his or her mind. Words not recognized can be checked with others for validation. Note the differences between the languages. The medium also describes the guides and how they assist the recipient. Take turns working.

EXERCISE 12

Spirit Sing

Participants pair up, hold each other's hands, and attune to the spirit world. Allow a spirit connected with the recipient to communicate eventual details and practical guidance. Instead of speaking the message, the medium sings the entire message from beginning to end without regard for quality of voice. Take turns working.

EXERCISE 13

Poetic Address

All members of a mediumship development group take turns with this exercise. The medium stands in front of the audience and connects with his or her spirit teachers, who inspire a subject matter for the medium to speak on. The entire address should be spoken in rhythm or prose for at least two to three minutes. The duration of the talk can increase with this exercise as the mediumship abilities of the students increase. The topic of the address can also be chosen by the audience.

EXERCISE 14

Musical Notes

Participants pair up, hold each other's hands, and attune to the spirit world. The medium receives the entire communication in the form of songs and music, which is interpreted as necessary. Absolutely no other information is permitted. The spirits convey the information in this exercise primarily using clairaudience. However, the song or music may be conveyed mentally in the form of an image, feeling or idea associated with it. Take turns working.

EXERCISE 15

Humor Does Not Die

Participants pair up, hold each other's hands, and attune to the spirit world. Allow a spirit connected with the recipient to come through and emphasize his or her sense of humor. Allow the spirit to tell a joke in the first person to the recipient. Take turns working.

CHAPTER 2

The Six Major Problems That Affect Accurate Mediumship

There are six major issues that affect accurate mediumship. A medium who knows these issues can better identify and address each area of concern. As a mediumship teacher for many decades, I offer practical solutions for students of mediumship to integrate into their training.

Problem: Lack of Confidence

Many individuals lack confidence and self-esteem for a variety of reasons because of past experiences. In mediumship development circles, they unfavorably compare themselves to others in the group, and often hold back from sharing in fear of getting something wrong. Individuals need encouragement at all stages of development. Many novices amid those more experienced naturally feel intimidated. The slightest error or lack of success greatly affects such students and contributes to further erosion of their confidence.

It is beneficial for a practicing medium to possess a strong, healthy sense of self. Lack of confidence and insecurity are qualities that need to be overcome. Over the years, I have noticed how ego-driven many mediums are in regards to their work. While it is a good thing to want to be the best possible medium, the motivation should be to serve God and help others in need both in the material world and the spirit dimension. Many mediums want to outdo other mediums and receive adoration from others over their marvelous psychic powers. The amount of jealousy and conflict between mediums within the Spiritualist movement is astounding.

A Reiki master enrolled her brother in a mediumship development course that I taught on Saturday mornings many years ago in Massachusetts. The brother contributed much as a student to the group, as he already was familiar with hands-on healing, after studying Reiki with his sister. After two classes, without contacting me, he abruptly stopped coming to class. I figured that it was because of his busy schedule as a tractor-trailer truck driver. The following class I asked his sister, who explained that he left the class because he felt that the others in the group did better than him in a psychometry exercise.

Psychometry or object reading is an excellent approach for students to learn to connect psychically with the energy of physical objects as well as link with the spirit world. The brother actually performed quite well in doing that particular exercise. His feelings of inadequacy existed completely within his mind, and led him to wrongly conclude that he lacked the potential to cultivate his psychic abilities. I would never have known what happened to him or his reasons for dropping out if I had not been able to ask his sister. It is a priority for me as a teacher to create an educational environment, where all students feel supported and encouraged with their growth.

Lack of confidence results in the medium needing external validation from others for his or her work. For example, when delivering spirit communications, the medium will continually ask the recipient for validation of the information coming through. Often this will come in the form of asking unnecessary questions, instead of making direct statements. "Did your father drive a car? Why am I seeing a hammer? Did your grandfather work with carpentry? " Asking questions is completely unnecessary and makes the medium appear as though they lack confidence with their abilities and that they are fishing for information. A skeptic, who completely disbelieves in the concept of spirit communication, will conclude that the medium is engaging in cold reading, a technique used by fake mediums to elicit responses from recipients to trick them into believing that they are receiving genuine spirit communications.

The voice vibration of the recipient strengthens the link and enables the spirit communicator to come in stronger. It is also good for a medium to know if the recipient understands the information that is coming through. Many mediums are taught to elicit responses from recipients, as others present will feel included and convinced of life after death by the survival evidence delivered. The problem that many novice mediums experience is that because of their lack of confidence, they automatically lose their mental link with the spirit world and engage their analytical mind in response to the recipient. Although spirit messages pass through the medium's mind, the medium needs to keep his or her analytical mind out of the content.

All mediums must overcome feelings of fear and doubt. These include fear of being incorrect and doubts about their ability to receive accurate information from the spirit world. The recipient of a spirit message may respond negatively and state that the medium is wrong or that he or she does not understand the information. He or she may even get angry with the medium for not bringing through what he or she wants to hear.

Student mediums need to cultivate detachment and absolute trust in the spirit world. There is nothing wrong with a medium receiving validation from the recipient in either a public demonstration or a private session. However, mediums should focus as much as possible on staying in the power and stating what they are receiving. The body language, facial expressions, and verbal responses of a recipient easily affect a novice medium. The lack of confidence that some novice mediums feel results in continual analyzation of spirit messages, even after receiving positive feedback and validation from recipients. Lack of confidence is an issue with the medium's ego. In order to overcome a lack of confidence, a medium must remain neutral and detached from what the recipients and others say or think in regard to their mediumship.

A recipient may massively praise a medium. "You are the most amazing medium in the world. Thank you so very much for that fantastic, evidential communication from my mother. You provided twenty-seven pieces of evidence in two minutes. You are the best medium I have ever seen. You are incredible, and a special angel sent by God. You should have your own television show. You are so wonderful." A recipient may also severely criticize a medium. "You are the worst medium I have ever seen. I don't understand anything you said. You couldn't even bring through my mother. She comes through with all the other mediums. You are a total fraud. I want my money back." In either case, a medium must remain neutral and true to his or her spiritual work. Praise easily inflates the egos of insecure mediums needing validation. Criticism traumatizes under-confident mediums, making them doubt their abilities even more.

How to Improve Confidence

Positive feedback from recipients and encouragement from peers and mentors are important, but ultimately mediums must do the inner work necessary to transform limiting belief systems and patterns of thinking. Therapy and support groups such as Twelve-Step-based programs are excellent in helping heal past wounds and dysfunctional behavior, all of which contribute to a lack of confidence.

The Power of the Unconscious Mind

The key to achieving happiness does not involve external changes, but requires work on both emotional and spiritual levels. Wrong beliefs such as low self-esteem and lack of confidence are due to faulty programming within the unconscious mind.

Hypnosis is Dynamic

My teacher Sylvia's son, who attended medical school at the time, told me that I should also study hypnosis as it would assist with my mediumship unfoldment. As a result, I studied hypnotherapy with Dr. Masud Ansari, who practiced hypnosis in Washington, DC. Hypnosis is a natural, deeply relaxed state of consciousness in which the unconscious mind is completely receptive to external influences and suggestions. As a modality, hypnotherapy works with reprogramming the unconscious mind from disharmonious patterns of thought or behavior. Common issues assisted with hypnosis include smoking cessation, weight control, phobias, addictions, and self-confidence.

As a hypnotherapist, I combine hypnosis technique with my mediumship assisted by spirit healers in the spirit world. The hypnotic state is the same as the altered states of consciousness involved in mediumship. All mediumship involves trance or altered states of consciousness in varying degrees. Trance is different from the process of mediumistic entrancement or control exerted by spirit operators.

Franz Anton Mesmer (1734-1815), an innovative German physician, developed a system of healing known as *Mesmerism* that utilized the altered state in the healing process. Many pioneers of the modern Spiritualist movement that started in 1848 studied and worked with Mesmerism prior to their involvement with mediumship. Self-hypnosis is a powerful approach for mediums to gain greater confidence with their mediumistic abilities. It is also beneficial for assisting mediums in getting the analytical mind out of the way and achieving a deeper trance state for their mediumship.

Program the Mind for Health, Happiness and Mediumship

Affirmations are short, positive phrases that are repeated to reprogram the unconscious mind in a harmonious way and overcome negative beliefs and harmful habits. Chanting affirmations are a powerful technique for mediums to use to increase confidence and strengthen their connection with the spirit world.

Affirmations for Mediumship

I am a clear and accurate channel for the spirit world to work through.

I allow the spirit world to use me as their instrument.

I let go and allow the higher spirits to speak through me.

I am capable and confident as a medium.

My mind is clear and at ease.

I am comfortable and powerful as an instrument for the spirit world.

I am divine spirit; I radiate the Christ light.

Problem: Inability to Distinguish Genuine Mediumistic Impressions From One's Own Thoughts

A major concern for novice mediums is the inability to distinguish their own thoughts from mediumistic impressions conveyed by the spirit operators. There is a fine line between the imagination and information coming into the mind telepathically transmitted from the spirit world. In the beginning, the analytical mind is predominant for most individuals. Information is conveyed telepathically from the spirit operators to the medium. The spirit operators generally extract material from the medium's mind for the content of clairvoyant messages. The medium's unconscious mind stores all information from the medium's entire life experience that can be drawn upon as a source.

Many novices have misconceptions about the process of mediumship and do not know what to expect in terms of receiving spirit messages. They expect that the images conveyed by spirits should be as distinct and vivid as on a color television. In some cases, clairvoyance is extremely vivid and intense, but most of the time the images are not much different than the ordinary thoughts originating from the unconscious mind.

I remember the first three weeks of sitting in a mediumship development circle. Although I had plenty of previous direct contact with the spirit world, I did not know what to expect in terms of receiving messages in the circle. During the meditation I observed many images in my mind, but dismissed them as having no significant meaning. One afternoon, I was hanging out with my friend Hugh from the circle, who mentioned that he had to get home for his piano lessons. At that moment, I remembered that an image of Hugh playing the piano appeared in my mind at the development circle during the meditation. I realized immediately that this image had been clairvoyance.

After this I began to pay closer attention to the images inside my head when I was sitting in mediation at development circles. So many thoughts flowed into my head. While some images randomly appeared, the majority of images flowed together through my mind like a film, each blending in with one another. The images in my mind were almost transparent and certainly did not seem to originate from my memory bank, and most did not appear to have any significant meaning. As I progressed over the next few months, I easily recognized clairvoyant images as separate from thoughts originating from my own mind.

How to Tell the Difference

A clairvoyant image stands out strongly sometimes, in most cases on a subtle level from regular images. Clairvoyant images possess a distinct feeling, unlike regular images, and stand out from other images within the mind. A novice may sit in meditative silence and dismiss such images as products of his or her own mind. However, a clairvoyant image will continue to reappear, no matter how much the medium diverts his or her attention to other thoughts. The spirit operators are persistent in their efforts to make a novice medium aware of such messages.

No matter how seemingly trivial or insignificant, novice mediums should share all of their experiences during the meditation. In a circle, all participants learn from each other, and sharing is a major part of this learning process. Sharing also helps the novice mediums get in touch with their inner minds and differentiate between their own thoughts and those conveyed by the spirit world. Sharing also lets the spirit operators know that the image is noticed. If the novice medium says nothing, they will not assume that it was not noticed. Mediumship is teamwork. Both the medium and his or her spirit team are learning to work with each other.

As novice mediums gain experience in connecting with the spirit world and delivering messages, they receive feedback and validations from the recipients of such communications. As a result, novice mediums learn to recognize the subtle differences between their own thoughts and spirit messages. A novice medium also increases awareness of the spirit presence within his or her energy field and the exhilaration of channeling information from the spirit world. The spirit operators will increase the volume or intensity of the feeling associated with genuine images. The images stand out from other thoughts and seem to possess an almost luminous energy. The quickest method to learn to distinguish your own thoughts from mediumistic impressions is regular meditation. Sit in the silence and observe your inner thoughts. It takes patience and constant practice to notice the subtle difference.

A novice medium often feels as though he or she is making up the message as it feels so much like the imagination. Many years ago, I facilitated a weekly mediumship development circle at a Spiritualist church in Massachusetts. I asked another medium named Daniel Duffy (1947-2000) to teach my class while I was out of the country working. Daniel did a great job. One of my students told me about a particular exercise that Daniel shared with the group that helped her considerably with her unfoldment. Daniel told the students, instead of attempting to receive a spirit message, to use their imaginations and make up a fake spirit communicator. I included this exercise in my first book, *Mediumship Mastery: The Mechanics of Receiving Spirit Communications: The Ultimate Guide.* This approach worked marvelously for my students, especially those with massively analytical minds, by making them aware of the subtle difference between the imagination and mediumistic impressions.

Problem: Getting the Analytical Mind of the Way

The greatest challenge for many mediumship students is learning how to successfully get the analytical mind out of the way during the process of receiving and delivering spirit communications. Everyone has an analytical mind, which serves a purpose in applying logic to gather data and make decisions based on intelligence. At my lectures, I sometimes jokingly ask my audiences if anyone present is an engineer. I follow this by asking if anyone in the audience is married to an engineer. Usually, a hand or two goes up. I mention how engineers can be very uptight and rigid with their thinking because of the nature of their profession, which requires much use of the analytical mind.

Hair Stylists

In my talks on mediumship, I often ask my audience what they think is the number one profession held by mediums before getting involved in studying and working with spirit communication. Hands will go up with participants sharing their views. Common answers include teachers, artists, and nurses. I know thousands of mediums, both male and female, from all over the world. The major occupation held by mediums before developing their mediumship is hair stylist. An active intuitive mind is required to properly work with mediumship. Cutting hair is more than a vocation; it is an artistic skill. What typically takes place when individuals go to get their hair cut? They sit in the chair and talk about their personal problems and issues. "My husband has run off with a cab driver, I'm devastated." At the same time, the energy fields of both the hair stylist and the individual receiving treatment blend. A healing naturally takes place. It is at this time that the guidance from the spirit world is impressed upon the mind of the hair stylist, who gives the advice to the recipient. Most hair stylists do not even realize that they are receiving information from the spirit world while they cut hair.

Successful mediumship requires an active intuitive mind. Most mediums utilize their intuitive minds in creative endeavors involving art, music, or writing. For some students, especially those involved in the arts, opening up to the spirit world is relatively easy. Other individuals coming from backgrounds in which the analytical mind is used more find the process extremely challenging.

A Few Suggestions

Work with art as a hobby. Take a formal class or attend life drawing sessions. Don't worry about technical ability. The objective is letting go of the tendency to analyze and pick things apart. Art is a fun activity that frees up the intuitive mind. The more a student of mediumship can integrate art into his or her schedule, the better. Creative activities and artistic expression loosen the mind up and free it from the tendency to over analyze. The analytical mind serves a purpose in mediumship for the discernment of what is taking place.

However, too much analyzation is a student medium's worst nightmare. An overactive analytical mind adversely affects the development of mediumship. As a result, it will be difficult for mediumship students to quiet their minds. In this way, the student medium's mind will not be receptive to the impressions conveyed by the spirit operators. In a similar manner, when the student mediums receive clairvoyant images, they automatically begin to analyze what they are seeing and pick it apart. This results in the student medium blocking the connection with the spirit operators and the flow of thoughts from them. It also results in the student medium changing the content of the message.

The time a student medium spends in meditation is invaluable in learning to detach and not interfere with the information coming through from the spirit world. An undisciplined mind is the worst enemy for this process, but through patience and regular practice, the control over the inner mind is cultivated. Buddhist silent meditation practices such as Vipassana, which emphasizes awareness of the inner mind, are excellent for self-growth as well as mediumship development. I spend about two hours daily doing mantra meditation, which I count on wooden prayer beads. Too many mediums fail to integrate a strict meditative practice into their lives, which contributes to a lack of discipline and harmony in their lives.

Problem: Mistranslation of Information Received.

A major issue affecting mediumship is that information is easily delivered incorrectly. Why does inaccuracy with spirit messages take place? Is it because the psychic conditions limit or prevent a clear or strong connection? Are the spirits responsible for giving wrong information to the medium? Is the medium at fault for getting his or her mind in the way and delivering the message incorrectly? Let us examine each of these questions in detail.

The psychic conditions at the time of a session greatly affect the quality of the mediumship. Harmonious, positive conditions assist the process of spirit communication. Negative vibrations do the exact opposite. Mental mediumship is telepathic in nature.

Lethargic, unenthusiastic, skeptical individuals are always difficult to work with compared to those sympathetic to mediumship. Information often is conveyed in a round-about way. If the energy is not strong, the content of a message tends to be less detailed and vague. It is also harder to receive the communication if sections are incomplete or unclear.

However, the psychic conditions are generally not the reason for the inaccuracy of some spirit messages. Spirits can certainly provide incorrect information. What comes through during a session is generally accurate at the time it is given. However, there is always freewill and, as a result, conditions can change depending upon the actions of individuals.

It is not that the higher spirits are infallible, but they are truthful and provide accurate information. Undisciplined mediumship opens the door for dishonest and unevolved spirits to come through. In most cases inaccurate information is the fault of the medium. A medium can interfere with the content of a spirit message in a number of ways.

Misinterpretation of the Information

The medium's mind is involved with the process of mediumship. Due to the mechanics of telepathic communication, much information cannot be directly conveyed. It is expedient for the spirit operators to utilize symbology for clairvoyant imagery.

The spirit team develops a vocabulary of symbols used to convey the messages. The spirit operators utilize information from the memory bank of the medium as a frame of reference for communications.

The interpretation of a particular symbol depends upon what the image means to the particular medium. Literal images are also conveyed. In some cases, a clairvoyant image, both literal or symbolic, is multi-layered in terms of meaning. Clairvoyant images always are accompanied by a feeling. It is important that mediums learn to trust what a symbol means to them, along with the feeling that comes with it. Although using symbols is an efficient and effective means of communication, it is relatively easy for a medium to misinterpret the image and deliver the message the wrong way.

The analytical mind of the medium can get involved and pick apart the meaning of the clairvoyant imagery too. A novice medium often cannot recognize when his or her analytical mind involves itself with the content of a spirit message. It is important for mediums, regardless of experience, to immediately shift focus on their attunement with the spirit operators and the mental impressions transmitted. A medium, in the process of receiving spirit messages, experiences great exhilaration along with a feeling of timelessness and being in the presence of a greater power. The more that mediums get out of the way and connect with this power, the less that misinterpretation of messages will take place.

Assumptions About the Recipient in Relation to the Information Received

I always tell my clients to never feed me information or tell me things about themselves before and during the session. I want my client to test the spirit world and me. During a session, the medium should be the one doing the most talking with the recipient's verbal responses or input minimal. I always tell my clients to stop me if they do not understand something as this way I can receive clarification. I do this for two reasons. It is more evidential for recipients receiving information from a medium who does not know anything about their lives. It also makes it easier to keep myself out of the session. The less of the medium and the more of the spirit world, the better.

Sitters love to talk during a mediumship session. Unfortunately, individuals generally don't test the medium or the spirit world. They also often react to the information coming through with all sorts of facial expressions and body language. Mediums should never allow their clients to influence them with what they say or through body language. When this happens, a medium starts to get his or her analytical mind involved with the session. This is when doubts and assumptions creep in and the potential for inaccuracy with the information conveyed to the recipient increases.

It is easy to look at the external appearance of people and make assumptions. Mediums should focus completely on the connection they have with the spirit world and deliver the information coming through exactly as they receive it. Sometimes the information coming through from the spirit world appears to contradict assumptions of what a medium knows about a particular sitter. This is when substantial errors take place that destroy the accuracy of an otherwise successful session.

A medium may assume that a sitter is uneducated and financially suffering because of his or her inarticulateness and tattered attire and hesitates when information comes through that indicates otherwise. In reality, the sitter may possess a doctoral degree and be a multimillionaire. The best defense for mediums against making assumptions about those they do mediumship sessions for is to know absolutely nothing about their sitters. Don't ask the sitter any questions, other than an occasional request to confirm that the individual understands the information coming through.

Learn to trust the higher spirits as they will never let down a sincere medium motivated by the desire to serve and help others. Focus completely on what the spirits say for the recipient and keep assumptions and knowledge about the sitter out of the spirit messages.

Some mediums will not do mediumship sessions for family members or close friends because they do not want to allow their knowledge of such sitters to affect their work. I think mediums should work with family members and friends as much as possible. The spirit operators will come through with relevant information and details beyond what is known about a familiar sitter. It is also a good opportunity for mediums to practice getting out of the way should they find their knowledge of a sitter entering into the session.

The Medium's Mind Goes on a Tangent and Adds Information to the Message

A medium can also add information originating from his or her own mind into the content of a spirit message. The flow of a spirit message is linear, with occasional pauses between subject matter, but more often than not communications are an ongoing flow of information that is best articulated by the medium immediately as it is received. It is within these brief pauses that a medium may insert additional information to the communications. This information may originate from the unconscious mind of the medium or result from assumptions or analyzation of the communicated information. It takes much discipline to recognize and prevent this from happening. Many mediums do not recognize when embellishment takes place.

There is a fine line between information, visual or otherwise, from the spirit world, and thoughts from the mind of the medium. Sometimes embellishment occurs because a medium feels an unconscious urge to answer a sitter's questions or feels that more information should be forthcoming. Although the stream of thought flows through his or her mind, the medium needs to learn when to pause or stop verbalizing the message. A spirit message may be short and to the point. Mediums must know when to stop talking and know that the spirit message is complete.

Problem: Leaving Parts of the Message Out

Mediums also leave parts out of the message due to uncertainty of accuracy and inability to discern their own minds from genuine mediumistic impressions. I can think of many occasions while doing a mediumship session that the spirits presented content that seemed to not fit in with the rest of the information coming through. Uncertainty about the interpretation or relevance of a clairvoyant image should not prevent sharing it with the recipient. Don't let doubt or fear of inaccuracy get in the way.

A medium's responsibility is to deliver the spirit messages as accurately as possible. Sometimes mediums are uncertain about receiving names, especially common names such as John or Mary. When this happens a medium's analytical mind kicks in and he or she thinks ", Who doesn't know someone named John in the spirit world? I can't say that". A medium also hesitates to share because he or she is concerned that the name is not from the spirit world but is merely a random thought from his or her own mind. Don't hesitate when a common name is heard. Share the name immediately. Stay connected to the power when the analytical mind gets involved as described above.

Don't judge the content. While receiving a less common name is extremely evidential, it does not mean that receiving a common name is inferior. What matters is delivering the messages conveyed from the spirit world accurately. It is certainly important for mediums to evaluate their mediumship and expand with their abilities. However, it is an ego issue when mediums focus on evaluating their mediumship based on what they consider valuable or superior. This mentality generally is influenced by the opinions of others and often results in comparing the abilities of mediums.

Share the pieces of information that don't seem to fit in with the rest of the content. Often the recipient understands the meaning and how it relates to his or her life or the lives of the spirit communicators. Besides dismissing such information, too many mediums will question the recipient about its meaning. "Why am I seeing a glass of water? Does this have any meaning to you?" Don't ask questions. Focus on delivering the message.

A novice medium is more likely unable to distinguish the origins of such information and exclude it from the content of the communication.

However, experienced mediums are not exempt from this taking place. Don't worry about inaccuracy. Deliver the information to the recipient as accurately as possible. Remember, seemingly insignificant information is often extremely evidential and meaningful for the recipient.

Problem: Holding and Strengthening the Connection with the Spirit Communicator

Another problem that affects novice mediums is their inability to strongly maintain a link with spirit communicators. A novice medium lacks sufficient discipline over his or her mediumship gained by years of meditation and practice. It takes time for them to properly attune to the spirit world and connect with individual spirit communicators. Although a novice medium may make a link, he or she may experience difficulty holding the connection for a long period. As an experienced medium, I can hold a connection with multiple spirits for long periods of time. As long as the energy is present and the spirits can come through, such a process is easy. A novice medium often finds that his or her links with a spirit communicator result in incomplete information. Low vibrations make maintaining a link for long periods especially challenging for any medium regardless of experience.

The practice of regular meditation assists mediums in raising their own vibrations, a necessary skill for quality mediumship. While the purpose of meditation is realization of self and God, byproducts include the ability to raise one's personal vibrations and greater mental discipline. Daily practice makes raising one's own vibration second nature. Mediums who regularly practice meditation will easily maintain links with spirit communicators for long periods.

Meditative practices create discipline and control over the mind. The mind can be your best friend or worst enemy. An untrained, undisciplined mind is never an asset to mediumship. The study of traditional martial arts, when I was younger, installed much mental control that I otherwise may not have developed. My Sensei Sara Grimes ran her dojo with an iron fist, yelling at students and hitting their physical bodies with a bamboo sword. Such hardcore training greatly strengthened my mental discipline.

Problem: Generalized Spirit Messages

A novice medium's learning process involves receiving spirit messages that contain vague and generalized information. Generalized information is easier to telepathically transmit and receive. "I see a little old lady with white hair and glasses who is sitting by the fireplace knitting," "I feel a fatherly spirit around you who passed over with a heart attack," "I see a woman who wore a dress and drove a car." Novice mediums should not feel disappointed with these types of messages as they serve as a foundation for future, more specific communications.

A message that appears generic to outsiders may be extremely evidential and significant for the recipient. No matter how trivial or vague a message may seem, never judge or evaluate spirit messages for other individuals as you do not know the whole picture and how that information relates to the recipients or may benefit them. Mediums often keep their mediumship on a surface level and fail to expand upon the information received. An experienced medium needs to advance past this and provide more detailed evidential descriptions.

Generalized information is usually nonessential. Many elderly women are white haired with glasses and knit, but an elderly woman who smoked a pipe and collected bottle caps is distinct. Learn to focus on specifics about the spirit communicators. The spirit team that works with a medium will make sure such information comes through. Mediums need to do their part and actively work with their teams to receive greater details with their mediumship. Many experienced mediums do not progress past receiving generalized information with their mediumship and deliver messages such as "Does anyone here know someone with the letter 'E' in their name? " "Who here can place an older fatherly man who passed over from a stroke?" "I have a man here in the spirit world who liked to eat food."

Traveling Clairvoyance

Traveling clairvoyance is the psychic perception of scenes at a distance. The modern parapsychological term for traveling clairvoyance is *remote viewing*. Remote viewing has been used by the United States government for international espionage. Remote viewing differs from astral travel because it does not involve the projection of consciousness. The medium is able to discern through his or her psychic senses scenes at a distance in the physical world as well as in the spirit world. The great Swedish mystic Emanuel Swedenborg (1688-1782) in 1759, while eating dinner with others in Gothenburg, allegedly described a large fire taking place at that moment hundreds of miles away in Stockholm. It took days for news of the fire to reach Gothenburg, but it was found that Swedenborg's vision of the fire occurred at the precise moment he had described it taking place.

Let the spirit communicators show memories of their former physical lives. Experience the memory through the eyes of the spirit. Involve all the senses-seeing, hearing, sensing, tasting, smelling, and knowing. Mediums who work this way greatly enhance the evidentiality of their mediumship. The medium feels as though he or she is reliving the memory through the eyes of the spirit communicator. This approach to mediumship is extremely powerful and vivid.

Telescopic Clairvoyance

A medium can also focus their attention on any aspect of what they are shown and like a telescopic lens zero in specific aspects of what they are experiencing. For example, a spirit grandfather presents a memory of his backyard with a swimming pool and fruit trees. Much evidence is revealed by observing the details presented. However, the medium can receive even more information through moving his or her perception into the memory through the eyes of the spirit communicator.

The medium can feel as though he or she is in the backyard, sit in the swimming pool and relive the memories associated with it. The medium can also look close up at objects and describe them in greater detail. For example, if a spirit uncle shows the memory of a box of rare comic books from his collection, the medium can be shown a specific issue along with its distinct features. "I am seeing a copy of *Action Comics* number one. I see a child colored on the top two panels in green crayon on page thirty-two."

The medium feels, in the manner of psychometry or object reading, the comic book and the story with it.

"I feel that this item was stolen by your Uncle Zachary from a used comic book shop in New York City. I feel the owner of the shop was a hippy named Norman who wasn't paying attention when the theft took place. The coloring with the green crayon happened later. I feel a little girl named Sally did it." The medium needs to learn to move their awareness into the memories of the spirit communicators on both an overall level as well as with specific components such as objects and locations. Don't settle for vague messages. Start paying closer attention to the information that comes through.

Use Clairsentience

Don't keep spirit communicators at an arm's-length away. Let the spirits come close and blend their energies. Mediums should feel the spirit's presence within their own physical bodies as the spirit personality's mind and energies overshadow them.

Many mediums surprisingly feel uncomfortable when spirits closely connect with them. Mediums who observe spirits at a distance can be accurate with the details they observe and feel. However, I always instruct my students to blend with the spirit personality as much as possible and allow themselves to feel as though they have become the spirit. Mediums should use clairsentience to describe the character and personality of the spirit communicator. They will sense the physical attributes of the spirit within their own physical bodies, including the manner of passing and distinct traits. I encourage my students to move like the spirit and make the same gestures and mannerisms. Mediumship involves all the senses. Many mediums not only keep the spirits at a distance but focus exclusively on receiving clairvoyant imagery. Clairvoyance is always accompanied by a feeling.

I instruct my students to involve all their psychic senses when working. Student mediums see symbolic messages and feel their meaning, but what do they smell or taste when observing the information? What sensations do they feel within their own physical body? What do they hear? The spirit operators communicate messages telepathically, which are received in a linear manner by the medium. A medium easily can miss part of the message for this reason.

Enhancement Exercises

EXERCISE 16

Missing Kids

This is a group exercise for mediumship circles.The teacher divides the class into equal numbered groups and gives each group a photograph of a child or children. The teacher explains that the children are either murdered, abducted, or safe. The objective is for the individuals in each group to work together and see what they receive from the spirit world in regard to the subjects. Are the kids alive or deceased? Are there details presented from the spirit world that indicate where they are located or about what happened to them? These cases are either cold or solved cases. The teacher should be familiar with the details of such cases. In addition, one group should receive a photo of children who are physically alive and known by the teacher.

The objective of this exercise is for students to learn the importance of accuracy, and not allowing their imagination to get in the way. This is especially true for the group with the photograph of the physically alive children. It is very easy to make incorrect assumptions by looking at the photographs. After all the groups share their results, the teacher provides feedback about the children in the photographs.

EXERCISE 17

Messages Around the Clock

Each member of the circle gives a brief spirit message to the individual sitting on his or her left, one at a time, going clockwise around the circle, taking turns.

CHAPTER 3

How to Receive More Than Generalized Spirit Messages

In the last chapter, I addressed the major issues affecting accuracy in mediumship including generalized spirit messages and offered practical suggestions to overcome this problem. In this chapter, I elaborate upon this issue and provide more in-depth approaches for receiving specific details from the spirit world. A major concern for many mediums is that the information they receive from the spirit world is often vague and generic in nature. Skeptics who analyze the content of messages delivered through mediums often emphasize in their debunking of mediumship the fact that the content of most spirit messages is generalized information that could apply to many people.

Mental mediumship involves telepathic communication. Telepathy is a natural process. We do it all the time. People mentally pick up on the thoughts of others, especially when a strong emotional connection exists between individuals such as family or close friends. Generalized messages such as a shape, emotion, or color are easy to mentally convey and receive. More abstract or detailed messages are harder to transmit and receive.

Clairvoyant development can be compared to the creation of a representational painting. The artist initially establishes the overall composition on the canvas and gradually develops its details. The spirit team trains mediums by first transmitting generalized messages, followed by messages of increasingly greater sophistication. Unfortunately, many mediums fail to challenge their abilities and never proceed past receiving basic information. The spirit operators approach presenting messages in two ways, both of which largely depend on the training and approach of the medium.

Observing

Many mediums are trained to observe the clairvoyant messages they receive and keep spirit communicators at an arms-length or further away. The clairvoyant messages can be literal or symbolic in nature. Clairvoyance is always accompanied by a feeling that relates to the meaning of the images presented. Many novice mediums cannot properly translate or interpret information. However, in time, such mediums generally develop a good working relationship with their spirit team and learn to trust their clairsentience and accurately deliver the messages.

Many mediums feel uncomfortable allowing spirit communicators to step in close. Hence, they keep the spirits at a distance instead of allowing closer contact to take place. This approach to mediumship is not wrong, as accurate descriptions of spirit communications along with personal guidance can effectively be conveyed. The problem that arises with this approach is that many mediums focus completely on the clairvoyant imagery and do not pay attention to the other ways that information can be received. It is as if the medium is wearing blinders and can only see straight ahead.

A clairvoyant view from medium to far range is limited. An overall, general description can be presented of a spirit communicator or other scenes, but the message may overall be deficient in substance. "I see an older gentleman from the spirit world who feels like a grandfather. He is wearing a green uniform, which looks like he worked as a janitor. He is smiling and holding a broom."

The basic information presented with the above message may be adequate for identification purposes. However, the message is still surface level and lacks detail. How can a medium receive greater details in the clairvoyant messages that he or she observes?

Positioning of the Spirit

A system of communication can be established with the spirit team that indicates the side of the recipient's family the spirit is from based on their position relative to the medium or recipient. The positioning of the spirit communicators can be observed or felt by the medium. For example, spirits on the left side are on the father's side of the family, and spirits on the right side are on the mother's side of the family. A spirit in front of the recipient indicates that the spirit is younger, while those behind or higher indicate an older generation.

Zoom In

The other method of improving clairvoyant observation is for the medium to zoom in with his or her vision and observe closer details of the spirit communicator.

"I see your maternal grandfather who stands behind you on your right side. He wears a green janitor's uniform. His last name was Tanner, as I can see it embroidered on his chest. He worked for Govinda's Custodian Service, as I can read a small red patch with the company name on his left shoulder. The brush on the head of the broom looks extremely worn, which indicates he worked very hard. It also indicates that the firm exploited him as an employee and provided him with inadequate equipment. When I see his smile, I am aware that many of his front teeth are discolored and missing. He had poor dental hygiene and because of this lost many of his teeth. I see a small heart with the name Miriam tattooed on his left arm. I feel this is the name of your grandmother."

A medium who closely observes details of the images presented will easily deliver messages containing greater evidence and substance. It is important that clairsentience is integrated in with the clairvoyance.

Share Space With the Spirit

The other way in which mediums commonly receive communications is accomplished mainly through clairsentience. Instead of relying on his or her observational skills as with clairvoyance, the medium allows spirit communicators to move in close and blend their energies within his or her energy field. This process of blending leads to overshadowing. The medium will feel in his or her body the character and personality of the spirit, conditions of physical death, and mannerisms and body language. The more a medium gets out of his or her way, the greater the spirit will be able to express his or her messages through the medium.

A clairsentient medium is able to impart an extremely detailed visual description of the spirit communicator. Clairsentience within itself like clairvoyance is limited. Clairsentient mediums can improve their abilities by deepening their altered state and allowing spirits to directly express their ideas. Instead of the third person, the medium will speak in the first person. Overshadowing often gradually leads to entrancement of the medium by the spirit operators who speak through the medium's voice box.

The most effective way for mediums to receive specific details is to combine clairvoyant observational skills with clairsentient overshadowing. The clairvoyance can include observation of spirit communicators and scenes from far away to extremely close up. At the same time, mediums need to allow the spirits to step into their personal space and directly express their personality and messages.

In addition, mediums should utilize the other modes of receiving information. Besides seeing and sensing within his or her own physical body, a medium must be aware of what he or she is smelling, tasting, and hearing. Information through claircognizance also can be downloaded into a medium's mind as he or she is working. All the psychic senses function together.

"I see your maternal grandfather who stands behind you on your right side. He wears a green janitor's uniform. His last name was Tanner, as I can see it embroidered on his chest. He worked for the Govinda's Custodian Services. I can read a small red patch with the name on his left shoulder. The brush on the head of the broom looks extremely worn, which indicates he worked very hard. It also indicates that the firm exploited him as a worker and provided him with inadequate equipment. When I see his smile, I am aware that many of his front teeth are discolored and missing. He had poor dental hygiene and because of this lost many of his teeth. I see a small heart with the name Miriam tattooed on his left arm. I feel this is the name of your grandmother. I sense that your grandfather was a very angry man at times and stubborn. I feel a great amount of pain from my shoulders down to my arms, I feel he suffered from crippling arthritis. I also am feeling massive pain in my lower abdomen, which indicates that he suffered from stomach cancer. I feel this illness was prolonged with much physical discomfort. I feel as though I am holding a broom and I want to hit my boss with it as I was very angry with how I was treated as an employee (Medium makes physical motions as though they are sweeping with a broom and using it to hit someone with).

I have received healing in the spirit world. I am no longer angry. I love you very much and want you to control your anger. (The medium shifts speaking from third to first person)."

Generalized messages serve as a foundation for future, more elaborate communications. Mediums at all levels of unfoldment should prioritize strengthening their attunement through regular meditation and sitting in the power. In this way, mediums will achieve a stronger connection with the spirit world and receive more sophisticated and detailed messages.

Spirit Awareness of Our Daily Lives

EXERCISE 18

Wallet Content

Participants pair up, hold each other's hands, and attune to the spirit world. Allow a spirit connected with the recipient to show the content of the recipient's wallet or pocket book. Note any items present such as ticket stubs and receipts. Count the currency inside, noting the denominations of the notes and the total amount that is present. Take turns working.

EXERCISE 19

Credit Cards

Participants pair up, hold each other's hands, and connect with the spirit world. Allow a spirit linked with the recipient to show a credit or bank card within the recipient's wallet or pocket book. The medium describes the card with details of the name on the card and its number and expiration date. Include the pin number for bank cards. Take turns working.

EXERCISE 20

Currency Serial Numbers

Participants pair up, hold each other's hands, and connect with the spirit world. Allow a spirit linked with the recipient to show the currency within the recipient's wallet or pocketbook. Zoom into one of the currency notes. Read the serial number of a currency note and describe specific details about the note. Take turns working.

EXERCISE 21

Count the Change

Participants pair up, hold each other's hands, and connect with the spirit world. Allow a spirit linked with the recipient to show the change in the recipient's wallet or handbag. Count the change. What is the total amount? What types of coins are there? Describe how many there are of each. Take turns working.

EXERCISE 22

Rare Coin

Participants pair up, hold each other's hands, and connect with the spirit world. Allow a spirit linked with the recipient to show the change in the recipient's wallet or handbag. Count the change. Zoom into a specific coin. Describe its features. What is its date? Take turns working.

Precision Exercises

EXERCISE 23

Phone Number

Participants pair up, hold each other's hands, and connect with the spirit world. Allow a spirit linked with the recipient to provide a recognizable phone number associated with his or her former life in the physical world. The medium should receive all the numbers either with clairaudience or clairvoyance.

EXERCISE 24

Invading Space

Participants pair up, hold each other's hands, and connect with the spirit world. Clairvoyantly observe a spirit connected with your partner. Describe details about the physical appearance of the spirit-his or her physical attributes and garb. Invite the spirit to move close so that his or her face is directly in front of your face. Observe all the details of the spirit's facial features and describe prominent characteristics. Take turns working.

EXERCISE 25

Observing Facial Features

Make a point of observing the facial features of those around you. Note hair styles, shape of head, facial structure. Distinct birthmarks, use of cosmetics, etc. Conscious observation in daily life leads to awareness of such information in mediumistic communications.

EXERCISE 26

Overcoming Generalized Messages

Participants pair up, hold each other's hands, and connect with the spirit world. Each medium works for a half-hour. Combine telescopic clairvoyance with clairsentient overshadowing simultaneously with other psychic senses to receive specifics. In addition, move gradually from a light to a deeper level of control.

1. Attune to the spirit world and step into the power.

2. Connect with a spirit communicator. Observe the spirit from medium range and describe their appearance and features.

3. Zoom in close with your clairvoyance and describe details.

4. Allow the spirit to step into your space. Blend minds and energies. Allow yourself to feel as though you are the spirit. Feel and describe the spirit's character, personality, attributes, and more within your own mind and physical body.

5. Simultaneously utilize and express information received through your other psychic senses-hearing, smelling, tasting and knowing.

6. Allow the spirit to express his or her messages through you in first-person. Dissociate from the physical body even more and get out of the way.

Take turns working.

CHAPTER 4

Levels of Spirit

In my Father's house are many mansions...
John 14.2 KJV

All the world's religious traditions include a belief in the existence of a heaven or spirit realm, where departed souls continue to live after physical death. While theology teaches the theory of an afterlife, the practice of mediumship provides evidence of the reality of such nonphysical dimensions. Atheists along with narrow religious zealots enter into the spirit world unprepared for what awaits them. Disbelief does not change spiritual truth, nor does blind adherence to rigid doctrine. I have learned so much from the thousands of spirits who have communicated through me in the decades that I have worked as a medium. The spirits pull no punches in their descriptions and narratives about their former lives in the physical world and present existence in the spirit dimension.

The known physical universe is vast with untold billions of galaxies, each containing billions of stars. Life exists in all environments-physical, subtle, and spiritual. Beyond the physical universe are subtle and spiritual dimensions containing many worlds. Souls occupy temporary subtle and physical bodies based on the development of their consciousness. Although nonphysical, the inhabitants of the spirit world reside in communities and engage in activities with others. They don't lose their individuality or merge into a formless, impersonal force. Many regions exist in the spirit world populated by numerous spirits uniformly grouped with others of like consciousness.

Different Categories of Spirits

A medium experiences different categories of spirits who come through for recipients.

Family

This includes both the mother's and father's side of the house, as well as the families of present and former spouses and partners.

Friends and Acquaintances

There are varying gradations of friendship and acquaintanceship, involving both people we are close to and people we know.

Spiritual Guardians and Guides

These spirits may assist an individual for life or for a short length of time. Their functions, abilities, and levels of consciousness vary.

Spirit Teachers

A teacher brings enlightenment and higher understanding. There are gradations of teachers in the spirit world.

Helpers

A helper functions as part of a medium's spirit team. There are many helpers who specialize in many different aspects of mediumship and healing.

Learn to Differentiate the Spirits

A medium must learn to accurately differentiate the various spirits coming through during a session. This is accomplished by the visual depiction and positioning of the spirits along with the feeling that they bring. In the past, some mediums identified the function of spirits and the spiritual plane they were from by the color of their energy field. Trust your feelings. Various spirit relatives feel differently from each other and from spirit friends or acquaintances. A close friend feels different from a casual acquaintance. A guide feels different from a family member. A neighbor feels different from a colleague or classmate, and so on. The differences are subtle, so learn to pay attention.

A medium will also feel differences in the various spirit team members based on their personality and function. The energy of a spirit healer differs completely from a spirit involved in teaching higher philosophy. Spirit guides and helpers generally feel as though their energy vibrates at a higher frequency than family or friends. A master teacher brings in a greatly refined, pure energy significantly higher than the typical spirit helper or family member does. Some novice mediums cannot differentiate between spirits coming through from the spirit world, and individuals physically alive connected to the recipient. I have observed such mediums ask the recipient of a spirit message to tell them whether the individual they are describing is in the spirit world or in the physical world. Spirits coming through all bring a unique, identifying energy.

The Skyscraper

I often use the analogy of a skyscraper to explain the different levels of the spirit world. I explain to my student mediums that they can envision God living in the penthouse on the top floor. On the Eighth floor are Jesus, Buddha and other God-realized masters. Chief Bacon Rind, a Native American teacher, resides on the Fifth floor with less evolved helpers and guides living on the Fourth floor. A devout Roman Catholic grandmother inhabits the Third floor and on the Second floor, an aunt. The aunt was a pleasant woman, but not very developed spiritually. On the First floor is a former employer who was extremely nasty and selfish in his relationships with others. The basement is populated by ignorant, selfish and low-level spirits such as murderers, rapists, and pedophiles.

I explain to my students the importance of prayer and meditation as part of a medium's daily routine. I teach my students as mediums to always attune to God or the top floor first and then work one's way down. Many mediums focus primarily on bringing through spirits living on the first few floors or the astral levels of the spirit world. The average spirit relative resides on such a level. Mediums of a similar mentality are a good fit for such spirits to communicate through. Telepathic communication requires harmonious conditions. A spirit on the same mental wavelength as a medium will naturally find it easier to communicate through him or her. Not every medium is the best fit for all spirits. This is why some spirits come through more fully with certain mediums over others.

The higher spirits on the upper floors set the agenda for any session with a trained medium. They determine who will come through and what major points will be emphasized. In most mediumship sessions several spirits will communicate, although many spirits are present. A spirit grandmother coming through may not be so evolved spiritually. However, she will still convey higher guidance for the recipient as an intermediary for guides in the higher levels. A group of intoxicated teenagers playing with a Ouija board at a party at 4 am will generally open up to the basement. Mediums need to learn to increase their rate of vibration and always connect with God and the higher spirits. Going to the top floor first makes working the other levels of the spirit world much easier.

The higher spirits often utilize guides with a lower vibrational frequency as intermediaries in the process of mediumship. With any mediumistic communication, much thought goes into the agenda of the session. The higher spirits prioritize the content for any communication in terms of what is said and who comes through. The one or two spirits who come through during a typical mediumship session generally speak on behalf of many more who do not directly communicate. For example, the grandmother of the recipient will come through, as the communication will help both her and the recipient with their healing and soul progression. The grandmother shares evidential information for recognition along with personal messages. The grandmother may also provide spiritual guidance beyond her level of spiritual development that originates from the higher guides in charge of the recipient's soul progression.

In many cases, the spirit control who entrances the medium acts as a third party by conveying messages from other spirits who lack the skill to directly come through. Even in situations when a fully conscious medium describes a spirit communicator, such intermediaries facilitate the process. A spirit teacher such as Silver Birch, Zodiac, or White Eagle, who entrances his or her medium often represents a larger group of spirits who work with the medium.

Work Only With the Highest and the Best

A medium's spirituality will automatically attract personalities in the spirit world on a similar wavelength. Mediums should aspire to only work with the higher level spirits in a disciplined and structured manner. A trained medium only connects with the spirit world under the right circumstances, and the rest of the time remains closed down. Many individuals open up as mediums with inferior or insufficient training. In some cases, such mediums may even consume alcohol or smoke cannabis while they are working as mediums and conduct frivolous or promiscuous seances. Such undisciplined mediums do not regulate their mediumship and are susceptible to the influence of unreliable and unevolved spirits.

A medium I knew lived in a fifth-floor apartment in the worst section of a major city in the United States. Homeless drug addicts and assorted derelicts defecated and tossed their used syringe needles on the sidewalk outside of his home. I was surprised at the content of the mediumship session that I did for him. The higher spirits showed his entire apartment filled with lower level spirits whose former physical lives had been like the homeless drug addicts who populated his neighborhood's streets.

The higher guides told me that he was not practicing his mediumship in the disciplined manner that he had learned in his training as a medium. They showed me that because he was not working under the right conditions, the lower spirits in his apartment had been providing false and inaccurate information that he had been giving to his mediumship clients. In addition, they explained that many of the medium's clients were getting upset as the guidance he had been providing them turned out to be incorrect. The medium did not realize that this was happening and believed the spirits giving him information were advanced guides. The higher guides revealed to me that they had cleared out the lower spirits and were protecting him from further interference. However, they emphasized that he needed to work with his mediumship properly and under the right conditions. The medium understood the message completely and vowed to adjust his approach accordingly.

Sex With Disembodied Spirits?

Is it possible for an embodied individual to maintain a sexual relationship with a discarnate lover in the spirit world? Most people would think this idea to be totally insane. An elderly woman consulted me for a mediumship session. In her younger years, she had been an exceptionally attractive and successful fashion model and performer. She explained to me that she wanted to establish contact with her spirit lover, an extremely famous Country and Western recording artist and television personality.

According to my client, she connected daily with this deceased musician, who telepathically communicated with her and although disembodied, sexually stimulated her on a physical level. At night, she experienced the sensations of her lover physically on top of her, sensually caressing her body and penetrating her. She explained that she had met this individual many years ago when she performed onstage at a music industry symposium in Nashville, Tennessee. For the past two years, although he had physically died, they had developed an intimate relationship.

As I listened to my client's story, my initial reaction was disbelief and skepticism. The entire concept of sexual intercourse with spirits seemed farfetched. I also thought it sounded low-level for any spirit to be interested in physical sense gratification. I figured that my client must have been totally deluded.

My skepticism, however, changed completely after beginning the mediumship session, as the deceased musician came through, strongly relaying many evidential details about his former physical life including his physical description, significant memories, personality and character. All of this my client unreservedly recognized as being accurate. The individual was intensely charismatic, strong willed and excellent as a spirit communicator. He related his enduring love for my client and devotion to her. He also throughout the session made many inappropriate sexual comments and jokes, which my client recognized as being indicative of his personality.

My client was determined to "materialize" her spirit lover, so she could engage in the experience of sexual intercourse with him more fully. As a result she questioned me about physical mediumship and methods for achieving her goals. I suggested that she consult a colleague residing at a major Spiritualist camp, who specialized in holding seances involving physical phenomena. She followed my advice and attended several of his development classes and open Friday evening seances, which involved the medium sitting in a spirit cabinet and channeling his spirit guide for the participants.

My client contacted me again wanting another session and explained how the medium threw his arms up and exclaimed how her spirit friend had blocked his guide from coming through. The medium had been very upset and brought the séance to a close. As soon as the lights were switched on, my client saw the form of her friend near the cabinet along with a group of other young male spirits. The forms were as solid and real as being physically present. She felt that her friend had materialized and wanted to know how to go about making it happen again. At the same time, she was completely turned off by the medium and did not want to return to his sessions.

I explained to my client that she had experienced objective clairvoyance which differs from the commonly experienced subjective clairvoyance impressed within a medium's receptive mind. The visions experienced in objective clairvoyance seem as though they are viewed with the physical eyes. However, I explained that only the medium would experience the vision. Physical mediumship such as with spirit materialization is objectively experienced by everyone present through their physical senses. Mental mediumship involves the intuitive mind of the medium.

I did a phone session for my client and again strongly connected with her lover in the spirit world. He again emphasized his possessiveness and love for her. He encouraged her in her pursuit of opening up her own psychic abilities for communication with him. He also emphasized that, although he greatly liked me as a medium, most mediums were phony in trying to come across as more than what they were.

Hick Guides

He described how the guides connected to the medium whose seances she had attended were a bunch of hicks and had prevented him from participating. I was shown the medium's band of spirit helpers symbolically resembling uncultured Hillbillies and lacking intelligence and sophistication. These guides had barred her friend from participating in the séance. However, he explained how he was part of a society or group of spirits, whose focus was on looking for individuals in need on the physical world and doing good deeds by assisting them with their situations. With the help of this group of spirits, he had barged into the séance, overriding the spirits in charge, and made an appearance so that my client could view him.

He did not like the medium, who he felt was backward and ignorant. Furthermore, he stated that the spirits providing guidance through this medium were also unintelligent and lower-level. He told my client to stay away from that medium and that she would be meeting mediums of a higher vibration more compatible for channeling him. He said that she would be meeting a female medium who, although less experienced than many of the mediums she had consulted, was much more compatible energetically. According to her friend, this medium also taught classes with many women students who were also very harmonious as a group.

As the session continued, my client further inquired from her friend about ways in which he could materialize for her. He explained that he had been barred by the higher spirits from coming through this way once they understood his motivation as they did not feel that such an action was right. Furthermore, the higher spirits had blacklisted him with other spirits who specialize in such work to prevent them from assisting him. He explained how he needed the help of other knowledgeable spirits to be able to materialize. He related how he was looking into connecting with other unauthorized, knowledgeable spirits, who could help him accomplish this goal.

He also emphasized to my client that the sexual aspect of their relationship was superficial compared to the deep emotional bond of love between them. My client also connected her spirit lover's elderly girlfriend with me for a phone session. His girlfriend, who had lived with him for many years, was extremely happy to communicate with her former boyfriend and receive highly evidential details validating his survival of physical death as well as invaluable personal guidance.

Lust After Physical Death

This account demonstrates that sexual desire does not instantly disappear after physical death and that sexual interaction can take place between the inhabitants of both dimensions. I had another client in New England, who also similarly engaged in an intense, sexual relationship with a lower-level spirit who in his former physical life had occupied her present physical residence. This client had been sexually promiscuous in her younger years and delighted in the erotic exchanges that also involved the sensations of her spirit lover physically on top of her and virginal penetration.

M. Lamar Keene (1936-1996), author of *The Psychic Mafia*, includes an entire chapter documenting how many fake mediums deliberately held special seances for lonely elderly clients to engage in sex with deceased lovers or fictitious spirit lovers.[1] Genuine mediums work on many different levels with spirits of varying degrees of intellect and spirituality. The medium's intellect, morals, and spirituality are essential for attracting the highest and best spirits to assist in all aspects of mediumistic communication. A well-trained, disciplined medium is able to work with spirits of all types and qualities.

Differentiating the Levels and Types of Spirits Exercises

EXERCISE 27

Feel the Spirit Team

This exercise can be done alone or directed by a teacher in a development group. Go into deep meditation and attune to the spirit world. Mentally call in your spirit team. Request a helper to step forward and to touch one of your shoulders. Ask this helper to step back.

---

[1] Keene, M. Lamar, *The Psychic Mafia,* Dell Publishing, New York, 1976, pp. 127-137.

Mentally request another helper to step in and touch the other shoulder. Ask this helper to step back. Call in the whole spirit team, and feel their presence and power.

EXERCISE 28

Compare and Contrast

Participants pair up, hold each other's hands, and connect with the spirit world. Make a mental link with a spirit guide and a deceased loved one, and also allow the spirits to describe an individual in the physical world who is around the recipient. Note the difference in energy and the feeling involved between the spirit guide and spirit loved one in the spirit world and the individual in the physical world. Take turns working.

EXERCISE 29

Family Feelings

Participants pair up, hold each other's hands, and connect with the spirit world. Bring in a spirit relative on the mother's side from the recipient's family, followed by a spirit relative from the father's side of the recipient's family. Note the difference in energy and the feeling involved between the mother's side and the father's side of the family. Take turns working.

EXERCISE 30

Buddies and More

Participants pair up, hold each other's hands, and attune to the spirit world. Bring in a close friend in the spirit world, connected to the recipient. Next, bring through an acquaintance in the spirit world, connected to the recipient. Note the difference in energy and feeling involved between the close friend and the acquaintance. Take turns working.

EXERCISE 31

Friends and Family.

Participants pair up, hold each other's hands, and connect with the spirit world. Bring in a friend in the spirit world, connected to the recipient. Next, bring in a member of the recipient's family in the spirit world. Note the difference in energy and feeling involved between the friend and the family member. Take turns working.

EXERCISE 32

Contacting Former Teacher

Participants pair up, hold each other's hands, and attune to the spirit world. Allow a school teacher involved in the recipient's education to come through. The teacher will present memories of his or her former academic career, including the institutions he or she taught at, the subjects he or she instructed, and the recipient's performance as a student. In addition, the teacher can present evidential information about his or her personal attributes and former physical life. Take turns working.

EXERCISE 33

Contacting Former Neighbor

Participants pair up, hold each other's hands, and attune to the spirit world. Allow a neighbor who resided near the recipient to come through. The neighbor will present memories of his or her former place of residence, including a description of the location, the street address, and connections with the recipient. In addition, the neighbor can present evidential information about his or her personal attributes and former physical life. Take turns working.

EXERCISE 34

Contacting Former Workmate or Colleague

Participants pair up, hold each other's hands, and attune to the spirit world. Allow a former workmate or colleague connected to the recipient to come through. The spirit will present memories of his or her professional life and connections with the recipient. In addition, the spirit can present evidential information about his or her personal attributes and former physical life. Take turns working.

EXERCISE 35

Contacting Former Classmate

Participants pair up, hold each other's hands, and attune to the spirit world. Allow a classmate who attended school with the recipient to come through. The classmate will present memories of his or her academic life and connections with the recipient. In addition, the classmate can present evidential information about his or her personal attributes and former physical life. Take turns working.

EXERCISE 36

Spirit Specialists

Participants pair up, hold each other's hands, and connect with the spirit world. Bring in three specialists, who are members of the recipient's spirit team. Describe each specialist, and his or her function in regard to the recipient's mediumship. Note the difference in energy and feeling involved with each of these three spirit helpers. Take turns working.

EXERCISE 37

Spirit Band

Meditate and connect with the spirit team. Note the various individuals in the spirit world who are working with you as a medium and healer. Using a sketch pad and pastels, draw a silhouette outline of a form on a page. The form represents you. Connect with your spirit team and draw images of five members on the page above the silhouette form, and note their functions in relation to your mediumship.

EXERCISE 38

More Spirit Band

Pair up with another student who has also drawn their spirit team. Connect with the spirit world. Using a sketch pad and pastels, draw an outline silhouette of each other's form. Depict five helpers in each other's spirit team and their functions relating to mediumship. Share the results with each other. See if the five helpers depicted for each other match the helpers previously drawn individually.

EXERCISE 39

Connecting with Spirit Team Individually

Go into a deep meditative state and expand your energy field. Be mentally aware of the four corners of the room or physical space. Mentally attune to each corner and be aware of a spirit helper in each corner who is part of your spirit team. Move your awareness to the front left-hand and right-hand corners and behind to both the left-hand and right-hand corners.

EXERCISE 40

Connecting with Spirit Team with Partner

Participants pair up, hold each other's hands, and connect with the spirit world. One partner goes into a deep meditative state and expands his or her energy field. The partner mentally is aware of the four corners of the room or physical space. He or she mentally attunes to each corner and is aware of a spirit helper, who is part of his or her spirit team in the front left- hand and right-hand corners and behind in both the left-hand and right-hand corners. At the same time, the other partner tunes in and mentally connects with four members of his or her partner's spirit team in each of the four corners. Describe what is received. Both partners should discern the same spirits. Take turns working.

EXERCISE 41

Connecting with a Spirit Helper Individually

Go into a deep meditative state and expand your energy field. Ask a spirit helper to step in close within your energy field. Be aware of the presence of the helper and details for recognition.

EXERCISE 42

Connecting with a Spirit Helper with Partner

Participants pair up, hold each other's hands, and connect with the spirit world. One partner goes into a deep meditative state and expands his or her energy field. The partner requests a spirit helper to step in close within his or her energy field. He or she is aware of the presence of the spirit helper and details for recognition. At the same time, the other partner tunes into the spirit helper and describes the spirit helper. The details should be the same. Take turns working.

EXERCISE 43

Identifying Spirit Helpers Individually

Go into a deep meditative state and ask one of your spirit helpers to step in close within your energy field. Feel the presence of your spirit helper and details for recognition. Mentally ask this spirit helper to bring another spirit helper who you do not know to step in. Feel the presence of this new helper and details for recognition. Note the difference between the energies of both spirits.

EXERCISE 44

Identifying Spirit Helpers with Partner

Participants pair up, hold each other's hands, and connect with the spirit world. One partner goes into a deep meditative state and asks for one of his or her spirit helpers to step in close within his or her energy field. This partner feels the presence of his or her spirit helper and details for recognition. The other partner tunes into this spirit helper and receives details for recognition.

The first partner mentally requests the first spirit helper to bring in another spirit helper who he or she does not know. The partner feels the presence of this new spirit helper and receives the details for recognition.

The other partner tunes in and connects with the second spirit helper and receives details for recognition. This partner shares information about both spirit helpers with his or her partner. The information about both spirit helpers should be the same for both partners. Take turns working.

EXERCISE 45

Drawing the Aura and Spirits.

Participants pair up, hold each other's hands, and attune to the spirit world. Both sides work at the same time or take turns. Using a sketch pad and pastels, partners draw each other's energy fields around an outline form of his or her partner drawn on the page. Partners observe the colors of each other's energy field and depict it on the paper. Draw a spirit loved one who is present on the left side of the page. On the right side of the drawing, draw a healing guide.

EXERCISE 46

Drawing Both Sides of the House.

Participants pair up, hold each other's hands, and attune to the spirit world. Both sides work at the same time or take turns. Using a sketch pad and pastels, partners draw an outline of each other's form on the page. Partners observe the colors of each other's energy field and depict it around the outline on the paper. On the left side of the form, draw a recognizable spirit relative from the father's side of the family, and on the right side of the form, draw a recognizable relative from the mother's side of the family.

EXERCISE 47

Going Deeper on Both Sides of the House

Participants pair up, hold each other's hands, and attune to the spirit world. Both sides work at the same time or take turns. Using a sketch pad and pastels, partners draw an outline of form on the page. Partners observe the colors of each other's energy field and depict them on the paper. On the left side, draw a recognizable spirit relative from the father's side of the family, and on the right side, draw a recognizable relative from the mother's side of the family. Receive from the spirit world the names of both spirits as well as the names of a place or location for both sides of the family.

EXERCISE 48

Doubles

Participants pair up, hold each other's hands, and attune to the spirit world. The medium links with a spirit who provides his or her name and other evidential information. Next, the medium asks the spirit to assist another spirit, whom he or she was connected to in his or her former physical life and has reconnected with in the spirit world, to step in. Allow the second spirit to give his or her name along with other evidential information. Both spirits can share details about their relationship. Take turns working.

EXERCISE 49

Two Generations

Participants pair up, hold hands and attune to the spirit world. The medium links with a spirit loved one who was connected to the recipient, such as a mother or father, and provides his or her name and other evidential information. Next, on the same link, the medium connects with a second spirit loved one connected to the recipient, who is of the same gender as the first spirit but from the previous generation, such as a grandmother or grandfather, who also provides his or her name and other evidential information. A father should precede a grandfather. A mother should precede a grandmother. A grandmother should precede a great-grandmother, etc. Note the difference in vibrations between the two spirits on a personal level and also generationally. Take turns working.

EXERCISE 50

Three-Story House

See in your mind a transparent three-story house with a basement. Each story of the house represents a level of the spirit world characterized by a particular vibration and color.

First, allow a spirit helper from the third floor to come close and blend with you energetically. Using clairsentience, note the less dense, higher frequency of this spirit along with his or her function within your spirit team. Clairvoyantly be aware of the vibratory color accompanying this spirit. Allow this spirit to step back.

Next, request a spirit helper from the second floor to come close and blend energetically. As with the first spirit, use clairsentience to feel the slightly denser vibrations of this spirit helper, along with his or her function within your spirit team. Use clairvoyance to view the vibratory color associated with this spirit. Allow the spirit to step back.

Next, allow a third spirit from the bottom floor to come close and blend energetically. As with the previous two spirits, use clairsentience to feel the dense, heavier vibration of this spirit along with his or her function within your spirit team. Use clairvoyance to view the vibratory color that this spirit brings. Allow this spirit to step back.

Finally, allow a lower-level spirit connected to the recipient from the basement to come close and blend energetically. Sense the heavy, dense vibration of this individual along with the issues affecting his or her soul progression. Use clairvoyance to view the vibratory color this spirit brings. Allow this spirit to step back.

Compare and contrast the differences in vibratory frequency between the four spirits and the levels of the spirit world they represent.

EXERCISE 51

In My Father's House

Participants pair up, hold each other's hands, and connect with the spirit world. Allow a spirit connected to the recipient to come through and present evidential details about his or her former physical life. Next, allow the spirit to show his or her present location in the spirit world and to describe his or her activities there. Allow yourself to feel the energy of this location and observe in detail the environment. In addition, allow the spirit to relate the progress he or she has made in overcoming personal defects and cultivating spiritual qualities. Take turns working.

EXERCISE 52

Spirit Team Architecture

Mediums pair up, hold each other's hands, and connect with the spirit world. One medium goes into a deep meditative state and expands his or her energy field. The medium mentally is aware of the four corners of the room or physical space. He or she mentally attunes to each corner and is aware of buildings or architecture connected with the former physical lives of four spirit helpers, who are part of his or her spirit team. The four spirit helpers are positioned in the front left-hand and right-hand corners and behind in both the left-hand and right-hand corners. The four spirit helpers only present a building or architecture for identification. The medium feels the history of the architecture in relation to the spirit helper's former physical life.

At the same time, the other medium tunes in and mentally connects with four members of his or her partner's spirit team in each of the four corners. The medium should also only see a building or architecture connected with the former physical lives of each spirit helper. Both partners should share what is received and receive information from the same spirits. Take turns working.

EXERCISE 53

Tuning In Below

Participants pair up, hold each other's hands, and attune to the spirit world. The medium senses the spirits connected to his or her partner, positioned beneath the floor or ground. The medium provides evidential details about the spirits. Take turns working.

EXERCISE 54

Twelve Spirits

Sit comfortably and mentally attune to the spirit world. Focus awareness on spirit helpers positioned on three levels in each of the four corners of the room. Start with the front left-hand corner and feel a spirit positioned beneath the floor or ground. Next, sense a spirit positioned on the same level as yourself. Lastly, feel a spirit positioned on the level above your head. Note, any differences in the vibratory rates, attributes and functions of each spirit. Repeat this process with the front right-hand corner, the back right-hand corner, and the back left-hand corner.

Physical Mediumship

Physical mediumship is dependent upon the chemistry of the medium, along with the psychic force created by those present. In most cases, an individual already considerably developed as a mental medium can easily cultivate phases of physical mediumship.

Physical phenomena are objectively experienced through the five physical senses and include many types, such as materialization, transfiguration, table tipping, spirit photography, and many more. Unlike mental mediumship, physical mediumship is rare. Few mediums possess the necessary chemistry for the production of physical manifestations. However, the development of physical mediumship is possible with the proper approach and maintaining the right conditions.

Questions to Consider About Physical Circle Participants

Careful evaluation of potential sitters in a physical circle is important. Be selective with who you allow to join. Physical mediumship is a serious endeavor with success dependent upon creating and maintaining the proper conditions. Too often mediums permit friends and acquaintances, who best should be excluded, to participate in a physical group. Choose your sitters wisely and trust the intuitive guidance you receive from your spirit teachers.

Are potential sitters psychologically balanced?

Serious mental illness does not mix with mediumship development. An individual with severe psychological issues might become even more imbalanced, as the psychic energies involved stimulate the unconscious mind, releasing unresolved emotions and problems.

Any psychic development requires that all participants are of sound mind, and able to discipline themselves in working with the energies.

Are potential sitters experienced sitting for development in other circles or working with mediumship and healing? If yes, what is the extent and nature of their experience and abilities?

Different mediumship development circles accommodate participants with different needs and abilities. A physical circle in general is best suited for sitters possessing a background in mediumship and healing. Of course, what matters most is the mental and energetic harmonious alignment of each sitter with other participants in the group. An experienced sitter generally provides better energy than the typical novice. However, any individual, regardless of experience, who possesses the right chemistry for the production of physical manifestations, and whose energies harmoniously blend with the others in the group, is ideal.

Does the potential sitter possess discipline? Is he or she committed to attending weekly séance sessions without absence?

Self-discipline and dedication are essential. All sitters in a physical circle must be committed to attending the sessions weekly. Without this consistency in attendance, the psychic conditions necessary for producing manifestations will be adversely affected.

Do the energies of the potential sitter harmoniously blend with the others in the group?

It is important that the chemistry of the group is harmonious, and blends together cohesively. Any disharmony between participants is counterproductive for the development and demonstration of physical mediumship. Remove disharmonious sitters from the circle.

Cleanliness is Next to Godliness

Sitters must refrain from consuming alcoholic beverages or other mind-altering substances the day of the session. Intoxication creates the wrong kind of energy for any type of mediumistic session. It is amazing how many mediums partake of intoxicants such as alcohol or cannabis regularly and even before working with the spirit world. Purity of mind, body and spirit is essential for connecting with the higher levels of the spirit world. In the past, Spiritualists would attend mediumship circles freshly bathed with clean clothes. In fact, sitters in some physical circles would wear the same clothes each session, as it was felt that the clothes would retain the vibrations conducive for producing physical manifestations.

Although physical mediumship is dependent primarily upon the chemistry of the medium, the mental and spiritual atmosphere of the session is still a major factor in the quality of the communications obtained. The *Law of Attraction* that like attracts like is a direct factor in any session regardless of the phases of mediumship demonstrated. Mediumship is not a game or a form of superficial entertainment. Reverence for the sacredness of the process is essential. At the same time, it is important that physical sessions should be conducted in a fun and relaxed manner. Unnecessary rigidity and uptightness create vibrations that are detrimental for the successful development of physical mediumship.

The Séance Room

First, a clean, clutter-free environment is the best physical environment for any development circle. A well-ventilated, temperature controlled space ensures comfort for participants, regardless of time of year. A room used only for spiritual purposes is ideal, as it ensures that the psychic atmosphere contains positive vibrations. A room with low ceilings and compact space is most suitable for physical mediumship, as the energy is better contained. Any windows in the room should be completely covered to prevent the intrusion of regular light.

The more natural the environment is, the better. Large plants and flowers bring considerable power to the séance room, and sufficiently enhance the conditions. As a measure to prevent fraud, place plants all over the séance room floor. This way, an individual moving about in the dark will stumble over the plants. A basin of water left in the séance room greatly assists physical manifestations. The spirit chemists store helpful chemicals in the water that they use for the production of physical phenomena. Sitters should also bring their own containers of water to consume at the conclusion of the session. The spirit doctors infuse such water with beneficial chemicals and healing energies.

It is good to place objects, or props, such as spirit trumpets, or musical instruments, in the middle of the circle for telekinesis or levitation to take place. Position a soft red or blue light in the séance room in order that all sitters can observe what is taking place. A dimmer is also good with any lighting, as this way it can be better controlled.

The Cabinet

If necessary place a spirit cabinet in one section of the room for the medium to sit in or use an appropriately sized closet. A cabinet is a curtained off area of the séance room or a specially constructed enclosure in which the medium sits. The interior of the cabinet concentrates the psychic force around the medium for the production of physical phenomena. Building a spirit cabinet is relatively easy. I have known many mediums who constructed portable cabinets out of plastic piping and other materials. The seat for the medium is generally positioned inside the cabinet. A cabinet is not necessary for the development of all phases of physical mediumship, but it is essential for concentrating the psychic energies involved in physical manifestations. Wooden chairs make excellent conductors for psychic force. In the séance room, avoid heavy curtains, couches, and seats constructed with padding, as such material absorbs power.

Seating Arrangements

Unless instructed otherwise by the spirit teachers, seat participants in the same positions and exact same physical chairs each week. The seating arrangement of the sitters requires careful consideration on the part of the circle leader or teacher. Generally, it is ideal to alternate the position of participants by gender. Of course, not all groups contain an equal number of male and female participants. Women tend to be more involved in mediumistic unfoldment than men. The circle leader needs to trust his or her intuition, along with the guidance of the higher spirits as to where to position sitters. Obviously, some individuals make better batteries than others as they exude a greater abundance of positive psychic force.

Experiment and see what seating position works best. It is always valuable to spend as much time as necessary, at the beginning of the first session, to examine possible arrangements, and feel which one is the most conducive for generating power. Once the best positioning is determined, keep the seating arrangement for future meetings. For physical and trance groups, I like to position sitters in a horseshoe formation and sit in the open section. With a larger group, I use the same seating arrangement, with double or more rows of chairs. After I intuitively assess the participants, I alternate sitters by gender, and position those most powerful as batteries accordingly.

It is always good as a medium to position sympathetic colleagues or students in proximity. This is especially true for mediums holding seances for attendees who are skeptical or disharmonious energetically. Adversity in any form is detrimental to the production of physical phenomena. It is best for sitters to avoid mental tension and maintain a relaxed, yet enthusiastic disposition toward the proceedings. The most important ingredient for achieving successful results with physical mediumship is harmony.

A common seating arrangement for a physical circle entails that the participants sit in a circle holding hands with the medium. The sitter's hands are positioned with their left hand up, and right hand down, which enhances the flow of psychic force, clockwise around the circle. In physical circles, in which the medium sits in a cabinet, the sitters are arranged in a horseshoe formation with the open section facing the medium, while holding each other's hands. The psychic force is pulled from the participants into a reservoir of energy about the medium.

It was a common practice in many seances to hold hands in this manner for the lengthy duration of the séance. Although this approach builds power and also helps to prevent cheating, its benefits are outweighed by the discomfort experienced by participants holding hands for long periods. In my physical circles, participants hold hands for a short period in the beginning to establish a harmonious flow of energy. It is more productive for participants to place their hands in their laps or on their knees without any physical contact. Although mediumship is scientific and operates according to established laws and conditions, flexibility is more important than rigid adherence to protocol. What matters the most is doing what works, as the chemistry within each group and the gifts of individual mediums are unique.

There is no correct way of positioning the medium or conducting the session. It is always important to experiment and inquire from the higher spirits directing the session. Maud Lord Drake (1852-1924), a prominent American Spiritualist medium, held physical seances with herself positioned in the middle of the circle.[1]

Sing Loudly

Mediumship is often approached in a frivolous and superficial manner. I always emphasize to participants at my mediumship meetings the sacredness of spirit communication. Every session needs to begin with an opening prayer or invocation as this creates a mood of reverence for the meeting. Fast, repetitive, loud singing is a proven method to build the powerful vibrations necessary for physical phenomena to take place. Singing in general is a good practice for creating a psychic atmosphere conducive for mediumship. A traditional Spiritualist séance or circle in the nineteenth and twentieth centuries always included singing for this purpose. Many contemporary mediums and séance attendees feel inhibited about singing with others. As a result, many mediums and circle leaders neglect singing as a means to build the power in their seances and circles.

Mediumship is scientific and functions according to established natural laws. The best results for physical mediumship are obtained through maintaining favorable, harmonious conditions. The spirit chemists draw psychic force and substances from each sitter to mix with those of the medium. A spirit chemist is a specialist who works with the energy of the medium for producing physical phenomena. The ideal physical mediumship circle is composed of seven or eight participants, and run by a competent leader or experienced medium. It is always advisable to audio record the proceedings, and, if possible, visually record with infrared devices. Recording the seance helps to prevent fraud and document any physical manifestations that take place. The development of any phase of physical mediumship is a long process and requires patience on the

[1] Fodor, Nandor, *Encyclopedia of Psychic Science*, University Books, Inc., 1966. p. 206.

part of all involved. It may seem sometimes that absolutely nothing is taking place in terms of development.

Séance Sensations

There is an intensity in sitting for physical mediumship that surpasses the faster sensations associated with mental mediumship. The spirit operators work directly with the medium and other participants, by drawing psychic force from their physical bodies and the physical environment around them. The sensations are often intensely physical, and not merely energetic on a subtle level. The subtle bodies interpenetrate the physical body and serve as a blueprint for what takes place in regard to the medium's physical health. The development of physical mediumship is holistic and involves both the physiological and subtle systems.

The production of physical phenomena requires the extraction of tremendous psychic force from the medium's physical body. A depletion of various nutrients takes place with physical mediumship that potentially results in many physical mediums developing diabetic and thyroid conditions. The unhealthy lifestyle choices of many mediums do not help. Mediums need to care for their physical bodies through regular exercise and a proper diet. Although mediumship works regardless of the foods we eat, a vegetarian or vegan diet is healthier than diets that include animal flesh. A vegetarian or vegan diet also typically vibrates at a higher spiritual frequency than the flesh of dead animals and assists individuals cultivate the qualities of compassion and mercifulness.

In some cases, it is possible in physical circles for empathic individuals to acquire unpleasant conditions, due to their inability to establish energetic boundaries and properly manage the intense flow of psychic force through their physical bodies. This is especially true for novices who are easily susceptible to the toxic energies of others. I did a mediumship session for a woman once in Massachusetts who I invited to attend an open development circle that I taught at a nearby Spiritualist church. She complained later to me how she was overwhelmed by the negative energies of a man sitting next to her and felt her entire solar plexus filled with horrible vibrations. I explained to her that the man's energies were fine, but since she was inexperienced, she was affected by the strong psychic force generated during the meditation.

In physical circles, a strong pull is often experienced by sitters in the solar plexus. This pull of psychic force is occasionally accompanied by feelings of extreme nausea, which compares easily with the morning sickness felt by women in the early stages of pregnancy. It is also not uncommon for participants in a physical circle to taste salt, sugar, or even aluminum on their lips. A sitter who eats a heavy meal prior to attendance at a physical circle will also likely experience nauseous feelings in the solar plexus. A light meal two hours prior to the physical circle is ideal, as a heavy meal weighs down the sitter, whose energies are concentrated upon the process of digestion.

The Touch of the Spirit Chemists

The spirit chemists perform many actions in the physical circle, both leading up to the phenomena, and, during the manifestations. It is common for sitters to directly experience this activity as temperature changes, psychic breezes, and the extraction of psychic force and ectoplasm from their physical and subtle bodies. As the spirit chemists withdraw the necessary substances, participants experience various situations in different parts of the physical body. The location of such sensations relates to the chemistry of the substance extracted. Obviously, the production of different physical manifestations requires specific types of chemicals taken from the physical bodies of those present and the material surroundings.

The spirit chemists diligently work to produce physical phenomena over a period of time with the circle participants. It is all about teamwork and cooperation for the desired goal. A sitter in a physical circle feels many peculiar sensations in various locations around his or her physical body that may occur separately, at the same time, or one after the other. It is a good practice in a physical circle for mediums to clairvoyantly observe the activity of the spirit chemists as they work with members of the group. Mediums will also clairvoyantly be aware of the colors of the energies present at the session.

As the spirit chemists blend their energies with the sitters may experience a variety of common sensations, including severe burning in the hands and arms, cold energy emanating from the pores of the skin, and the draining of masses of translucent substance from the bottom of the spine and abdomen area. In addition, a sitter in a physical circle may literally feel the spirit chemists pull material from various sections of his or her physical body. These sensations range from cold to intense heat. In some cases, the extraction starts as intense heat and diminishes to a cool feeling or the action begins as a cold energy and changes to a burning sensation. Bleeding from the nostrils may even be experienced. Pulling, burning actions are because the spirit chemists are exacting material from the upper surfaces of the skin and other bodily systems. Substances and gases are emitted in every sitting, which result in the séance room smelling like a chemical factory.[2]

Psychic Breezes, Lights, and Odors

A cool force or wind may be felt moving around the circle along with masses of concentrated cold. Physical odors are another phase of mediumship that is commonly experienced by those sitting for development. At times, clouds of a cold substance that emits distinct odors, such

---

[2] Vickers, Ernest, *The Development of Physical Mediumship*, Spiritualist National Union, Ltd., Manchester, UK, 1935. pp. 7,9,11.

as perfume, may manifest in the séance room. Such nasty and nauseating smells such as rotten eggs, soot, and iodine can also be produced.[3]

The Extraction of Ectoplasm

Ectoplasm is a term coined by French Nobel Laureate Charles Richet (1850-1935), discoverer of the X-ray, to describe the substance utilized by the spirit operators for the production of physical phenomena. Ectoplasm is living matter drawn from the physical bodies of the medium and others in attendance at the session. Although impalpable and invisible, the spirit chemists can manifest ectoplasm, in many forms-solid, liquid, and vaporous-for the production of physical mediumship.

Distinguished scientists involved in psychical research have successfully obtained plaster casts, and fingerprinted ectoplasmic spirit hands. In addition, they have cut small samples of ectoplasm from materialized spirits, and analyzed its chemical composition. As a substance, the ectoplasm is extracted by the spirit chemists from the pores and orifices of the medium. The spirit chemists are masters in the science of producing physical manifestations. They are able to construct ectoplasm rods for the telekinetic movement of physical objects such as spirit trumpets and furniture. Sitters observe such rods protruding from the area of the spleen and solar plexus of the medium, and attach to a physical object for levitation or movement.

Ectoplasm appears in many colors and degrees of density as solid as a physical chair or as intangible and invisible as mist. Ectoplasm is used in the production of raps and percussion as well as the production of spirit voices and other sounds heard by séance participants. In addition, the spirit chemists can materialize partial and full spirit forms and less dense, etherealized spirit forms. They can also transfigure the features of the spirits over the medium's face and physical body.

---

[3] Ibid. pp. 13, 15.

Ectoplasm is generally used as a term to describe all material withdrawn from a medium's physical body. However, Ernest Vickers, a British physical medium, detailed three distinct substances extracted from his physical body, as part of his process of development for physical mediumship-psychic force, psychoplasm, and ectoplasm. Vickers relates the nature of each of these substances as follows:

Psychic Force

In every sitting, the psychic forces exude from the physical body in a fluid and gaseous state invisible to the physical eye. Although this energy is invisible, it is experienced as a cool sensation. This psychic force is the first withdrawn, and the last reabsorbed. At the conclusion of the sitting, it is important to remain in the séance room to allow this force to adequately reabsorb back into the physical body.

Psychoplasm

Psychoplasm is the consolidation of gaseous psychic force with material drawn from the bones. It is cold, lacks moisture, and is malleable like dough.

Ectoplasm

The temperature of ectoplasm is often warm and contains moist content. It is similarly derived from the psychic force and is soft and mailable and drawn mainly from the abdominal region.[4]

My First Experience With Ectoplasm

The concept of mental mediumship is an easier concept for most individuals to intellectually accept. Physical mediumship, however, is

---

4 Ibid. pp. 18-19.

generally approached by many individuals with suspicion and skeptical disregard. As a medium, I have observed ectoplasm stream from my physical body, and felt it with my hands. My first experience with ectoplasm took place many years ago. At the time, I regularly practiced mantra meditation in the evenings, followed by a period of qi-gong exercise, involving movement and breathing. I also used this period to connect with my spirit teachers and helpers, who assisted me with my mediumship development.

As I performed the qi-gong exercises, I felt the subtle energy flow through me and build up as a ball in the palms of my hands. Suddenly, I experienced intense vibrations surge throughout my physical body and move down through my forearms and hands. I observed and felt a thin, vibrant substance simultaneously move from both my palms, and momentarily join between them, before retracting back into my palms. This experience happened extremely quickly. I remember thinking at the time that the substance must have been ectoplasm.

At a Spiritualist conference in the UK, I shared this account with an Australian medium, who immediately accused me of lying, because, according to her, it was impossible for ectoplasm to appear in regular lighting. I explained to her that this occurrence took place in dim lighting and that historically many accounts exist of physical phenomena taking place with dim or regular lighting. The Australian medium had attended seances with several phony physical mediums, all of whom emphasize to sitters at their seances that ectoplasm can only manifest in the dark. These same mediums refuse to allow infrared devices and even red lighting at their seances claiming that they will potentially be harmed. Physical phenomena can take place with red, dim, or even regular lighting with the right conditions. Sitters should beware of mediums who conduct seances in the dark with inadequate test measures in place.

The Australian medium was correct in stating that the production of ectoplasm is adversely affected by white light, and that physical medium-ship is better developed in the dark. This does not mean, however, that physical phenomena only occur under such conditions. A seed requires darkness to germinate, and the absence of light is necessary for the chemical process of developing film. Similarly, an environment free from white light enhances the production of physical phenomena. It is for this reason that physical mediumship circles are held in the dark or subdued lighting. Red or blue lights are also used for physical seances. In this way, participants can observe what is happening without adversely affecting the conditions.

Many documented accounts exist that detail sessions in which white light unexpectedly introduced into the session violently reacted back into the medium's physical body, resulting in shock and internal hemorrhaging. For example, Helen Duncan (1897-1956), a controversial Scottish physical medium, suffered internal bleeding after local police shone a flashlight in the middle of a materialization séance. The police thought that the ectoplasm was a white sheet and attempted to grab it. However, the ectoplasm retracted rapidly like an elastic band back into her physical body. It is for this reason that sitters at a physical circle, unless given permission by the spirit operators, should never touch the medium or ectoplasm.

Writing On the Skin

Saint Francis of Assisi (1181 or 1182-1226), Saint Padre Pio of Pietrelcina (1887-1968) and many other devout Christians experienced the phenomena of Stigmata in which markings and sensations appeared in locations on the body associated with Jesus the Christ's crucifixion wounds. This phase of mediumship, or dermography, also manifests in the séance room in the form of small, red inflamed areas on various locations of the body. Charles Foster (1838-1888), an American medium from Salem, Massachusetts, exhibited the names of spirit communicators written on his forearms in blood red letters. Maud Lord Drake (1852-1924), another famous American physical medium, also demonstrated this unusual type of mediumship. Séance attendees should pay particular attention to the consistent appearance of small inflamed areas on the body, as this may lead to words or other images produced on the skin.

Dark Seances

Although sitting in the dark is conducive for the production of physical manifestations, physical mediumship circles should work toward sitting in dim lighting or with a red or blue light. Avoid holding seances in complete darkness, unless stringent test measures are in place. The prevalence of dark seances in the nineteenth century resulted in much fraudulent mediumship. The same remains true today. Test both the medium and the spirits.

The Demise of Physical Mediumship

There are several reasons why there is less physical mediumship demonstrated in this modern era compared to its heyday in the nineteenth century. First, physical mediumship is rare, as mediums possessing the right chemistry are few and far between. Also, the development of physical mediumship often entails years of sitting with the same group, under the same conditions, without much seemingly taking place. Few individuals possess the discipline, dedication and patience necessary for this. In addition, in this fast-paced, modern age, there is less leisure time for people to devote to sitting for mediumistic unfoldment. Contemporary sitters are generally oriented toward cultivating their own spiritual gifts, instead of sitting solely to assist another medium's development, as was common in the past.

Another major reason is that many people are mainly interested in experiencing phenomena on a superficial level. Such individuals are attracted by the inherent sensationalism and entertainment value of physical mediumship, which leads to fraudulence and trickery by charlatans, as well as mediums who are unable to produce genuine phenomena on demand. The higher spirits are also more interested in enhancing the moral and spiritual development of individuals than providing entertainment. The higher spirits, because of the prevalence of education and the hectic lifestyles of the present, currently focus more on developing students as mental mediums and healers.

Séance Exercises

EXERCISE 55

Nice Rice

Evenly spread uncooked grains of rice on half the surface of a tray positioned in the center of the séance room. Sit individually or with a group in the dark or with a red light under séance conditions. Talk with the spirit chemists and ask them to move or produce messages with the rice. At the end of the session, examine the tray for possible movements of the rice, including writing, shapes, or symbols.

EXERCISE 56

Flour Messages

Evenly spread white floor on a tray positioned in the center of the séance room. Sit individually or with a group in the dark or with a red light under séance conditions. Talk to the spirit chemists and request they produce phenomena with the flour. Pay attention to what takes place during the séance and, at the end of the session, examine the flour for possible writings, shapes, or symbols created with the flour.

EXERCISE 57

Flowers Seance

Place a variety of freshly picked flowers on a flat surface or arranged in a vase in the center of the séance room. Sit individually or with others in the dark or with a red light under séance conditions. Talk to the spirit chemists and ask them to produce phenomena with the flowers. Pay attention to what takes place during the séance and afterwards examine the flowers for possible movements.

EXERCISE 58

Flour and Flowers

Break apart a variety of freshly picked flowers upon a table or tray positioned in the center of the séance room. Mix and thoroughly coat the flower pieces with the flour. Sit in the power individually or with a group in the dark or with a red light under séance conditions. Ask the spirit chemists to move the flour and flowers. Pay attention to what happens during the session and afterwards examine the flour and flowers for possible movements.

EXERCISE 59

Objects to Steal

Place a variety of small items such as jewelry, coins, etc., on a table or tray positioned in the center of the séance room. Sit individually or with a group in the dark or with a red light under séance conditions. Ask the spirit chemists to move the objects around the surface or dematerialize and teleport the items to another location. Pay attention to what happens during the session and examine the table or tray afterwards for possible movements or missing items.

EXERCISE 60

Spirit Music

Place a variety of smaller musical instruments such as bells, tambourines, rattles, harmonicas, etc., on a table positioned in the center of the séance room. Sit individually or with a group in the dark or with a red light under séance conditions. Ask the spirit chemists to move or produce sounds with the musical instruments. Pay attention to what happens during the session and examine the instruments afterwards for possible movements.

CHAPTER 6

Dynamic Spirit Manifestations

Mental mediumship provides the energetic foundation for the unfoldment of various physical phases of mediumship. Physical phenomena rarely take place, even if a medium deliberately sits to develop it. Physical phenomena often take place when it is least expected to occur. The spirit operators produce physical manifestations with specific spiritual objectives in mind. Physical phenomena can be compared to fireworks in that people are momentarily excited by the explosions in the way many people are thrilled by spirit manifestations.

The spirit operators will only produce physical phenomena when it serves a higher purpose. They want to enlighten people and assist in their process of soul growth. The higher spirits will not waste their time developing mediums whose main desire for mediumship unfoldment is financial gain or impressing others with their abilities. However, a humble service oriented medium with the right conditions and chemistry can potentially develop physical mediumship.

Materializations

The materialization of spirits is a spectacular event to experience. In most cases, a materialized form will appear either invisible and fully solid or visible but impalpable like a mist. In addition, many material-ized forms lacking substance may appear partial or incomplete. A fully materialized spirit is rare because of the psychic force necessary for such a complete manifestation. The materialized spirits can interact with séance participants and engage in conversation. A spirit cabinet is recommended for materialization seances as it helps concentrate the power needed for the manifestation. Materialization is best developed in the dark because of the detrimental effect of regular light upon ectoplasm.

The spirit chemists make the materialized bodies using the elements of the medium, sitters and surroundings. They draw pigment from the furnishings of the room to color the garb worn by the materialized spirits. The medium during materialization is typically placed in a deep unconscious trance by the spirit operators. A materialization medium experiences weight loss during the séance. Researchers have documented the changes in weight for materialization mediums before, during, and after the séance. In order to produce the materialized form, the spirit chemists create a soft covering of ectoplasm around the medium, which is projected away from the medium and draped around the spirit communicator. At the end of the session, the ectoplasm is naturally reabsorbed back in the physical body of the medium.

Personation

Several types of mediumship lead to materialization, which, although clearly designated, blend into each other. The first involves overshadowing, in which the spirit's energy and mind blend with the medium. The medium feels the spirit's physical characteristics and personality within his or her physical body. A medium may utilize clairsentience during overshadowing to describe what he or she is experiencing. As control deepens, the intonation of his or her voice changes and his or her gestures and mannerisms resemble that of the controlling spirit.

The controlling spirit does not have to speak through the medium for others to recognize the visible changes taking place. This is known as personation, which, along with clairsentience and trance speaking, is a mental phase of mediumship. However, the physical features of the medium gradually change as the personation of the spirit communicator occurs.

Transfiguration

Transfiguration involves the construction of an ectoplasmic mask over the medium's face, which is molded to resemble the features of the spirit communicator. Overshadowing and personation can gradually lead to physical transfiguration with the changes in the medium's features observed by all present. Those to the side of the medium will see the ectoplasmic mask over the medium's face. Transfiguration is a popular phase of physical mediumship, yet at the same time it is greatly misunderstood. I have attended numerous transfiguration seances over the years, which rarely resulted in genuine phenomena.

How to Do a Transfiguration Seance

Position sitters in a horseshoe formation with the cabinet in the open section. The medium sits in the cabinet and goes into a deep altered state. Singing loudly always helps to build considerable power. In some cases, the medium may be controlled by various teachers and other guides, who impart philosophy or even personal messages to those present.

Place a red light beneath the medium in order for those in attendance to have a full view of the medium's face and upper body during the proceedings. A small red light with a dimmer is ideal, as the intensity of the light is adjustable during the session. The light should not cast shadows across the face of the medium.

In 1997, at an International Spiritualist Federation (ISF) week at the Arthur Findlay College in Stansted, England, I watched Jean Skinner, a noted British transfiguration medium, demonstrate transfiguration before an audience of at least a hundred people. During the séance, Skinner's guides controlled her and brought through evidential messages for several of those in attendance, while their loved ones transfigured over her face. Séance attendees often mistake shadows cast across the face of the medium for transfiguration. This sort of delusion is common in many circles due to light playing tricks with people's eyes. Genuine transfiguration does not resemble such imaginary faces caused by the dim visibility in the séance room. Mediums sitting for transfiguration should be careful not to distort their faces as they mentally sense the spirit faces overshadow their own. A medium sitting for transfiguration feels the buildup of the energy along with the presence of the spirit operators within his or her energy field.

Sitters will see the medium's features manipulated into the faces of various spirit personalities. A medium may experience the ectoplasm softly flow from his or her eyes, nose, and mouth and even feel cobweb-like sensations over his or her face. Ectoplasm as a fluid-like substance creates an easily pliable mask over the medium's face. Sitters will observe the medium's face seemingly dissolve as his or her facial features change to those of discarnate personalities. Séance attendees should quietly observe the process and provide energy. If a recognizable face transfigures, the sitter will vocally acknowledge this and greet the spirit. Welcoming the communicating spirits builds power and assists them to come in stronger through the medium. The spirit may also entrance the medium while the transfiguration is taking place. In addition, the medium's spirit control may function as an intermediary and describe the transfiguring spirits and relay messages from them. Mediums can also retain more control during the session and bring through messages from the spirits transfiguring without their spirit controls directly speaking. Mediums do not need to be in a deep trance for transfiguration to take place. My teacher Sylvia took a field trip with other members of her home circle in Virginia to the Lily Dale Assembly in New York. Although I could not travel with them, they told me about the remarkable phenomena that took place. Inspirational Stump is a large, concrete-encased stump, where public Spiritualist services and demonstrations of mediumship are held twice a day. In the past, mediums actually stood on the stump to deliver spirit messages to the crowds of hundreds seated before them in the forest location. In order to prevent deterioration, the stump is encased in concrete, and mediums currently may not stand on it while giving spirit messages. Sylvia led the group to the stump around midnight to practice giving messages in the moonlight. The circle members took turns standing on the stump and attuning to the spirit world. When Elizabeth, a wonderful healer from Ghana, stood on the stump, the entire group observed her features transfigure into the face of a guide.

Impersonation

Impersonation differs from personation in that the spirit chemists drape ectoplasm over the entranced medium's body and mold into the spirit's form. This is similar to transfiguration and occurs when there is insufficient ectoplasm to create a materialized form.

Etherialization

Etherialization occurs when the ectoplasmic substance is insufficient to create a solid form. The etherealized forms appear white, semi-transparent and vapory. The forms can be partial or full and often self-illuminated by an almost phosphorescent light.

Amazing Action in the Séance Room

Materialization may initially involve the contact of invisible hands and gradually result in partial or incomplete materializations of hands or sections of the body. Séance attendees may also experience the physical touch of spirits during a physical séance. The editor of a leading Spiritualist publication in the UK attended a dark séance conducted by a popular physical medium. The editor simultaneously felt the alleged spirit control's hand upon his head, and someone wearing shoes stepping on his sock clad foot. The editor, a veteran of many genuine physical seances, was not convinced that the phenomena was authentic as the medium was the only individual in attendance wearing shoes.

Materialized forms often are partial and incomplete. A materialized form may appear to glide across the floor and lack solidity in the lower part of the body. The materializations of animals and objects can also appear in the séance room. A materialization séance generally takes place in the dark since regular light affects the production of ectoplasm. However, materializations can take place in dim lighting or even full light on occasion. Don't let anyone tell you anything different. While materialization in regular light is rare, it does take place under the right conditions. Anne Gehman, a prominent American Spiritualist medium, shared with me her experience of the materialization of her older sister in broad daylight, a year after she had passed over. Horace Leaf (1886-1971), a well-known British exponent of mediumship in the twentieth century, also experienced materializations in full light.

A Veteran Spiritualist's Eyewitness Account

Materialized forms can instantly appear and disappear, or they can gradually build up and dissolve. I conducted an interview many years ago with the late Reverend Joseph Merrill (1903-2001) who served as President for the National Spiritualist Association of Churches (USA). Joseph shared with me the following account of a materialization séance he attended in the 1920s in Boston, Massachusetts.

> *I sat in a darkened room with soft lights on. Present were 32 people with chairs against the wall on three sides. The mother of a friend of mine had passed away about a year before this happened. The chairs we sat on were the wooden folding type that had a crossbar underneath. We*

were up against the wall. If a medium wanted to fake this operation, we would have seen so. He would have to go behind the chairs and into the wall. Neither could they crawl under the chairs.

I felt a nudge at the foot of the chair, so I looked. Right at the floor by the foot of the chair was a white substance the size of a golf ball. I said to my friend; "Oh, something wants to manifest. Let's try to give it room."

We tried to move the chairs, but couldn't. By then the golf ball was seen by everybody in the room. Soon the golf ball started to expand. It grew to the size of an orange. It continued to grow in size; and wax; it took form and had arms and limbs which moved. It was a woman. She moved in circles around my friend's back so that the spiritual form was in the wall. It was his mother, who was recognizable to all present. I could not say, "That was fake."

Table Mediumship

An easy form of physical mediumship for groups to explore is table mediumship involving the use of a wooden table. Sometimes known as table tipping or tilting, the spirit operators utilize the movements of the table to communicate with recipients. Although cumbersome in execution, table mediumship is a dynamic and fun approach to spirit communication. Large, heavier tables are best avoided as they require considerable power to move. Smaller, lightweight wooden card tables and circular tables with three legs are the easiest models to manage and the most ideal for the production of physical movements.

The late Barbara Thurman (1933-2004), a Spiritualist minister and medium, invited me to her weekly development circle that consisted primarily of table mediumship. The closed group met in San Francisco's Japantown and used a small wooden card table for the meetings. I was impressed with the strong psychic force generated by the group and the many evidential messages received. The main drawback to table mediumship is that it is a time-consuming process. I remember as I took part in

Barbara's circle thinking how much easier it was to mentally receive spirit messages compared to the length of time involved in table mediumship. At the same time, I highly recommend mediums experiment with table tipping as the power created leads to the unfoldment of other phases of physical mediumship.

How to Do a Table Tipping Séance

During the session, participants sit around the table with their palms placed lightly upon the surface. Experiment with the positioning of the participants' hands. Allow the thumbs of participants' left and right hands to touch, while the pinky fingers of participants touch the pinky fingers of those on either side of them.

At a physical mediumship workshop that I taught, participants attempted to communicate with the spirit world through table tipping. The excited students, in their enthusiasm to connect with spirit loved ones, unwittingly applied force upon the table, and genuinely believed that spirit power caused its violent movement.

Is physical contact with others around the table absolutely necessary, or are more favorable results achieved without physical contact? It is advisable for groups to experiment with what feels natural, comfortable and, most importantly, produces results. Large groups with a small table can experiment by taking turns during the session. See what arrangement is most effective for obtaining intelligent communications.

Participants not sitting directly around the table function as batteries for the manifestations. A séance involving table mediumship follows the same general procedure for physical circles. Start with an invocation or prayer followed by loud, fast-paced singing. Happy, upbeat songs work best for creating the psychic force necessary for physical manifestations. Often, the table movements begin while the singing is taking place. Participants will feel the power surge from the table up through their hands and arms. Initially, sitters feel as though their hands, which are lightly placed on the table, are floating upon a liquid, flowing surface.

Talk to the spirits and ask them questions. Establish a system of communication with the spirits and wait for their response. One movement for "yes", no movements for "no". As the circle leader or medium slowly recites the alphabet, the spirits move the table when the correct letter is called. In this manner, the spirits transmit detailed, evidential communications to circle participants.

The spirit operators also may produce raps that are created independently from the table. The raps may be extremely loud or soft and emanate from various locations around the room. If a spirit trumpet is present, small taps or percussion may be heard from within the device. The same approach for communication used for table movements should be applied to raps. The raps produced have distinct individuality reflecting the spirit communicator.

The communications obtained through table mediumship is dependent upon the psychic conditions and force available. As with any form of mediumship, the quality and nature of the communication is largely determined by the mentality and intentions of those involved. Table mediumship is not a game or frivolous entertainment. The sensational nature of table tipping attracts many people to this type of mediumship. The purpose of spiritual mediumship, regardless of the mediumistic phase, is to assist recipients with their enlightenment and soul growth.

Levitation

In order to levitate a table, the spirit operators utilize an ectoplasmic rod that exudes from the medium's physical body. It is supported by thinner ectoplasmic threads from the sitter's physical bodies and attaches to the table. The ectoplasmic rod often can be observed connecting to the base under the table. It is not uncommon during a séance for telekinesis or levitation to take place with both large and small objects. Nettie Colburn

Maynard (1841-1892), President Abraham Lincoln's medium, reports a séance in which a grand piano levitated with Lincoln and several other individuals sitting upon it.

The spirit operators also occasionally levitate individuals. Indridi Indridason (1883-1912), a remarkable Icelandic physical medium, demonstrated the levitation of his body many times during his physical seances. The famous nineteenth century Scottish-born American medium Daniel Douglas Home (1833-1886) is best known for this phase of mediumship. Home, in front of witnesses, levitated out a window and reentered the room from another window. The spirit operators levitated world-renowned American mediums Ira Davenport (1839-1911) and William Davenport (1841-1877) on numerous occasions during their extraordinary physical seances. Often, the seances of the Davenport Brothers included the levitation of a spirit trumpet for direct voice and multiple musical instruments played by discarnate musicians. Their younger sister Elizabeth "Libby" Davenport also held seances in which levitating musical instruments would play and move above her head and about the room as she sang in tune.[1]

Slate Writing

Slate writing is a popular physical phase of mediumship that involves the spirit operators producing writing or drawings between two closed slates. A piece of chalk or slate pencil is placed between two pieces of blank slate, which are bonded together, leaving enough space for movement. A question written by the sitter can also be placed inside the slates. The procedure for slate writing varies between mediums. The slates can be placed under or on top of a table during the session, with or without the physical contact of the medium. During the session, scratching will be heard from between the slates as the spirits produce the message. Both

[1] Heagerty, N. Riley, Wizards of the North, The Brothers Davenport, Tempestina Teapot Books, 2019. p. 158.

the writing and drawings that appear on the slates, besides containing highly evidential details, may resemble that of the spirit communicator. Colored chalk is always nice to use. Slate writing is relatively easy to fake. Hereward Carrington (1880-1958), a British psychical researcher, documents several dozen methods of producing fraudulent slate writing utilized by bogus mediums.[2]

At the Wigwam Spiritualist Camp in Onset, Massachusetts, there are several slates on display with drawings and writing in colored chalk that were done in seances held on boats by the Spiritualists generations ago. At one point the entire town was a Spiritualist Mecca with thousands attending the summer camp meetings. Onset was known for materialization seances and many world-renowned mediums served there. Physical seances were also held on Wicket's Island in the bay. Although the town is no longer a Spiritualist camp, the First Spiritualist Church of Onset founded in 1903 and the Wigwam Spiritualist Camp erected in 1894 still hold regular meetings. I love serving both organizations as the spirit energy in Onset is especially powerful.

Precipitated Art

Precipitated Art is an amazing phase of physical mediumship in which the spirit artists produce images on canvas, paper or other material without using brushes or other implements. A blank, stretched canvas or paper are placed on an easel or flat down on a table encircled by the medium and sitters. Paint, ink, or crayons are positioned nearby along with a basin of water to provide power. The colors from the paint, ink, or crayons are gradually precipitated directly upon the surface, with séance participants at times able to observe the procedure take place. Precipitated art commonly depicts portraits of deceased loved ones and

[2] Carrington, Hereward, The Physical Phenomena of Spiritualism, Fraudulent and Genuine, Dodd, Mead & Company, New York, 1920.

spirit guides. However, the spirit artists can precipitate other subject matter such as landscapes or even abstract imagery. A close examination of genuinely precipitated paintings should reveal no brush marks. Maud Lord Drake (1852-1924) experienced the precipitation of spirit faces composed of early morning frost that appeared on the bedroom window. The amazing images naturally disappeared as the frost thawed.

The Campbell Brothers, Allen Campbell (1833-1919) and Charles Shourds (?-1926) and the Bangs Sisters, May (1862-1917) and Elizabeth (1859-1920) are the best-known mediums who worked almost exclusively with precipitated paintings. Examples of precipitated portraits produced through their mediumship are on display at the Lily Dale Assembly in New York, Chesterfield Spiritualist Camp in Indiana, and other locations. Many bogus mediums in their seances manifest phony precipitated art on notecards or silk. At Camp Silver Belle in Ephrata, Pennsylvania, and similar establishments, fraudulent mediums would iron images soaked in ammonia on silk to produce phony precipitated spirit pictures. I was always amused how so many people could believe such nonsense when the faces on the silk resembled photos cut out of magazines.

More Séance Exercises

EXERCISE 61

Transfiguration

Set up the cabinet with a red light positioned, so that the face of anyone sitting in the cabinet is properly observed, without excessive shadows over his or her face. The teacher has members of the group take turns sitting in the cabinet, with others observing and acting as batteries. The power is built up. As circle members sit one at a time in the cabinet, voice any observations of physical transfigurations as well as clairvoyant impressions of spirits. Overshadowing likely will take place. Note other phenomena and conditions that take place such as changes in temperature.

EXERCISE 62

Table Tipping

Sit with a group for table communications. Experiment with the seating of participants around the table. Develop awareness of the distinct vibrations necessary for this phase of mediumship. Connect with spirits and work on receiving evidential messages from them.

EXERCISE 63

Precipitated Painting

Place a clean canvas, stretched over wooden frames, face up upon a table with a palette of paints containing all the colors of the spectrum on a nearby surface. A basin of water can be included to assist with the power. Participants sit around the table with their hands gently touching the edges of the canvas or flat down on the table. Attune to the spirit world and allow the spirit chemists to work with the group for at least an hour. Check the canvas for results.

EXERCISE 64

Precipitated Cards

Distribute blank notecards to participants, who mark their cards for identification. Place the marked notecards along with an assortment of colored crayons, colored pencils, and magic markers in a basket, covered and positioned in the center of the circle. Attune to the spirit world and allow the power to build for at least an hour. Uncover the basket and check cards for results.

EXERCISE 65

Precipitation Box Fun

Build or acquire a precipitation box composed of durable material such as wood Place an open artist sketch pad at the bottom of the box and layer with an assortment of magic markers, colored pencils, and pastels representing all the colors of the spectrum. The box should close at the top so that the interior remains completely dark. Sit daily with the box for the unfoldment of precipitation mediumship. In addition, take the box to any development circles or séances and regularly examine the paper for possible markings. Talk with your spirit chemists daily and follow their suggestions. Ask them to produce markings with specific colors.

EXERCISE 66

Slate Messages

Participants sit around a table with two blank slates with chalk fastened together. The slates are held by the medium against the bottom of the table. Attune to the spirit world and allow the power to build for at least an hour. Open the slates and check for results.

CHAPTER 7

Independent Voice and Trumpet Mediumship

*A*nd when the voice of the trumpet sounded long,
and waxed louder and louder, Moses spake, and God
answered him by a voice. Exodus 19:19 *KJV*

Voice mediumship is a highly evidential expression of physical phenomena that is generally preceded by telekinetic forms of mediumship, such as table movements and the production of rapping and percussion noises. The sounds produced in this dynamic phase of mediumship are objectively heard by the physical ears of those present, who are able to engage in conversation with the communicating spirit personalities. This phase of mediumship is called direct voice, when the sounds emit through a spirit trumpet, and independent voice without the use of such a device.

The sounds produced with independent voice mediumship are heard from all locations within a room, and sometimes in the area of the medium's solar plexus. Direct voice mediumship involves the use of a spirit trumpet, a cone-shaped device, composed of one or more sections, used to direct and amplify the sounds produced.

Leslie Flint (1911-1994), a remarkable British independent voice medium, as a young man in the 1930s, was regularly quieted by other movie attendees, who heard whispers and voices around him in the cinema's darkness. As Flint was not making any noise, at first, he did not understand their accusations. The absence of light is especially important for the unfoldment of voice mediumship. Flint realized his spirit operators had worked on developing his voice mediumship as he sat in the movie theater.[1]

The spirit operators utilize two methods to produce voice phenomena. The first is the manufacturer of an apparatus composed of ectoplasm drawn from the medium, for the purpose of amplifying the spirit voices.

Although this apparatus is usually referred to as an artificial voice box, in reality, it bears no physical resemblance as photographs obtained by psychical researchers investigating Margery Crandon (1888-1941), a controversial Boston, Massachusetts, medium indicate. The apparatus functions in the manner of a microphone and amplifies sounds produced within the medium's subtle body. In the early stages of development, it is common for the voices to resemble those of the medium, because of the source of ectoplasm used to construct the apparatus. The spirit operators extract long strands of ectoplasm from the medium which are positioned on the floor of the séance room around the feet of the participants. The strands are molded into the apparatus used for voice production. The strands connect to the medium, who supplies the vibrations necessary for creating the phenomena. The dark interior of the trumpet can be used to mold the apparatus used in direct voice communication.

The other method that the spirit chemists employ to produce voice phenomena is accomplished through the manipulation of sound vibrations created by the medium and the others present, such as singing and speaking. Here too, the voices produced in the early stages of development, also may resemble those of the medium and others present at the

---

[1] Flint, Leslie, *Voices in the Dark*, Psychic Press Ltd., London, United Kingdom, 1988 Edition. p. 73.

session. In such cases, the strongest evidence is the information and details provided by the purported spirit communicators.

In the beginning, the voices produced typically are faint whispers emitted from within the trumpet or around the room. Slowly, as development continues, the indistinct and muffled voices increase considerably in volume and duration. As proficiency increases, the spirit operators perfectly duplicate the voices of spirit personalities, who can speak in their native tongues and even engage in conversation with sitters fluent in such languages. Unlike a speaker or singer inhabiting a physical body, the sounds produced through voice mediumship do not involve the use of the respiratory system. A voice communication can be lengthy and straight forward without any pause for breath.

Although some voice mediums in the initial stages of development are put into a state of deep trance, it is generally not necessary with this phase of mediumship. Most voice mediums remain completely conscious during the phenomena and can fully take part in the séance, and interact with the communicating spirits. Sensations indicating voice mediumship include drawing sensations in the areas of the throat and solar plexus, combined with a dull pain in the back of the head. In addition, a voice medium's hands in the dark emit strong visible emanations from the fingertips of both hands.

At a voice mediumship session, the sounds are typically whispers or mumbled words and sentences that increase in volume and clarity as séance participants respond with energy. While some voice mediums are limited to the production of only one spirit voice during a session, others possess sufficient power to enable multiple spirit communicators to speak, in some cases, at the same time from various sections of the séance room.

The Spirit Trumpet

A developed telekinetic medium may easily levitate tables and other material objects, but never demonstrate voice mediumship. However, a direct voice medium is always potentially a good telekinetic medium as evident with the levitation of the trumpet.

As previously noted, the spirit trumpet is a device used for the production of voice phenomena, and functions as a sort of psychic megaphone by directing and amplifying the spirit voices to the recipient. A spirit trumpet is generally made out of aluminum or plastic, and constructed in one or more sections. An ectoplasmic apparatus is built by the spirit operators within the darkness of the trumpet, which also serves to stabilize and hold the structure together. This is an ideal environment, as the formation of ectoplasm is hindered by regular light. In addition, the interior of the trumpet concentrates the psychic force for the production of the voice phenomena in the same manner as a spirit cabinet does for other physical manifestations.

Raps and table movements often proceed the production of voice mediumship. Often, tiny raps and percussion are heard within the trumpet followed by whispering and mumbling inside it, or sometimes in the medium's proximity. Ectoplasm for any phenomena is drawn from, and returns to, the body of the medium and is influenced by the subconscious of the medium. The ectoplasm used for voice mediumship is generally drawn from the throat or solar plexus areas of the medium.

Slight movements of the trumpet are followed by full levitation over the heads of circle participants and around the room at great speeds. The trumpet may gently tap seance participants or even forcefully hit them in the head should they attempt to disrupt the session. Kenneth Custance (1904-2003), who with his wife Gladys Custance (1900-1989) taught my teacher Pauline Hathaway, told me the story of a trumpet séance in the 1940s, during which his skeptical father-in-law stood up to grab the levitating trumpet, only to be hit in the head and forced to sit back down. In some seances, there is sufficient power for spirits to simultaneously speak through two or more levitating trumpets in different locations in the room.

It is believed by many Spiritualists that the development of voice mediumship is influenced by climatic conditions, as evidenced by the many voice mediums from the Great Lakes region in the United States and Canada. The Niagara Falls area in particular has produced many mediums with this ability. Physical mediums, in general, also tend to be highly emotional. As such, a medium's temperament greatly affects the production of physical phenomena as his or her energy is directly utilized to create the manifestations.

Tips for Developing Trumpet Mediumship

Sit with the trumpet regularly alone, and with a harmonious circle composed of sympathetic friends.

Never allow others to handle your trumpet.

Sleep with your trumpet and carry it with you as much as possible, so that it is satiated with your vibrations.

Run cold water through the trumpet regularly, especially prior to séance sessions. Don't dry the trumpet after rinsing as the droplets of water are used by the spirit chemists.

Keep a large basin of saline water by the trumpet in the séance room, and add more to it prior to every session.

How to Hold a Physical Circle for Trumpet Mediumship

The same general guidelines for conducting physical circles should be applied for trumpet seances. A spirit cabinet is unnecessary for trumpet mediumship, but it is good to experiment and see what conditions produce the best results. A small room that is adequately heated and ventilated is best. In the beginning, make sure that regular light is completely absent. Completely cover windows and any smaller openings to prevent the inclusion of regular light. Total darkness is best for the initial development of trumpet mediumship. However, consult the spirit operators regularly for instructions on any modifications that need to be made. A potential voice medium will exhibit thin emanations from the tips of their fingers in the dark. The thickness of these emanations will grow thicker overtime as the unfoldment of voice mediumship takes place.

Place the trumpet upright upon a small wooden table in the center of the circle or on the floor. Alternately, position the trumpet sideways on a table with the large section facing the medium or hang the instrument sideways from the ceiling. Hanging the trumpet ensures that energy is saved that otherwise might have been used to levitate the trumpet. In addition, carefully mark the outline of any upright trumpets to document possible changes in position that take place. It is good to paint the trumpet with phosphorescent paint or attach luminous bands around it. That way its movements are observable in the dark.

A medium friend of mine in Massachusetts once attended a physical séance conducted by a noted physical medium from the UK who refused to allow phosphorescent bands to be placed around his trumpet or even brought into the séance room. According to the medium, the light on the bands would interfere with his trance. The séance was held in complete darkness, with no safeguards to prevent fraud and to validate the alleged phenomena taking place.

Trumpet in the Light

A developed voice medium is able to work in regular lighting with his or her mediumship. There is sufficient darkness within the trumpet that enables the spirit operators to create an ectoplasmic apparatus inside that is suitable for communication. Follow the same seating arrangements and procedure for working with the spirit trumpet in full or subdued light. The medium holds the trumpet in his or her palms with the smaller section held up to his or her ear by the recipient. In other cases, the recipient holds the small end of the trumpet with no contact with the medium or the trumpet is positioned sideways on a stand or table. The voices produced in this manner with favorable conditions will be as strong as those produced in the dark.

The extraordinary direct voice medium Elizabeth Blake (1847-1920) held most of her trumpet sessions in the light at her cottage in rural Ohio. The recipient would hold the small end of the trumpet to his or her ear with Blake holding the other end or placing her fingers upon the device to give power. Recipients reported feeling as though the trumpet increased in weight immediately before the voices commenced speaking. Blake also conducted dark seances where direct voice and other phases of physical mediumship took place.[2]

Another noted American direct voice medium Mrs. Cecil Cook (later Mrs. N. S. Themelis) , regularly conducted trumpet sessions in the light for her many clients. She relates, "During one of these bright-light seances, sometimes as many as thirty or forty or even fifty voices will come through, each different. Perhaps four or five will sing."[3]

Maud Lord Drake (1852-1924) was another incredible American physical medium recognized for the demonstrations of voice mediumship in both dark seances and bright daylight that occurred in her presence. Drake's clients included such notables as former US President Ulysses Grant, Leland Stanford, founder of Stanford University, Dr. Julius Seelye, the President of Amherst College, and many others. The spirit phenomena reportedly took place, even while she slept, with her spirit guides loudly singing and carrying on conversations with each other.[4] The remarkable Icelandic physical medium Indridi Indridason's (1883-1912) powerful voice mediumship similarly took place in both the dark

[2] Heagerty, N. Riley, *The Direct Voice, The Mediumship of Elizabeth Blake,* Tempestina Teapot Books, New York. 2017.

[3] Cook, Cecil M., *The Voice Triumphant, The Revelations of a Medium,* Alfred-A-Knof, New York, New York, 1931. p. 225.

[4] Lord-Drake, Mrs. Maud, *Psychic Light, The Continuity of Law and Life,* The Frank T. Reilly Publishing Company, Kansas City, Missouri, 1904.

and regular lighting. Indridason like Lord Drake also exhibited voice phenomenon while he slept with multiple spirits singing and carrying on conversations with each other in both Icelandic and other languages.[5]

The sounds produced through voice mediumship are not limited to human voices, but include explosions, barking dogs, and other sounds. Henry Olcott (1832-1907), a New York journalist, researched the physical mediumship of the Eddy Brothers, Horatio (1842-1922) and William (1832-1932), at their homestead in Chittenden, Vermont, for several months in late 1874. Olcott reported hearing the sounds of an ocean storm, with the whistling of the gale and the force of the waves, at an Eddy family physical séance.[6] The Eddy Brothers were best known for their sensational materialization seances in the dark as well as the light.

A Few Remarkable Displays of Spirit Power

At my teacher Sylvia's home circle, an interesting example of voice phenomena occurred that is worth noting. As I meditated in silence during the circle, I heard the distinct sounds of a rocking chair from a woman seated across from me. At first, I felt annoyed that she would deliberately rock her chair and disturb the others in the group. However, I soon realized, upon opening my eyes that she was sitting in a regular chair, and that the rocking sounds were spirit phenomena. The rocking sounds persisted for over five minutes. At the completion of the circle, the others in the group all reported hearing the same noise. Sylvia always tape-recorded her classes in order to preserve the trance lectures that she regularly channeled from her spirit teachers. Unfortunately, the tape contained no trace of the uncanny sounds on an otherwise perfect

[5] Haraldsson, Erlendur and Gissurarson, Loftur R., *Indridi Indridason, The Icelandic Physical Medium,* White Crow Books, Howe, United Kingdom, 2015. pp. 109-111.
[6] Olcott, Henry S., *People From Other Worlds,* American Publishing Company, Hartford, Connecticut, 1875. p. 111.

recording. At the time, I wondered whether the phenomena had been an example of collective objective clairaudience or independent voice mediumship. The fact that the rocking sounds did not record on the tape leaves this question open.

Another year, I held an informal circle with several of my students in the visiting medium's cottage at Pine Grove Spiritualist Camp in Niantic, Connecticut. As we sat in the power, I heard the muffled sound of heavy, labored breathing coming from one corner of the room.

The phenomena sounded as though someone on a respiratory machine, with extreme breathing problems, was attempting to speak. In addition, the breathing blended in with the sounds of a dehumidifier operating in the same part of the room. My students also heard the breathing and focused their attention upon it.

I told the spirit to move to another section of the room closer to where I was sitting. Immediately, the breathing shifted to that area, and continued for another five minutes before dissipating.

The late Betty Putnam (1905-2004), an outstanding Spiritualist medium, regularly demonstrated independent voice mediumship while she delivered spirit messages from the platform. The spirit voices, fully audible to all, emanated from her solar plexus. Unfortunately, at the auditorium service I shared with Putnam at the Lily Dale Assembly, the voice phenomena did not take place.

At a Spiritualist church in Chicago, I received a small section of a spirit trumpet, which I brought with me to Sylvia's home circle in Virginia that week. I placed the trumpet by my feet as I comfortably sat. Sylvia's husband Joseph Giunta (1937-2009) facilitated the guided meditation that evening for the circle. I heard what sounded as though there was a radio turned on from the space above his head. As Joseph spoke, it sounded as though a recording of Joseph's exact words repeated at a much lower volume. This phenomenon went on for around five minutes. At first I suspiciously wondered whether Joseph somehow was fraudulently producing the sounds. As I analyzed the situation, I concluded that the only explanation was that genuine voice mediumship was taking place. Unfortunately, we did not tape-record this amazing manifestation.

Additional Séance Exercises

EXERCISE 67

Sand Gazing Messages

Fill a glass with grains of colored sand. Sit daily with the glass and take with you to any development circles or seances that you attend. Talk to your spirit chemists and ask them to produce symbols or write names with the sand. Examine the sand regularly for such manifestations.

EXERCISE 68

Egg White Messages

Place the white of a fresh egg in a glass. Sit with the glass by yourself or with a group. Allow the spirit chemists to produce shapes and symbols with the egg white, which can be interpreted by yourself or other mediums. The egg white will change into a colorless fluid and should only be used once.

EXERCISE 69

Trumpet Movement

Position a spirit trumpet with luminous bands, upright on a small table or on the floor, in the center of the séance room. Place a sheet of paper underneath the trumpet and draw its outline. Ask the spirit chemists to work on moving the trumpet. Darken the room and sit by yourself or with others for an hour. Examine the trumpet for possible movement.

EXERCISE 70

Solar Plexus and Throat for Physical and Trance

The medium sits comfortably in a chair with his or her spine erect and his or her arms and legs uncrossed. The medium uses deep breathing to progressively relax his or her physical body and attain a deep meditative state. Next, the medium focuses his or her awareness on the solar plexus, followed by shifting his or her awareness to the throat. The medium brings awareness back down to his or her solar plexus and then back up again to the throat. The medium should repeat this pattern at least a dozen times, while dissociating from his or her physical body and energetically blending with his or her spirit control.

CHAPTER 8

Rescue Work

The rescue circle is a specialized circle focused on providing healing treatments to troubled spirits and helping them move on to a higher level. There are many levels of consciousness in the spirit world. After physical death, spirits travel to a region of the spirit world that corresponds to their level of consciousness. We create our life in the spirit world by our thoughts and actions throughout our physical plane life. It is not as though a recently departed soul is instantly enlightened after leaving his or her physical body. A recently departed spirit brings both positive and negative attributes to the spirit world.

Dysfunctional patterns of behavior and thinking, along with personal defects, are contained with the subtle bodies that interpenetrate the physical body. I often joke that if an individual needs forty years of psychotherapy and does not receive it here, he or she will need to get it in the spirit world once he or she passes over. There are healers and therapists in the spirit world, who assist individuals with emotionally healing and working on their spiritual and moral development.

Thoughts are things as solid and real on a subtle level as material objects are in the physical world. Ugly, negative, materialistic, and selfish thoughts weigh the soul down. Individuals create their own heaven or hell through their own patterns of thinking. The spirit world is all around us and interpenetrates the physical dimension. The denser levels of the spirit world are closest and easiest to access. The lower spheres are inhabited by individuals whose consciousness is polluted by materialistic attachments and base desires.

Murderers, rapists, pedophiles, unremorseful criminals, emotionally imbalanced and other unevolved individuals wallow in the misery there.

The spirit healers and teachers on the higher levels make use of mediumistic rescue circles to help the inhabitants of the lower regions. It is easier for the spirit teachers and healers in the higher realms to utilize rescue circles to help such unevolved souls progress, as the physical plane vibrations are more in accord with the frequency of the lower regions. During a rescue circle, the higher spirits are able to direct troubled spirits to the meeting, where they are permitted to communicate with the rescue mediums. The others in the rescue group provide counseling and healing to the afflicted spirits in a nonjudgmental, therapeutic environment. At times, a rescue medium, with or without a rescue circle, can assist individuals obsessed by unevolved and ignorant spirits. The rescue medium may apply hands-on healing within the energy field as a means to dislodge the spirit.

Intense sexual perversion, hatred and greed attract lower spirits who feed off and encourage negative emotions and addictions. Drugs and alcohol also open the door to similar vibrations in the spirit world. The healthy energetic boundaries that are naturally present are broken by the ill effects of such substances. An individual suffering from mental illness should never get involved with any aspect of psychic and mediumistic development. Psychic unfoldment stimulates the unconscious mind and makes an unstable individual even more unstable, and unable to control his or her psychic sensitivity.

Over the years, I have worked with many mentally ill individuals, who heard voices and experienced severe imbalances. An unstable individual, possessing no protective boundaries, easily opens the door to the negative influences of ignorant, unevolved spirits. An unevolved spirit can naturally influence a weaker mind or a mind on a similar wavelength. There are both psychological and physiological reasons for mental illness.

The lower spirits, due to their lower vibratory frequency, are unaware of the higher spirits and healers who guide them there and work through the mediums in the rescue circle. In some cases, ignorant or imbalanced spirits psychologically influence individuals in the physical world and adversely affect their behavior and mental condition. For example, a spirit person attached to alcohol may decide to hang out around drunks and subtly influence them to continue with their self-destructive addiction. An individual in the spirit world, highly addicted to excessive sexual perversions, similarly may influence his or her victims in the physical world to watch pornography, and engage in perverted sexual acts. This type of situation is known as obsession and involves an unwanted, spirit influence, upon unknowing individuals in the physical world. A mind weakened through drug and alcohol abuse or psychological imbalances is extremely susceptible to negative, external energies and influences from both the physical and spirit worlds.

Many spirits in need of assistance are not necessarily on a lower level in consciousness. Spirits passing over suddenly or unexpectedly may find themselves disoriented upon their arrival in the spirit world.

Victims of wars or natural disasters, small children and others may arrive in the spirit world severely traumatized, unprepared and unable to accept the fact that they have left their physical bodies. In some cases, such individuals believe they are still physically alive, but feel confused as others around them are unable to notice or respond to their presence. A British medium, who performs much rescue work in her trance circles, told me that many of the spirits needing such assistance could not move on because they were waiting for someone.

After physical death, Andre Lutz, a highly materialistic medical doctor, spent many years in these lower hellish regions, before he progressed to a higher spiritual level. As a guide for Chico Xavier (1910-2002), a famous Brazilian medium, he produced many books through automatic writing that detailed his experiences in the spirit world. Lutz describes extensively the various regions of the spirit world, and the mechanics of all phases of mediumship, including rescue work. He also relates the massive relief work put into motion by the higher spirits to assist the large numbers of spirits passing over at the onset of the Second World War.[1]

Dr. Carl Wickland (1861-1945), a medical doctor, operated a clinic in Los Angeles, California, that specialized in the treatment of patients suffering from psychiatric disorders caused by obsessing spirits. During the treatment sessions, Wickland's wife, a developed trance medium, permitted the obsessing spirits to temporarily control her body, while her husband attempted to reason with them, and encourage them to ascend to higher levels. In order to dislodge uncooperative spirits, Wickland invented a static electricity machine, from which he used a short wand to apply low-level electrical shocks to the heads and spines of afflicted patients.[2] Wickland authored two classic books, *Thirty Years Among the Dead* (1924), and *The Gateway to Understanding* (1934), which document the successful and innovative treatments that took place at his clinic.

Rescue mediumship is a highly specialized application of mediumship that requires considerable hands-on mediumistic experience, impeccable morals and spiritual character, combined with expert counseling skills. A rescue medium needs to be comfortable working with denser psychic energies and assisting individuals suffering severe trauma and confusion. The vibrations experienced dealing with ignorant, unevolved spirits in rescue mediumship are rarely exhilarating. Many mediums hold circles

---

[1] Wickland, Carl, *Thirty Years Among the Dead*, Spiritualist Press, London, UK, 1924.

[2] Luiz Andree (Spirit) Received by Xavier, Francico Candido, Translated by Fernando Brito, *Nosso Lar by the Spirit Andre Lutz*, International Spiritist Council, Brasilia, Brazil, 2006.

for rescue work, or spirit release therapy, as the process is presently called, within the worldwide Spiritualist movement. In Brazil, the Spiritualists operate psychiatric hospitals which offer conventional medical treatments for mental illness, combined with mediumistic healing, past life therapy, and disobession treatments.

Some Spiritualists argue that the term rescue circle is a misnomer, since nobody needs rescuing in the spirit world. They assert that rescue mediumship is delusional, as all spirits ascend to the light after physical death. The truth of the matter is that many individuals do not immediately go to a higher level. While the doorway to reformation for all souls is never closed, spiritual enlightenment is not instantaneous. Prayers and healing directed to such spirits assist them considerably with their soul progression. This includes the counseling and support provided in rescue work.

A Brazilian medium occasionally attended my teacher Pauline's Friday evening development class at the Church of Two Worlds in Washington, DC. One evening, she was entranced by an unevolved spirit, who went on for a long time about his problems and how he had wasted his former physical life. At the time, I mainly worked directly with higher guides in my mediumship, so it was educationally beneficial to observe her work.

Frozen to Death

My first experience with rescue mediumship took place on a cold January evening, at my teacher Sylvia's home circle. A little girl, only two years old, entranced Sylvia, and emotionally conveyed to the group how desperately she wanted her mother.

The members of the circle carefully and lovingly addressed the toddler, telling her to go to the light. At the time, I worked in daycare with small children and naturally engaged in conversation with the little girl. I repeatedly encouraged her to go to the light. According to Sylvia, she responded favorably to my suggestions.

The emotional intensity of the little girl pervaded the room. The energy involved was not the higher vibrations associated with Sylvia's spirit teachers, who regularly delivered trance lectures through her. Everyone in the group psychically felt the vibrations. At the conclusion of the circle, Sylvia explained how she felt that the youngster somehow had gotten separated from her mother and had frozen to death.

Joseph's Conversion

When Sylvia dated her second husband, Joseph, she initially kept her mediumship a secret. Gradually, she introduced him to Spiritualism by taking him to a weekly mediumship development circle held in the residence of a medium at the Lily Dale Assembly in New York. Joseph, a medical doctor, worked in the emergency room of a hospital in the Buffalo, New York, area. Although as a physician, Joseph held reservations about the possibility of spirit communication, he investigated the subject with an open mind.

Late one evening, during his shift, at the hospital emergency room, ambulances brought in the victims of a horrific car crash, including a critically injured seventeen-year-old boy. The young man had lost a considerable amount of blood, and, if he was to physically survive, needed an immediate blood transfusion. The medical personnel, who frantically attempted to save his life, could not perform the procedure, because he was a member of the Jehovah's Witnesses, a Christian sect theologically opposed to blood transfusions under any circumstances. Legally, there was nothing that Joseph or the other attending physicians could do to administer treatment, and the severely injured youth passed over.

Joseph and the other emergency room staff were greatly disturbed by their inability to prevent the physical death of their patient. Joseph went home that evening distressed over the incident. He told Sylvia absolutely nothing about what had happened. The next evening, Joseph attended the weekly development circle at Lily Dale with Sylvia. At the circle, Sylvia was entranced by an extremely disturbed spirit, who was in great emotional turmoil over his recent physical death. It took a considerable amount of time and energy for the circle members to finally persuade the distraught spirit to look toward the light and let go of his attachments. Sylvia expressed to me that this rescue in particular was especially demanding. Before releasing control, and going to the light, the disturbed individual, through Sylvia, spoke a final pleading question to the group. It was the spirit's parting words that struck Joseph the most. "The blood-why didn't they give me the blood?" Joseph realized that this was the teenage boy who had passed over the previous evening. In retrospect, it was apparent to Joseph that this incident had occurred to demonstrate to him that it was possible for the dead to communicate through mediumship.

Healing Light for Troubled Souls

Rescue mediumship is healing work. A medium should be motivated by the desire to help others. Too often, people play around with spirit communication as evident with the Ouija board and similar games. A Ouija board is an excellent tool for obtaining quality communications from higher spirits. However, when used for entertainment, it opens individuals up to the spirit world in an unregulated, unsafe manner. Many individuals get into ghost hunting in order to free lost spirits from inhabiting physical locations. The spirit dimension interpenetrates the physical world. In some locations, there are many spirits present. This does not mean that the spirits are haunting the location, or are earthbound and at a lower level.

A director for the *Travel Channel* invited me to appear as a guest on a ghost hunting program with expenses paid for me to travel to a shoot taking place at an old farm house in New Hampshire. The house contained a rich history that dated from the Colonial period. In addition, its basement was used as a hiding place for escaped black slaves, as part of the invisible Underground Railroad. The television show focused on the stars investigating paranormal activity in different allegedly haunted buildings around the country.

The director explained to me how, often, demons, and negative spirits disrupted their shoots at various locations. In the house's basement, many spirits communicated to me associated with the location and the family that lived there. However, none of the spirits were earthbound, or unable to progress. Unfortunately, the entertainment industry, through sensationalistic movies and television programs, inaccurately portrays many aspects of psychic phenomena and mediumship.

At a hypnosis convention, I watched a demonstration of purported spirit release therapy, in which the presenter put a volunteer into a deep trance and asked the spirits afflicting her to speak. Her voice deepened, as the imagined spirits spoke, giving the number of attached spirits stuck in her aura from this life and past lives. I forget the exact number, but it easily was over one hundred and fifty.

I have met many individuals over the years who tell their clients that the reasons for their problems or issues stems from the attachment of negative entities stuck in their auras. While troubled spirit personalities mentally connect through the energy field, it is not as though they are trapped there. It is impossible for anyone to get stuck in anyone's aura. A dysfunctional spirit may psychically connect through an individual in the physical world's energy field, but he or she is not a prisoner of the situation and can leave at any point.

Spiritual healing involves the laying on of hands, and passes and sweeps through the energy fields of an inflicted party energetically breaking such dysfunctional connections. Dr. Carl Wickland's use of electric shocks accomplished the same thing.

Disobession treatments are never successful with only one party receiving healing. Both the spirit and those who are afflicted must seek improvement. The most important aspect of rescue mediumship is assisting the spirits in moving past their blocks and taking responsibility for their spiritual growth. In order for any lasting improvement, individuals must be willing to do their part.

Many times, as part of their growth, spirits will spend time around individuals in the physical world to learn from how they handle various situations in their lives. At many Spiritualist meetings, individuals from the spirit world attend for the purpose of personal enlightenment and healing. Most religious traditions encourage the practice of praying for the departed. In some cases such as Shintoism and similar traditions, ancestral altars are constructed with regular offerings made.

Moral Reformation

In the nineteenth century, it was common to attempt to educate ignorant spirits as they entranced their mediums by reading to them and even teaching them the proper use of language. Education is incomplete without including the development of moral character. It is not enough to learn mundane knowledge, as ultimately self-realization is the purpose of life. Rescue mediumship, and disobsession treatments, differ from exorcism as they are not limited to getting rid of ignorant spirits, but instead concentrate on bringing them healing and enlightenment. Many individuals waste their human lives focused on materialistic pursuits and sense gratification. As the experience of rescue mediumship indicates, our spiritual unfoldment and relationship with God is the most important aspect of our lives.

Rescue Circle Exercise

EXERCISE 71

Spirit Rescue

In this exercise, participants hold a spirit circle following standard procedures and structure. After the energy of the group is sufficiently raised, ask the higher spirits to bring lower level spirits in need of healing.

Participants connect with the spirit healers and the lower spirits receiving care. Compare and contrast the energies between the spirit healers and the lower level spirits. Also, note any details about the spirit healers or lower spirits.

CHAPTER 9

Predicting the Future

In the spirit world, there are guides who possess the ability to see the past, present and future. The skills necessary for accurate prophecy and predictions are not possessed by every guide. Predictions regarding more immediate events are easier to foretell. However, there are some higher guides who can accurately predict events many months and years into the future. The higher spirits possess greater spiritual realization and, as a result, are highly proficient in determining the probable future or karmic patterns of individuals. Some guides may work within the spirit team of individual mediums, who specialize in this aspect of spirit communication.

How do such predictions take place? The higher spirits can read the energy of the individuals involved and see their actions in the present. The complexities involved with individual actions make accurately foretelling future events difficult. However, the higher spirits possess greater spiritual realization and as a result are extremely proficient in determining the probable future or karmic patterns of individuals.

Our future is based on what we do in the present. All physical action begins in the subtle mind. Thinking, feeling and willing are the functions of the mind, which are followed by actions. For every action there is a reaction, such is the Law of Cause and Effect.

Predictions are either of a personal nature for the recipient of the communication, or broader in scope, affecting larger groupings of people and the world. Predictions within themselves are not going to enhance the recipient's spirituality or expedite his or her soul growth. This part of why information about future events is rarely given by the spirit personalities. Sometimes too, a recipient told of a positive future event, may be inclined to passively wait for the situation to unfold, instead of engaging in the actions necessary to bring the event to fruition. Higher spirits are there to provide support and guidance, but they do not interfere with our freewill and the, often, challenging lessons individuals endure within this material world. Mediumship is sacred and should never be confused with fortune telling or superficial information provided for entertainment.

At the Lily Dale Assembly in New York, a woman approached me one summer and stated that I had given her a reading five years before. She told me that at the time she did the session with me that she did not understand what I was talking about, and thought that I was completely crazy. She explained to me that several years after the session, all that I had said during the session came true. As such, she was very grateful for the session, although she did not appreciate it at the time. It is important for mediums to trust the expertise and wisdom of their spirit team, regardless of the reactions of recipients or their lack of understanding of the information conveyed.

A Chaotic Disaster Foretold

Generally, when predictions are conveyed during a session, it is for proving the power of the spirit world. Predictions can be about events in either the near or the distant future. A dynamic and startling example of spirit prediction took place on the evening of Wednesday, March 4, 1987, at my teacher Sylvia's home circle. Sylvia was a fabulous trance medium and facilitated incredibly powerful circles. After an opening prayer, participants were led on a guided meditation followed by an hour or more of sitting in the power, after which participants would share, clockwise around the circle, their experiences and spirit messages for others in the group. It was during the period of silence following the guided meditation that Sylvia would typically allow her spirit teachers to entrance her and speak philosophy to those in attendance.

When Sylvia was entranced, the entire atmosphere of the room dramatically changed. Participants strongly felt the distinct personalities and energies of the various spirit teachers as they worked through Sylvia.

Often, prior to Sylvia's entrancement, participants experienced the chilly psychic breezes associated with physical mediumship filling the room. In this particular class, Sylvia explained her guides had told her that they were going to be working more with bringing through the foretelling of future events.

During the meditation period, one of Sylvia's spirit teachers controlled her and delivered a brief talk. A period of silence followed, during which I could hear Sylvia's breathing, and feel the spirit power concentrated around her. Sylvia proceeded to speak in great detail about a vessel that was sinking and related the panic and chaos experienced by its passengers. In a deep altered state, Sylvia described, how it felt as though she was there as it was taking place, and that there were many people losing their lives. She could strongly sense their fear and terror. She specifically related how she felt it was occurring in the British Channel and off the coast of France.

Upon returning to regular consciousness, Sylvia explained how emotional and intense this experience had been. She felt that the disaster was something happening in the present or very near future, and that there was nothing that any of us could do to prevent it from taking place. Naturally, none of the circle members knew of the tragedy Sylvia had witnessed. The next two days were uneventful with the incident passing from my mind. Saturday morning, March 7, 1987, I saw the newspaper headlines, which described the capsizing of the *MS Herald of Free Enterprise* ferry off the coast of Belgium that resulted in the loss of 193 lives.

How are Such Predictions Beneficial?

Obviously, there was absolutely nothing that anyone in Sylvia's circle could have done to prevent this tragedy. However, the purpose of presenting this prediction was to demonstrate the power of the spirit. Many in Sylvia's group were relatively inexperienced, and such a prediction provided greater understanding and conviction in the reality of the spirit world.

For the same reason, the higher spirits will similarly convey details of events, unknown to recipients, in the present that are taking place at a distance. I describe in an earlier chapter, the Swedish seer Emanuel Swedenborg's vision in 1759 of a fire taking place several hundred miles away in Stockholm. A similar incident occurred in 1905 when a Dane named Emil Jensen entranced the famous Icelandic physical medium Indridi Indridason at a séance in Reykjavik and reported a fire taking place over 1300 miles away in Copenhagen. The details of the fires conveyed by both mediums, although unverifiable at the time, were later found to be completely accurate. A Spirit speaking through a trumpet at a séance held by the famous Davenport Brothers, Ira and William, in Chicago on April 12, 1861, conveyed news of the Confederate bombardment of Fort Sumter over 900 miles distant in South Carolina. An hour later, a telegraph arrived that confirmed the attack.[1]

As a medium, clients often ask questions about what is going to happen in the future in regard to situations in their lives. Mediumship is not fortune telling, but the higher guides provide information about possible future events based on the present circumstances. The higher guides want to encourage individuals to learn spiritual lessons, overcome defects of character and progress in our aspects of their lives. The higher guides are able to assess an individual's current situation, and based on the Law of Cause and Effect, determine probable future events.

[1] Heagerty, N. Riley, *Wizards of the North, The Brothers Davenport,* Tempestina Teapot Books, 2019. p. 155.

Because of freewill, there is always some flexibility. Individuals cannot necessarily prevent events from taking place, but they can choose how to respond to the situation. Each action made creates appropriate reactions. The higher guides see the overall picture in the lives of incarnate spirits. Often the most important aspect of a mediumship session is the guidance, encouragement and healing conveyed. The higher spirits will not interfere with the karma of individuals or take away burdens that are necessary for soul growth.

I Want to Know When My Husband is Going to Die

Many years ago, at a Spiritualist camp, a woman approached me after a church service for a private mediumship session. At the end of the session, I asked her whether she had any questions that she wanted to ask. "I want to know when my husband is going to die."

Part of me wanted to tell her, "Thursday, at 4:30 PM, this week." The husband of the woman was in better health than her. However, she was unhappy with the marriage and wanted to obtain his inheritance. A year later, she got her wish, and he passed over to the spirit world. Guess who showed up for another private consultation with me and wanted to communicate with him? In general, this is not the type of question to ask a medium for even if such information could be predicted accurately, how would such knowledge help the recipient?

Superficial Questions About the Future

"What color sweater will I wear tomorrow?", "What will I eat for tonight's dinner", "How many children will I have?" The higher spirits do not interfere with the decisions we make in our lives, especially those of a mundane and superficial nature. During a session, a woman asked a medium I know for the date of her physical death. In this case, the woman suffered from a terminal illness and wanted to get her estate in order. She was extremely grateful for the date that was given by the guides. The date that came through was accurate.

Mediums need to be careful in giving predictions as people commonly experience great disappointment when the information does not come true. I once referred a client in London to a prominent UK television medium whose reading included many predictions about future events in my client's life. She contacted me after the session to tell me how much she loved it. A few months later my client told me how angry she felt about the session as none of what the medium told her happened how he said it would. I don't know exactly what the medium told her, but I know that individuals often hear what they want to hear during a mediumship session and ignore the rest.

Individuals also do not always do their part to manifest favorable outcomes to the situations in their lives. The higher spirits teach personal responsibility and the need to learn from the challenges we experience. We create our own happiness or misery through how we live our lives. The more an individual lives his or her life in accordance with the laws of God, the more he or she will experience harmonious conditions and happiness. The higher spirits do their best to influence us to progress spiritually and overcome our defects of character. Individuals generally learn the most through hardships and suffering. When we experience personal pain and suffering, we are forced to turn to God for strength and comfort.

Prediction Awareness Exercises

EXERCISE 72

Phone Calls

Whenever the phone rings intuitively discern who is calling and why. Practice this regularly, so that the unconscious mind is programmed to accurately foretell this information.

EXERCISE 73

New Year's Predictions

This is a group exercise for mediumship development groups. At the beginning of the new year, a circle is held with a meditation to connect with the spirit world. Ask the higher guides to influence participants with accurate information predicting events for the new year. Participants write predictions for the year, which are placed in a sealed envelope. A year later, the group meets and the envelope is opened. Review the predictions and see what actually transpired. Then make a variety of new predictions for the coming year.

EXERCISE 74

Elections

Attune to the spirit world. Ask the higher guides to predict the results of upcoming elections in both local and national politics.

EXERCISE 75

Sports

Attune to the spirit world. Ask the higher guides to predict the outcome of athletic competitions for both individual athletes and teams.

EXERCISE 76

Spirit Forecasting

Participants pair up, hold each other's hands, and attune to the spirit world. The medium connects with a guide who provides a prediction about the recipient that will take place within the next three days. Next, the guide conveys a prediction concerning the recipient that will occur in three months. Finally, the guide makes a prediction for the recipient that will transpire in a year. Take turns working. Participants should carefully record the details of the predictions and share feedback with each other at the specified periods of time.

CHAPTER 10

Out-of-Body Travel Made Easy

O ut-of-body travel, or *Astral Projection*, is not a phase of mediumship, but as a practice quickly awakens dormant psychic abilities. As souls, we inhabit a temporary physical body, interpenetrated by layers of subtle coverings or bodies. After physical death, we vacate the physical body and continue to exist in the spirit dimension. We don't have to wait until we pass over to experience the spirit world and connect with our spirit loved ones and guide. It is easy to journey out of the physical body. All it takes is regular practice combined with a strong desire to succeed.

My first mediumistic experience at the age of two and a half occurred in a partial out-of-body state. My grandfather, on my mother's side, conversed with me with objective clairaudience. I could see and engage in conversation with him. It is extremely common for people to travel out of their physical bodies, in the manner of sleepwalking, while in the dream state. These experiences are generally remembered as vivid dreams entailing flying or meeting with deceased loved ones and spirit guardians.

Near-Death Experiences (NDE's) are an involuntary form of out-of-body travel that take place unexpectedly as a result of an accident or sudden shock. For example, an individual who is seriously injured in a car accident observes his or her physical body lying in the road.

In many Near-Death Experiences, the individual is told by higher spirit guardians that it is not his or her time to physically die and is sent back to his or her physical body. Individuals commonly undergo a great spiritual awakening because of such an experience, and some even find their psychic abilities heightened. Years ago, I headlined several mediumship presentations in California moderated by best-selling author Dannion Brinkley. In his books, Brinkley describes his Near-Death Experiences, his journey to the spirit world, and the interactions with angelic beings that took place.

The Thinker

My teacher Pauline recounted many personal experiences to me involving her mediumship, including a remarkable out-of-body experience. As a student medium, Pauline regularly attended a mediumship development circle at the First Spiritualist Church of Onset. At the time, Pauline suffered from a medical condition that required surgery. The hospital scheduled her for the operation on the same evening that the church development circle met. In the hospital, although Pauline received anesthesia for the procedure, she retained her consciousness and floated up toward the ceiling, above the operating table. Pauline looked down and observed the physician and nurses performing the operation on her physical body.

At the same time, Pauline simultaneously observed the activities taking place at a distance with the development group at the church, where the circle members chanted affirmations and directed healing energy to her and others. Pauline related to me how she watched the healing energy move from the circle and enter her physical body lying below her. She also observed a man in the spirit world, who sat with his fist on his chin, in a manner similar to the French sculptor Rodin's

The Thinker. The spirit stared into what resembled an older model computer monitor.

The man did not move or say anything. He merely sat there and looked at the screen. Pauline psychically knew that he was in the process of reviewing his life. He was thoroughly examining his entire life, and especially paying special attention to particular areas that he did not do well in. Pauline ascertained that this spirit was not being judged by any outside force, but was having to evaluate his own life. It was not as though the man had committed major crimes or injustices. Instead, it was the little things that he had done wrong that mattered the most, which he had to review more than once. In the spirit world, individuals often encounter deceased relatives and spirit guardians. In some cases, individuals experience a life review, in which they review and assess their actions throughout their entire physical life. A life review entails more than merely the experience of the individual, but includes the effect of his or her conduct upon others he or she has interacted with.

Easy Steps for Astral Travel

The practice of learning out-of-body travel is easy. In general, out-of-body travel takes place on an unconscious level for most people during the sleep state. The trick is learning to move from unconscious travel to conscious, deliberate projection. In order to induce a conscious out-of-body experience, I recommend focusing attempts prior to physically awakening. This way the physical body is relaxed with less unconscious bodily resistance.

Mental Programming.

Combine a strong desire for out-of-body travel with continuous practice of the out-of-body travel exercises in this book.

Lucid Dreaming.

Train the unconscious mind for conscious awareness in the sleep state.

Common Sensations Experienced.

Conscious out-of-body projection often starts out with the participant lying down. A half-asleep physical body is best. It is common to experience strong vibrations that start at the toes and surge up throughout the entire body. The vibrations are intense, like waves and quicken with intensity. If you are lying on a bed, it will feel as though the entire bed is physically shaking, although this is not the case. In most cases, the physical body is in a rigid trance.

An Interesting Experience

In one of my first conscious projection experiences, I felt waves of energy move from my feet up through my spine; I experienced an expanding feeling in the upper part of my body as my consciousness traveled up to my third eye. I perceived sparkles of pure white light directly in front of me. At the same time, it felt as though my entire physical body was shaking. I experienced myself move headfirst and literally pop through my third eye at my forehead. I floated slowly up toward the ceiling above my bed, where I viewed the close-up details of a poster hanging there. After this experience, it was fairly easy for me to induce the vibrations, and I regularly began to travel out of my body both consciously and unconsciously.

The Speed of Thought

Have you ever noticed a plane pass overhead and heard, a few moments later, the booming roar of its engines? The speed of sound is fast, and the speed of light even faster. The stars we see in the night sky are actually light years away. In the out-of-body state, an individual can travel faster than the speeds of sound or light. I remember traveling out of my body at a super speed with the surroundings on either side of me a blur, as I moved quickly forward.

Once, while traveling in this manner, I deliberately thought of going to another location, and, immediately, my flight came to an abrupt halt. I spun around before I regained my bearings and started up again. In terms of out-of-body travel, the process involves thought and intent on the part of the traveler. It is best for the traveler to focus on individuals that he or she is emotionally connected with over a physical location. In the subtle body, the individual possesses telescopic vision and is able to see distant scenes close up.

The Major Blocks for Out-of-Body Travel

Out-of-body travel is easy to induce with the right approach. It is essential for the individual to identify blocks that prevent the experience from taking place. Major Blocks for out-of-body travel include:

The analytical mind gets in the way.

This is a typical block that infers not only with astral projection, but other forms of psychic ability and mediumship. This block is best overcome by regular meditation and dissociation exercises. It is difficult to calm an untrained mind. However, the tendency to analyze gradually diminishes, as the student progressively learns to relax his or her physical body and mentally detach from uncontrolled thoughts within the mind.

Astral travel is best as a spontaneous occurrence. When the mind is focused elsewhere, and not in the way, dislocation of the astral body from the physical body, naturally takes place. While the physical body is asleep, out-of-body experiences occur with many people in a manner similar to sleepwalking.

Fears associated with being out of the body. Dying, not being able to get back in, fear of being in an uncomfortable environment.

Many students allow their fears, both conscious and unconscious, to adversely affect their ability to disconnect from the physical. Common fears include the concern that disconnection from the physical body will lead to physical death or an inability to reenter the physical body. Other common fears include feelings of discomfort associated with being in the out-of-body environment and contact with spirit personalities.

The best solution to alleviate such fears is to reprogram the mind using hypnosis and positive suggestions to anticipate and respond to the experience of out-of-body travel in a positive light. Fears often are deeply buried within the unconscious mind. It is important that such issues are constructively handled by the individual lest they adversely impact his or her psychic development.

The physical bodies built-in defense mechanisms which result in resistance.

Souls function in the material world through the physical body. Displacement of the subtle form from the physical form naturally results in unconscious defense mechanisms, or physiological reactions, to prevent such disconnection from taking place. Physical and mental tension prevents the movement of the subtle body from the physical. This is why out-of-body excursions frequently take place in extreme situations involving shock, such as with Near-Death Experiences, or while asleep. Regular meditation and exercises that result in deeper levels of altered states of consciousness and disassociation from the physical body are the best methods for overcoming such resistance. The practice of out-of-body travel, once mastered, enables the medium to consciously project from the physical body to interact with his or her spirit helpers and others in the spirit world. A byproduct of out-of-body travel is that it activates the psychic senses and opens the door for direct communication with the spirit world. Many mediums working in deeper levels of trance experience out-of-body travel. For example, Cora L. V. Richmond (1840-1923), world-renowned trance medium, often traveled to the spirit dimension while her spirit teachers lectured through her.[1]

Astral Travel Exercises

EXERCISE 77

Prelude to Blast Off

This exercise can be done alone or directed by a teacher in a development group. Lying flat on the back, progressively relax the entire physical body starting with the toes up to the top of the head. Feel as though the upper part of the physical body is expanding. Pick a point on the ceiling above and focus your vision and mind upon it. Mentally project your awareness, as though you are mentally going to the point. This exercise should be practiced repeatedly with both the eyes open and closed.

EXERCISE 78

Around the Ceiling

This exercise can be done alone or directed by a teacher in a development group. Lying flat on the back, progressively relax the entire physical body starting with the toes up to the top of the head. Feel as though the upper part of the physical body is expanding. Focus your gaze on the upper left-hand corner of the ceiling, from where you are lying, to up near the ceiling. Attempt to mentally project your awareness to it.

Next, shift your awareness across the ceiling to the upper right-hand corner in front of where you are lying. Again, project your awareness

---

[1] Richmond, Cora L. V., *My Experiences While Out of My Body And My Return After Many Days, Part I and Part II,* Modern American Spiritualism Publishing, St. Louis, Missouri, 2002 Edition.

to it. Continue by shifting your awareness back to the upper right-hand corner, behind you, and again projecting your awareness to it.

This is followed by again, shifting your awareness straight across to the left-hand corner behind you, by mentally projecting awareness to it.

Next, awareness is brought back to the starting point with focus to that point. Basically, the focus is shifted around the room from corner to corner from where you are lying. Movement around can be clockwise or even backward or counterclockwise. This exercise is perfect to do while lying in bed, early in the morning or late at night.

EXERCISE 79

Shifting Awareness

This exercise can be done alone or directed by a teacher in a development group. Lying flat on the back, progressively relax the entire physical body starting with the toes up to the top of the head. Feel as though the upper part of the physical body is expanding. Focus your gaze on the upper left-hand corner of the ceiling, from where you are lying, to up near the ceiling. Attempt to mentally project your awareness to it followed by returning back down to your starting point.

Next, shift awareness to the upper right-hand corner in front of where you are lying. Again, project your awareness to it followed by returning back down to your starting point. Bring your awareness back down to the starting point. Continue with shifting awareness behind you to the upper right-hand corner followed by returning to the starting point and finally back again to the upper left-hand corner and again to the starting point.

This movement should be done multiple times, both clockwise and counterclockwise. This exercise is perfect to do, while lying in bed, early in the morning or late at night.

EXERCISE 80

Astral Travel Dream Journal

Keep a journal of out-of-body experiences that occur consciously and on an unconscious level in the sleep state. Record any interesting dreams that stand out. Keeping a journal assists students in programming their minds for out-of-body travel. It also will assist with developing the ability to retain conscious awareness or lucid dreaming while in the sleep state.

EXERCISE 81

Moving Arms

This exercise can be done alone or directed by a teacher in a development group. Lying flat on the back, progressively relax the entire physical body starting with the toes up to the top of the head. Feel as though the upper part of the physical body is expanding.

Go into a deep altered state of relaxation, yet retain conscious awareness. While you are in this state, attempt to raise the arms of the subtle body. The physical arms along with the entire physical body should remain completely immobile. This exercise works best before falling asleep and early in the morning prior to fully waking and increases awareness and the subtle bodies.

EXERCISE 82

Stomach Rotation

This exercise can be done alone or directed by a teacher in a development group. Lying flat on the back, progressively relax the entire physical body starting with the toes up to the top of the head. Feel as though the upper part of the physical body is expanding.

Go into a deep altered state of relaxation, yet retain conscious awareness.

While in this relaxed state, practice rotating the subtle body over onto the side, followed by onto your stomach, and then back again. Attempt this exercise as much as possible on both the left and right sides. This exercise works best before falling and early in the morning prior to fully waking and increases awareness of the subtle bodies.

EXERCISE 83

Lifting Out Underneath

This exercise can be done alone or directed by a teacher in a development group. Lying flat on the back, progressively relax the entire physical body starting with the toes up to the top of the head. Feel as though the upper part of the physical body is expanding.

Go into a deep altered state of relaxation, yet retain conscious awareness. While in this relaxed state, attempt to project out of the physical body, moving underneath your prone physical body, instead of moving above it. Attempt this exercise as much as possible. This exercise works best before falling asleep and early in the morning prior to fully waking and increases awareness and the subtle bodies.

EXERCISE 84

Astral Visit

Pick a target individual you know and visit him or her in your astral body at a set, mutually convenient time, when he or she is either conscious or asleep. Make notes of your experience and get feedback from the target if he or she could sense your presence.

CHAPTER 11

Past Life Mediumship

*A*s a person puts on new garments, giving up old ones, similarly, the soul accepts new material bodies, giving up the old and
useless ones. Bhagavad Gita 2.22

Past life information is a dynamic aspect of spirit communication
that rightfully should be included within the typical mediumship session.
It is not uncommon for a medium to receive details about past physical
incarnations experienced by the recipient.

Many mediums trained in traditional Spiritualism are taught that
information about past lives should not be presented, as the purpose of
spirit communication is solely on providing evidential communication
that demonstrates the survival of the personality after physical death.

Furthermore, unlike evidential information, which in most cases may
be validated, descriptions and details about alleged past lives are generally
impossible to substantiate. The fact that these points are completely true,
however, does not prevent such information from coming through during
a session. It goes to reason that the higher guides, in charge of facilitating
the exchanges that take place during mediumistic sessions, feel that there
is a great need for certain individuals to receive such information. Those

who belittle the relevance of past life readings forget that a session with a trained medium is carefully planned and orchestrated by the higher guides, who put considerable effort into determining its content. It is important to remember that the higher guides set the agenda for every mediumistic session with what they feel is for the highest good of the recipient and the spirit communicators.

I have done mediumship sessions for decades for many thousands of people. Rarely are details about past physical incarnations the focus of the sessions. In most cases, the content for my mediumship sessions comprises both evidential details about the spirit communicators, along with practical advice and spiritual guidance for the recipient. Often, a particular spirit personality will come through the strongest with other communicators piggybacking off his or her energy. Although spirit communicators will impart evidential information to prove survival and for recognition, they will also offer their own opinions along with spiritual guidance provided by highly developed guides. The higher guides rarely come through during the typical mediumship session. Instead, they rely on intermediaries connected to the recipient to convey practical guidance and advice.

Invaluable Information

Mediumship students training to receive evidential spirit messages often do not recognize the value of a past life reading. Many mediumship students ask me how information about a previous incarnation benefits the recipient of a past life reading. I explain that the blocks and dysfunctional patterns that affect many people often originate from past conditioning either in this life or, in some cases, past physical incarnations. There are many therapeutic approaches that assist individuals achieve mental balance and overcome disharmonious thought patterns and behavior. As a medium, I learn much from the individuals who come to me for personal sessions. Often, the higher spirits impart much higher wisdom and guidance to assist those I am working with. As such, the healing and transformative power of a mediumship session is amazing.

The healing experience is not limited to evidential communications that comfort the bereaved, but includes the supportive guidance that enables individuals to identify and overcome personal blocks, and achieve a greater connection with God and themselves on a soul level. It is not uncommon for clients to relate the therapeutic benefit experienced in a single mediumship session as far greater than years of conventional psychotherapy or other psychological treatments. In order for a healing to be complete, past life information is an absolute necessity in many cases. Once we identify the reasons various unnecessary patterns of thinking or actions are in our lives, then we can apply appropriate means to reprogram ourselves in a healthier manner. If dysfunctional thinking or actions in our present are results of past life situations, it is imperative that such experiences are harmoniously resolved and replaced with positive thoughts and behavior.

A young woman consulted me for a mediumship session. The guides showed me a vision of her in a past incarnation as a tall, powerfully built, bearded male in robes with an extremely aggressive and authoritarian personality. The guides explained that the recipient still retained this forceful temperament and felt out of place in her petite female body. The woman could relate completely to this information as she understood that her physical body did not match her truculent personality.

In another session, I worked with a student of mediumship, who was Jewish by birth. The guides revealed to me that in the recipient's most recent past life; he had tragically died in a Nazi concentration camp during the Second World War. They explained how the recipient suffered severe trauma and reincarnated relatively quickly without receiving adequate healing.

As a result, the recipient continued to experience psychological imbalance in his present life. The details conveyed by the guides assisted the recipient significantly in his personal healing process.

A Past Life Animal Reading

I did a mediumship session once for a woman who included her small dog in the session. I held the small paws of the dog as she sat on my client's lap. The higher spirits showed the dog's past life as a lioness in Africa and that she was chained up and killed by people who feared that she would hurt their children. The lioness experienced great trauma and did not stay long in the spirit world. As a result, the dog is distrustful of people and becomes territorial and protective of the ones she trusts and loves.

The Soul is Transcendental

According to ancient Vedic scriptures, the eternal soul gradually transmigrates through numerous species of life until taking birth in a human body. The particular body we inhabit is based on the development of our consciousness. We receive a suitable material body based on the qualities that we cultivate. Our material desires and attachments determine what type of physical body we receive in our next birth. Souls are qualitatively the same regardless of species or temporary form. However, a soul in an animal body is locked into instinct and cannot think about God or the highest purpose of life.

Past Life Details

Many mediums at my workshops ask me how they should prepare to receive past life information. I explain that past life details will come through strongly during a mediumship session, if the knowledge of such information will enhance the spirituality of the recipient or assist in his or her personal healing. Tell your spirit teachers and those in your spirit team that you would like to receive such information. The content of the medium's mind is especially important for mental mediumship. The medium's education and overall life experience affect the nature and quality of potential mediumistic communications. This is especially true for evidential messages that focus on recognizable details pertaining to the spirit communicators. The spirit team extracts memories and knowledge, stored deep within the unconscious mind of the medium, and utilizes such information as frames of reference.

This process is also relevant with past life readings. Mediums who wish to unfold this aspect of their mediumship should attempt to study and learn as much about world history as possible. A medium with knowledge of historic events from a variety of cultures, countries, and time periods, holds an advantage in recognizing such details during a session. As a child, I was always extremely interested in history and spent hours reading books on the subject. I especially am fascinated with military and ancient history, and as a result, I am familiar with such details within the context of a mediumship session. For example, I can generally identify the rank, nationality, branch of service, and era of spirit personalities who present themselves to me wearing military uniforms. My spirit team regularly uses my knowledge of history for both evidential and past life communications.

It is highly beneficial for a medium to possess a basic understanding of world and regional histories. Ignorance of major civilizations, religions, cultures and historic trends is extremely detrimental for cultivating past life mediumship. What matters the most with past life information are the patterns or tendencies from those incarnations that are relevant in the present. Often, despite my extensive knowledge of history, I receive information about past life patterns and how they affect the recipient's present situation, without specific details about the historic period.

Objections to Past Life Readings

I know an ordained Spiritualist minister and medium who is aggressively opposed to the concept of reincarnation, and who angrily stormed out of a mediumship session in London when the medium described his alleged past lives. In his view, reincarnation, or physical rebirth, is impossible, and any information about past incarnations given during a mediumship session is completely rubbish. It is important for mediums to remember that the higher spirits, who orchestrate mediumship sessions, avoid including information that would upset or disturb the recipient. Obviously, in the above case, the medium's helpers should have kept their mouths shut.

The prominent American medium Anne Gehman vehemently opposed the inclusion of past life information in mediumship sessions. Anne told me that in her younger years she investigated the validity of reincarnation by receiving sessions from many of the leading past life readers. Anne explained to me that none of the details about her alleged past lives in various eras described by such psychics matched. Anne did not believe in reincarnation. She explained to me how souls in the spirit world would eventually lose their individuality and merge back into an impersonal ocean of spirit. New souls created from this vast reservoir could include the recycled memories of the lives of such spirits. Such information could be read by psychics.

Anne approached her investigation of past life readings intelligently. Were the past life readers she consulted fraudulent, deluded or unknowingly reading the recycled memories of spirits? Information given by a medium about an alleged past life should never be blindly accepted. The content of any mediumistic communication should always be scrutinized. The higher spirits will go out of their way to validate such details through other mediums or directly through past life recall. Talk with your higher guides and insist on such validation.

Past Life Reading Exercises

EXERCISE 85

Past Life Connections

Participants pair up, hold each other's hands, and connect with the spirit world. The guides show details about a family member or friend in the present life of the recipient, who was connected in a previous physical incarnation. The guides present details about this individual's role in this past incarnation and how this affects his or her present relationship. Both sides work.

EXERCISE 86

Past Life Health

Participants pair up, hold each other's hands, and connect with the spirit world. The guides show details about the physical health conditions and how this condition is a carryover from a past life situation. Take turns working.

EXERCISE 87

Past Life Patterns

Participants pair up, hold each other's hands, and connect with the spirit world. The guides show negative patterns in the present life and details about a past life that contribute to them. Take turns working.

EXERCISE 88

Past Life Blessings

Participants pair up, hold each other's hands, and connect with the spirit world. The guides present positive attributes and qualities of the recipient in the present life and details about a past life that resulted in acquiring them. Take turns working.

EXERCISE 89

Soul Objectives

Participants pair up, hold each other's hands, and connect with the spirit world. The guides show the soul development of the recipient, including patterns from past lives, and the many learning objectives for this life. Take turns working.

EXERCISE 90

History Lesson

Study history regularly in a broad sense, as well as focused on particular areas of interest. Spend time reading history online and in books. Learn about past cultures, religions and civilizations. Historic knowledge in the mind provides a frame of reference for the spirit guides to extract for past life readings.

EXERCISE 91

Past Fashion

Study the clothing of past and present civilizations and cultures. Familiarize oneself historically with military uniforms, indigenous fashion, costumes and dress. Historic knowledge in the mind provides a frame of reference for the spirit guides to extract for past life readings.

EXERCISE 92

Three Past Lives

The subject sits in front of a group. Individuals in the group take turns connecting to their guides and receiving information about three past lives of the subject in 1945, 1880 and two thousand years ago. Participants should not allow the information received by others influence what they receive and share. Are the lives described by the different mediums the same for the time periods? Take turns working. Allow each member of the group to be read by the others.

EXERCISE 93

More Past Lives

The subject is read privately in succession for ten minute sessions by multiple mediums from a group. Each medium describes three past lives of the subject from 1900, 1500, and 1000. Are the lives described by the different mediums the same for each time period? Take turns working. Allow each member of the group to be read in this manner by the others.

CHAPTER 12

Essential Practices for Dynamic Mediumship

Mediumship development is a lifelong endeavor. As a skill, there is always room for improvement. Mediums should also always strive to expand on a personal level. I have known many mediums from all over the world. Some mediums strive to grow on a personal level as well as attain greater proficiency with their mediumistic abilities. Other individuals are comfortable to stay where they are at and do not try to improve their lives or expand their mediumship. Personal growth and mediumship development cannot be separated. What essential practices can mediums do regularly to improve themselves and the quality of their mediumship?

Meditate

Meditation is communion with God and involves doing within. Where is God? God is all around us as an impersonal energy or universal force, but as a personality God is seated within our hearts. Meditation for realization of self and God differs from the process of sitting in the power. While sitting in the power involves connecting to the power of God and the spirit forces, its primary focus is on strengthening the connection between the spirit operators for mediumistic attunement.

Meditation is essential for self-growth and spiritual development. Psychic and mediumistic development within yourself differs from spiritual unfoldment. Spirituality is about our relationship with God and cultivating higher qualities and overcoming materialistic tendencies and imperfections.

I took part in my first meditation group as a child. I learned a yogic meditative process that involved silent mental repetition of a mantra. I instantly loved the practice, although the adults in the group did not like that I could not sit still in my seat and disturbed them by moving about. At the time, I wanted to be a yogi and appreciated meditation greatly as a practice. Later I studied traditional Shotokan karate, a meditative discipline and Japanese martial art, in which I gained great inner awareness and discipline over my physical body and mind.

Many systems of meditation exist and involve either the use of mantra or silence in their approach. Both silent meditation and mantra meditation are valuable for self-discovery and spiritual devotion. In silent meditation, practitioners go deep within their minds and learn to separate themselves as the observer from their thoughts. The presence of God is experienced when the excess clutter is removed. Individuals wrongly identify with the impermanent thoughts that come and go within their minds. The practice of silent meditation leads to greater clarity and calmness, qualities necessary for dynamic mediumship.

Mantra meditation involves the repetition of a mantra silently or aloud. The practitioner's mind easily wanders during silent meditation. The advantage of mantra meditation is that practitioners can direct their attention on the mantra should their minds lose focus.

I prefer chanting mantras aloud over silently in my mind. I also love singing mantras with others in a process called kirtan. Kirtan is especially powerful, as the Divine presence is always experienced even more intensely in the company of other lovers of God.

Meditation should be done daily. If we don't brush our teeth, they yellow and eventually decay and fall out. Meditation cleans the heart of unwanted qualities and obstacles on the path to God realization.

A medium at the Lily Dale Assembly was extremely jealous of his wife's excellent mediumship abilities. He desperately wanted to surpass her level of expertise. He was unemployed because of a workplace injury, with much time on his hands. He decided to meditate in his bedroom closet for ten hours a day to outdo his wife and gain greater psychic powers. His mediumship abilities, much to his disappointment, did not instantly improve. He eventually got bored and abandoned his pursuit. You cannot rush mediumship or force your development. Mediumship is natural and progressive and goes hand in hand with our emotional growth and spiritual evolution.

Practitioners of yoga perform their spiritual practices and meditation two hours before sunrise. The energy is purer at this time and easier for meditative practice. Mediums don't need to meditate early in the morning, but they should meditate daily, ideally at the same time. If possible, create a special space within the home for meditation and spiritual practice. Many mediums keep a séance room in their residences that they use only for spirit communication and healing.

An altar with pictures or deities of God and saintly teachers is also beneficial for focusing one's attention on the spiritual. Many Hindus worldwide keep altars in their homes for worship and meditation. The vibrations in a space that is used exclusively for spiritual growth exude the Divine presence. Spirituality is not about adherence to particular religious tradition or dogma; it involves awareness of our true identity as eternal spirits and our eternal loving relationship with God.

Make meditation a daily practice. Meditation as a process purifies our hearts and enhances our lives in many ways. A medium should not meditate solely for furthering his or her mediumistic abilities. However, the benefits of regular meditation are many for practicing mediums. Meditation helps mediums achieve a deep altered state, attain a calm receptive mind, increase their rate of vibration, and discipline their mediumship.

Sit in the Power

Sitting in the power, as previously noted, differs from meditation in that the focus is on strengthening the connection with the spirit world for mediumship development. A medium raises his or her personal vibration and mentally attunes to the spirit world. The spirit operators lower their rates of vibration and mentally and energetically connect with their medium. Sitting in the power should be done daily, along with prayer and meditation for self and God realization. Sitting in the power also takes place with others in a development circle. The increased vibration of the group creates a collective energy field in which the spirit helpers work with participants and unfold their mediumistic abilities. A medium should sit in the power daily for at least a half hour and at least once a week with a development circle.

The power builds overtime, and the medium's attunement to the spirit world is considerably strengthened. Make an appointment with the spirit world and keep it. Sit in the power at the same time each day. Sitting in the power allows the spirits developing a medium to work with his or her chemistry and unfold his or her spiritual gifts.

Pray

Meditation is listening to God. Prayer is talking with God. Pray all the time to God. Converse with God. Talk as much as possible with God. God is both impersonal and personal. You cannot talk with an impersonal force, but you can talk to a loving parent or a dear friend. God is not limited and responds to our devotion and love. Prayer opens the door to the higher spiritual dimensions. Mediumship is a two-way street. Individuals often focus on what they receive from the spirit world. Talk with the spirit operators as much as possible. You are not praying to them; you are building a relationship with them and strengthening the connection.

Love is expressed through what we do or our service to others. God works through his instruments. The higher spirits work through mediums. The Roman Catholic saint, Mother Teresa of Calcutta, said: "Prayer in action is love, love in action is service." Silver Birch, a spirit teacher who was channeled through the British medium Maurice Barbanell, stated: "There is only one prayer-that prayer is, 'Teach me how to serve." There is no greater work, no greater love, no greater religion, no greater philosophy than that you say ", I want to serve the Great White Spirit and His children.""[1]

Expand Your Frame of Reference

The spirit operators utilize the contents of a medium's mind as frames of reference for communications. The more substantial the content is, the greater their ability is to express themselves through the medium. A master violinist's music will still sound horrible if played on an instrument missing several strings. Fill your mind with knowledge and intellectually grow as much as possible. Mediumship requires dedication and teamwork. The spirit team is restricted in communication by the limitations of the medium. Make an effort to improve yourself and educate yourself past your present level. Read as many books as possible on a variety of subjects. Doing this will substantially improve the depth of your mediumship abilities.

Emotional Growth

Work on yourself emotionally. Stay balanced and harmonious in body and in mind. Mediumship development is connected to the

---

[1] Austin, A. W., *Teachings of Silver Birch,* Psychic Press Ltd, London, UK, 1983 Edition. p 79.

endocrine system. Mediums are highly sensitive, often experiencing massive mood swings. Many mediums are easily affected by the surrounding energies. In addition, many mediums and healers bring much baggage from the past into their development and work with the spirit world.

Psychic and mediumistic development is fine, but within itself it is incomplete without spiritual and emotional growth. A wounded healer possesses the insight and empathy to effectively ease the pain experienced by others going through the same or similar situations. However, an individual cannot save another from drowning if she or she is weighted down with their own issues. Wounded individuals often get involved with mediumship development as part of their healing process and journey of self-discovery. In addition, many individuals wrongly equate psychic and mediumship development with spiritual growth.

Many experienced mediums are mentally imbalanced and need therapy. The higher spirits work through our minds and subtle bodies. Emotionally healing clears negative patterns of thinking from the mind and removes unresolved traumas from the heart. Many mediums do not work with spiritual healing, nor do they receive it. Their thinking is not constructive, and their behavior greatly dysfunctional. Negative thinking and behavior can be changed. Mediums need to recognize their issues and do their part to heal. Ask God and the spirit healers for help. God will direct the right connections and resources in the physical world to help with the particular situations or issues.

Mediumship development is not about mastering techniques or reading books. The most important growth takes place because of how the medium handles the mundane situations in life. The spirit operators work through the energy fields and mind of the medium. A happy, stable mind is harmonious to work through. The spirit healers impart healing for broken physical bodies and minds.

The medium's emotional balance relates directly to his or her physical health and vice versa. A holistic approach is best for mediumship development. Right living and proper thinking create harmony. A poor diet destroys the physical body and mind. Unhappy individuals project their unhappiness toward others in the form of unkindness and negativity. This energy comes back to affect them in a disharmonious manner.

Many mediums are jealous of other's mediumship and display toxic behavior within their interpersonal relationships. An emotionally balanced individual is secure and appreciates the success of others. Mediums should instantly cancel negative emotions such as jealousy or animosity the moment they arise and replace them with constructive thoughts.

Moral and Spiritual Growth

Don't separate mediumship unfoldment from the application of spirituality and moral principles in one's life. Develop the highest level of spirituality and impeccable personal character. Mediums should put as much emphasis on their spiritual growth as much as possible in their lives. The higher spirits will influence mediums to conduct all aspects of their lives with truth and integrity.

The higher spirits know our weaknesses and imperfections. Ask God and the spirit teachers for assistance in overcoming faults and becoming a better individual. Spirituality is not an imposition, as it is our true nature. A medium's spirituality attracts similar minded souls from the spirit world to work through him or her.

How Individuals Too Open to the Spirit World Can Close Down

Some individuals are hyper-sensitive. Unlike most who gradually unfold their mediumistic abilities, some people are naturally open and unable to control their abilities. They receive unwanted communications from spirits at all times of the day and the night. Years ago, in

Massachusetts, a woman contacted me concerned about her openness and lack of boundaries with the spirit world. Spirits communicated with her all day at her retail job at the shopping mall. Although she possessed no formal mediumship training, she already was doing mediumship readings at her job in the mall. Her spirit father, she complained, influenced her to smoke two packs of cigarettes a day. She did not know how to turn her psychic abilities off.

I told her to attend my new series of mediumship development classes starting up the following week. I emphasized that she should only work with the spirit world at the development class, and the rest of the time stay psychically closed down. I explained that she needed to control her mediumship and not allow spirits to communicate with her at random times. I explained that as a novice she needed to learn the mechanics of the process before she attempted to give readings to other people.

She only attended the first class of the course and did not show up for the subsequent classes. About a month later, she called me in a distraught state of mind. She did not apply any of my advice, but she did the exact opposite. She continued to give readings to people during the day at her mall job. She felt completely alarmed and overwhelmed as she did not know how to stop the spirits from coming in.

There are many popular television programs that depict mediumship. Sometimes, the mediums in such shows accost individuals in public and give them spirit messages. Besides being unethical, this approach to mediumship leads to unreliable information coming through from dubious sources in the spirit world. Mediumship is not cheap entertainment. There should always be reverence for the process.

Discipline is essential for quality mediumship. Most individuals spend considerable time learning how to properly and safely open up and manage their mediumship. As a mediumship teacher, I find that fewer individuals are excessively open. The remedy for this problem is for students to control their mediumship.

Rules for Student Mediums for Attaining Higher Mediumship

Only open up in a circle or other structured times.

Do work with others until you are properly ready.

A qualified teacher can assess you and find out your level of development and abilities. Listen to his or her suggestions.

Mediumship is a sacred act. Reverence and higher purpose are important.

Stay clean. Alcohol, cannabis and similar substances do not mix with spirit communication.

Develop your moral and spiritual character. Remember like attracts like.

Mediumship Improvement Exercises

EXERCISE 94

Daily Word

Sit comfortably in a relaxed. Meditative state. Repeat the affirmations on page 20 with each slow inhalation and exhalation. The affirmations can be chanted either mentally or out loud.

EXERCISE 95

Affirmations Daily Intervals

Repeat the affirmations on page 20 at intervals during the day. The affirmations can be chanted either mentally or out loud.

EXERCISE 96

Fun Art

To help get the analytical mind out of the way,
purchase art materials and do art as much as possible.

EXERCISE 97

Life Drawing

Attend life drawing sessions on a regular basis. Learn to draw the human
form as well as portraiture.

This assists with getting the analytical mind out of the way for receiving
spirit communications and also assists with developing artistic skill
beneficial for spirit portraiture and mediumistic art.

EXERCISE 98

Sitting in the Power

Pray to God for the highest and best to work with you and through you.
Ask that they connect with you and help you unfold your mediumship for
the purpose of helping others. Quietly sit and focus awareness within. Pay
attention to the breath. Expand the energy field. Allow the spirit operators to come close and blend with you. Sit in the power for at least thirty
minutes or more. Feel their presence and the spirit power as it builds. Be
aware of mental impressions and sensations.

Altered States Exercises

EXERCISE 99

Deep Breathing

Sit comfortably with an erect spine. Inhale slowly and deeply into the
lower abdomen. Feel the lower, middle and upper lungs expand. Exhale

slowly. Place your palms on your lower abdomen as you breathe and feel it expand with each inhalation.

EXERCISE 100

Clock for Dissociation and Entrancement.

This exercise can be done alone or directed by a teacher in a development group. A student imagines that he or she is in the center of a round clock with the numbers 1-12, indicating the time, surrounding him or her. The student imagines that he or she is sitting facing the number 12. After going into a deep altered state, the student mentally dissociates and shifts his or her awareness, to the position of 12, followed by mentally returning to the center position. The student repeats this process with each of the 12 numbered positions. This entire sequence can be repeated by the student mentally positioning him or herself through dissociation several times around the clock. The student can start out clockwise and repeat the process counter-clockwise.

CHAPTER 13

Channeling Aliens and Animals

Many psychics involved in the New Age movement claim to channel an assortment of beings including Ascended Masters, nonhuman species of life, such as dolphins, elves, and even extraterrestrials, who transmit higher philosophy and wisdom through them. It is common for spirit animals to come through during a mediumship session, for individuals they were connected with in their physical lives. I have brought through, over the years, an assortment of spirit animals including; cats, dogs, horses, cows, pigs, monkeys, snakes, elephants, birds, and other species. Spirit animals generally make their appearance with human spirit personalities connected to them or the recipient of the communication and, like spirit humans, they always convey evidence to confirm their identity.

At a Spiritualist church service, as I delivered a spirit message, I felt a spirit dog urinating on my foot and leg. The message recipient identified the spirit immediately as a beloved family pet. Another time, in Austria, I watched a New Zealand medium I know, deliver highly evidential messages for recipients in a packed auditorium. All the spirit communicators were spirit horses, who were recognized by the recipients as connected to their families. I felt a small monkey on my shoulder during a mediumship session I did for a woman who had worked as a zoo keeper for many years. My client instantly recognized the communicator as a spider monkey who had passed over despite her efforts to save his life. In addition, I brought through a jaguar, several exotic birds and other animals, all identified by my client. I could see many spirit animals surrounding my client as many inhabitants of the zoo had physically died during her career.

Many Spiritualists in the past century believed that animals lacked an individual existence and merged into a larger group oversoul after physical death. This idea is completely false, as all souls, after the destruction of the physical body, continue to evolve in the spirit world, and, in most cases, take birth in another physical body again. It is not as though individuality is ever lost, and the soul dissolves into some vague cosmic oneness. The soul within an animal body is the same as the soul in a human body. A soul within an animal form of life is focused primarily upon eating, sleeping, mating, and defending. The difference is that humans can philosophize about their eternal spiritual nature and develop their relationship with God. Animals are locked into following their physical instincts, unlike humans who are able to cultivate God consciousness.

It is love that enables spirit animals to communicate with those they love in the physical world. A medium who loves animals will naturally attract such spirits and easily function as an instrument for them to come through. Animals emotionally communicate through transmitting their feelings and ideas. While it is possible to bring through mediumistic communications from spirit animals, what about channeling extraterrestrial personalities? In theory, it appears this is possible, since life exists throughout the universe, in countless forms, on both subtle and physical levels.

Over the years, I have read many transcripts of channeled teachings from space aliens, and observed individuals purporting to channel messages from extraterrestrial sources. In most cases, it was difficult to take such claims seriously, given the absurdity of much of the channeled material and the lack of genuine mediumistic connection taking place with the live channelings. It is common for many wannabe actors to move to the Los Angeles, California, area, hoping to make it big in the entertainment industry. The only problem is that for every job that opens up, there are countless unemployed actors seeking the same position. As a result, it is far easier to work as a channeler in Hollywood, and far more lucrative than waiting tables, or other menial jobs.

Delusion is also fairly common. Many poorly trained mediums cannot differentiate between their own imaginations and genuine psychic impressions. Although ill prepared, they engage in the practice of spirit communication, without properly understanding the mechanics of the process. As a trained medium, I observe the energy fields of other mediums as they work and observe the spirit personalities they are connecting with. I can accurately assess the way other mediums receive information from the spirit world. Most mediums are honest and sincere with the work they do. However, because there are dishonest mediums and deluded individuals, it is always a good practice to test both the medium and the spirit, and use one's common sense in regard to any purported spirit communication.

From Another World

At Cassadaga Spiritualist Camp in Florida, a woman traveled from out of state to attend several of my workshops on spiritual healing and receive a private mediumship session with me. Although I did not remember her, she explained that she had received a mediumship session with me several years before.

Although extremely positive and sincere, it was apparent that this woman lacked social skills in the strange manner that she interacted with others in the class. She frequently interjected irrelevant comments, and came across completely out of place with the rest of the group.

The first spirit personality who I brought through for her during her private mediumship session was extraterrestrial and motherly to her. The former physical body of the spirit was sturdy like a rhinoceros, but with lumpy protrusions all over. I do not always see the personal features of the spirit personalities vividly. Often, I receive a transparent image of the spirit communicator, within my inner vision, along with the idea of their physical features, character and distinct personality. The spirit alien mother told me that the recipient had previously lived on another distant planet and that her present incarnation was her first as a human on Earth.

The extraterrestrial used the analogy of her being like an exchange student. I received much information from the spirit world about why the recipient felt awkward for her entire life and did not fit with her family and society. During the session, other spirit personalities, including guides and members of both her birth family, and former husband's family, came through with much evidential information for recognition as well as both material and spiritual guidance. She was extremely satisfied with the session and could understand all the information completely.

Two years later, the same woman again attended my workshops at Cassadaga and scheduled a private mediumship session. The higher guides explained her extraterrestrial origins, with Earth being one of many physical worlds that she had experienced physical incarnations. They described how a group of spirit healers from her former planet assisted her in each of these incarnations. This healing team worked for God to spread healing light to many planets throughout the universe. The higher guides also related how these extraterrestrial spirit healers worked with other discarnate healers from Earth connected to my client.

I also felt the presence of a nonhuman personality who explained how he channeled strange noises, which resembled insect sounds, through her while she was doing sound healing. My client understood this completely, as the extraterrestrial healers made unusual sounds through her when she was performing healing treatments. My client cried as the higher guides related her lifelong loneliness and inability to fit in with others. They explained that on a soul level, she was mature and viewed the souls on Earth and similar worlds as little children. The higher spirits explained how humanity was spiritually backward and the purpose of her incarnation was to help such souls evolve.

My client describes her initial encounter with the extraterrestrial healers:

Previously I had channeled my healing angels, who were teaching me about my healing energy gifts. I assumed they had more information to share with me. I turned on my voice recorder, and next thing I knew I was channeling an energy that was completely unlike my healing angels. It was very high pitched and fast. It sounded like I was talking after having sucked on a helium balloon. Needless to say, I was completely freaked out! They told me that they had been with me for a long time and wanted to work with me when I was ready.

Decades before the above incidents, the late Bill Colvin of Toronto, Canada, a registered medium at the Lily Dale Assembly in New York, told me of a similar experience. A man consulted Bill for a mediumship session and explained that he wanted to know the reason that he had felt completely out of place for his entire life. During the session, the higher guides told the man that before this life, he had been incarnate as an alien on another planet. The man related to this information and felt completely relieved. As a medium for over thirty years, Bill explained to me that this was the only time something like this had happened in all the many thousands of mediumship sessions that he had done.

Channeling Enod

Is it possible for extraterrestrials to speak through an entranced medium? If so, how does it work compared to channeling deceased loved ones and guides? My teacher Sylvia and her husband Joseph spent a

Saturday doing mediumship sessions at a Spiritualist church in Norfolk, Virginia. At this church, a resident medium did a private mediumship session for Sylvia. A week later, at her home circle, Sylvia explained to me that this mediumship session had been the best reading that she had received in a long time, and that she could relate to everything that the medium had told her except for one part at the end.

Although the session contained much valuable spiritual guidance along with evidential messages, the medium also stated that she would be involved in channeling the Intergalactic Command. A highly rational and skeptical medium, Sylvia told me that this sounded like something out of a science fiction movie. She dismissed the information and soon forgot this part of the session.

About six months later, at her home circle, Sylvia's spirit teachers impressed her that they would work with her differently in terms of the information transmitted during entrancement. At this circle, an extraterrestrial intelligence communicated through her for the first time. After a brief philosophical address by a spirit teacher, the vibrations around Sylvia dramatically shifted as a different personality spoke through her.

The personality controlling Sylvia identified himself as Enod, who articulated his words in a quick, almost mechanical manner. As a medium, I ascertained that Enod operated on a much faster vibrational, less dense, frequency, than the other spirit teachers who regularly channeled through Sylvia. Sylvia explained to me that the mechanics of the channeling process remained the same with Enod.

Sylvia describes her experience as follows:

After a short pause, I saw what appeared to be a large group of spirit children entering the circle with my third eye. As they grew closer, I realized that they were beings from another dimension. As the leader of this group drew close to me, I was filled with intense heat and energy as I never experienced before. There clearly was a language translation difficulty which you can hear on the tape.(Sylvia taped the sessions so that the trance lectures delivered by the spirit teachers through her mediumship could be transcribed.)

"I have traveled from many, many thousands of miles from here to be with you this evening. My translation is not perfect. I will have problems for a time. I bring you love. I bring you friendship. I am Enod. I bring you light."

Many of the group members felt the intense heat and saw these beings as I did. I feel they will return.

Although alien, Enod, like other spirit personalities, lived in a subtle dimension. He was not a physical incarnate extraterrestrial, as depicted in popular culture, or, as likely, reside on other physical planets. The content of the information differed from that of other spirit teachers, as it focused on the help that Enod, and others with him, were bringing to humanity for greater global harmony. At the time, in September 1990, the first Iraq war was about to take place with the United States military preparing for an invasion.

The idea of channeling extraterrestrials is a difficult concept for many people to accept. Many individuals, including those involved with mediumship, would consider Sylvia either a fraud or severely deluded.

The mechanics of entrancement involve energetic control of the medium's nervous system, with telepathic communication conveyed automatically via the vocal cords. It makes sense that souls in humanoid life forms live on other physical and subtle worlds. Entrancement, as a process, is not limited to only channeling spirits from Earth. In the same manner, alien personalities operating on a subtle level can come through. The higher spirits facilitated such communication through Sylvia, who possessed great skill with her abilities as a mental medium.

Insect Aliens

I did a mediumship session for a young man in Peru, who struggled with an overwhelming feeling of estrangement from society and an inability to establish human relationships. My client was extremely easy to work with. I brought through various spirits who shared practical guidance to help with my client's situation. Suddenly, I heard a weird musical tone that I felt only insects could hear, and I saw ants crawling all over my client. "You can communicate with insects, you can read them," I stated. My client understood exactly what I was talking about.

Next, a guide connected to my client strongly made his presence known. I discerned with my clairvoyance a spirit whose subtle form resembled that of a giant antlike insect. The personality of this guide felt cold and alien. I knew that this spirit, in his former physical life, belonged to an intelligent insect species from another planet. My client's guide exuded a highly intelligent, yet impersonal and emotionless vibration, completely unlike the feelings associated with the typical deceased loved ones and guides that communicate through my mediumship.

The guide explained that most people could step on an ant and not think anything of it, but my client would think, "That's one of my brothers." The guide stated, "You are one of them. You identify with them. You relate to them."

My client's guide continued to impress my mind telepathically with information about the challenges my client faced in life, which I articulated as it was received. I told him how he connected with insects on a very deep level and would find an insect petting zoo emotionally gratifying and did not want insects to be caged in. I was also shown that my client would develop a relationship with a group of insects, who would actually respond to him. I explained to him that in the future he would acquire pet insects.

The guide told me that in his former physical life, he held a leadership position on another planet, where an insect species was predominant. He related to me how my client was learning insect language and making weird toning sounds that they could understand. He explained that my client, who, all his life, felt extreme discontent with people, somehow had contacted them. I told my client, "You asked them for guidance. They consider you one of them."

I explained to my client that regardless of his efforts, all of his human relationships would fall short. "You are not one of them, and you know it. It is like a bad experimental type of dream that you can't wait to get out of." The guide suggested that my client should think of his life on Earth as observational lab work. He explained that my client was in the dark and unable to see the full picture about his situation. I stated, "You won't be coming back to Earth after this life. You will go another planet when you take physical birth again." "It's like a big botch up. You're not one of us," I continued.

I was shown many references to creative works of science fiction, such as *Star Trek*. The guides said that if my client constructed a 3-D, conceptional model of an alien structure that "...it would be accurate and not just a product of your imagination." I stated, "You're getting stuff; you have been in touch with actual aliens. What might seem like a fictitious work would actually have many elements of truth to it."

I continued to convey information to my client from his guide. "You came into this life kept in the dark. It wouldn't work if you didn't think you were human. If you knew the full truth, you wouldn't be ready for it."

In regard to my client's strong inclination to end his physical life through suicide, I stated, "They want you to stay on Earth. They don't want you to leave."

"You ask: why do I want to stay alive? You feel like you are an old man and have been here a long, long time. What point is there for me to stay here?" The guide explained that all of this was positive and that my client was gathering information and experience that would be used in the future to help others.

Alien Healers

Another time, I did a mediumship session in Cassadaga for an elderly woman from Oregon who attended my mediumship development workshops at the camp. I brought through many of my client's deceased loved ones and guides who provided her with much soul guidance and practical advice. A guide stepped forward who showed me an image of my client vocalizing weird sounds and tones for healing. I did not see this guide, but sensed his personality and character. The guide's energy felt nonhuman and non-terrestrial and he explained he assisted my client with her healing work along with other spirit healers in her team. The guide described how he had traveled a long way and made me aware of a vast distance, far from Earth.

I did not know my client worked with sound healing. In fact, the reason she consulted with me was to ask her guides if she should continue using the unusual sounds she channeled while giving people sound healing treatments. The above example shows that the higher personalities who provide spiritual help, although in most cases have experienced incarnation as humans on Earth, can also be individuals from other physical worlds.

Spirit Animal Exercises

EXERCISE 101

Spirit Pets

Participants pair up, hold each other's hands, and connect with the spirit world. Bring through a spirit animal connected to the recipient. Describe evidential details. Take turns working.

EXERCISE 102

More Spirit Pets

Participants pair up, hold each other's hands, and attune to the spirit world. Bring through a spirit animal connected to a person in the spirit world. Describe evidential details. Take turns working.

EXERCISE 103

Advanced Spirit Pets

Participants pair up, hold each other's hands, and attune to the spirit world. Bring in the spirit person connected to the spirit animal brought through in the prior exercise. Describe evidential details. Take turns working.

EXERCISE 104

Pet Art

Participants pair up, hold each other's hands, and attune to the spirit world. Both sides work at the same time or take turns. Using sketch pad and pastels, draw a spirit animal or pet associated with the partner. Receive the names associated with the animal, or humans associated with the creature.

EXERCISE 105

Fish From Heaven

Participants pair up, hold each other's hands, and connect with the spirit world. The medium allows information about a fish or references to fish, either symbolic or literal, to be presented that relates to a recognizable spirit communicator. The medium should elaborate on the fish or fish references with evidential details about the spirit communicator. Take turns working.

EXERCISE 106

Animal Tags

Bring through a spirit animal wearing a collar with tags, who is connected to the recipient. Describe the communicator and relate details on the collar and tags such as names, addresses and phone numbers, etc.

CHAPTER 14

Using the Power of Sound With Mediumship

In the beginning was the Word, and the Word was with God, and the Word was God. —John 1.1 *KJV*

As a teacher of mediumship, much of my work involves assisting individuals in the development of their spiritual gifts. Many subtle worlds exist beyond this physical dimension populated by unlimited personalities, many of whom have experienced innumerable physical embodiments. The spirit world is not found in some distant location, but exists all around us at a much faster frequency of vibration. Mediumship requires proper mental attunement with the higher spirits who facilitate any communication that takes place. A medium must raise his or her rate of vibration and connect with the spirit operators who slow their energetic frequency to work through the medium.

While many people commonly describe God as light, few individuals understand that God also manifests as sound. According to the teaching of the ancient Vedas and other spiritual traditions, there is no difference between the holy names of God and the personal and impersonal energies of God. Yogis, mystics, and devotees from all the world's great spiritual traditions utilize the chanting and singing of select sacred prayers to attain higher, transcendental states of consciousness. The process of hearing and vocalizing spiritual sound vibrations is not mechanical or lifeless, but it is a blissful journey within the heart that leads to greater realization of self and God. The shamans and mediums of indigenous cultures worldwide have also always used sound as a medium to achieve altered states of consciousness for healing and connecting with the spirit world. All phases of mediumship involve levels of trance and dissociation from the physical body. My practice of mantra meditation since childhood has enhanced my abilities considerably as a medium and healer. Mantra meditation is unbeatable as a method for spiritual purification and effectively attaining the pure love of God. My disciplined, daily practice of mantra meditation has raised my personal vibration to a higher frequency and opened me up considerably as a channel for the higher spirits to work through.

All the phases of mediumship that can be cultivated are connected to the chakras or energy centers which are found within the subtle body and which relate to physical glands within the endocrine system. For example, clairvoyance involves the third eye chakra and the pineal gland at the forehead, and healing mediumship is connected with the heart chakra and the thymus gland in the center of the chest. Mediumship development results in subtle changes affecting the chemistry of the medium's physical body. The spirit chemists or doctors responsible for the psychic awakening of a particular medium work through his or her chakra and endocrine systems to accomplish the unfoldment of mediumistic ability.

Mediumship development is generally a gradual process. However, mediumship development is much quicker during puberty and menopause because of the natural hormonal changes taking place in these periods of life. The mental outlook, diet, lifestyle choices, and the spiritual practices of the medium all contribute to the process of mediumship unfoldment.

The effectiveness of sound as a tool for heightened mediumistic unfoldment cannot be overemphasized.

Mystic Siddhis

Chakra is a word from the ancient Sanskrit language that means *Wheel.* Seven major chakras function as part of the subtle body, along with additional minor chakras the hands and feet. Each chakra vibrates at a different frequency of sound and color. In the yogic tradition, specific mantras are used to awaken the individual chakras for higher realization, and in some cases the attainment of mystic powers or Siddhis. The use of specific sounds as a tool for mediumistic unfoldment stimulates the various chakras and facilitates development with the phases of mediumship associated with them. In addition, the power of sound raises the personal vibrations of the medium and the collective energy of groups sitting for mediumship development or communication.

Singing is a Doorway to the Spirit World

The home circles held by the early Spiritualists often included considerable time singing to harmonize the collective energy and raise the vibration. Singing also assists the medium to dissociate from the physical body and achieve a deeper meditative state. The more a medium can relax his or her physical body and get out of the way, the easier it is for the spirit operators to convey communications, impart healing, or produce physical manifestations. As I mention in the chapter on physical mediumship, singing upbeat peppy songs, contribute in building up the energy necessary for physical phenomena. Faster songs are great for mental mediumship circles too. If you are involved in a mediumship development circle, experiment with songs and see for yourself.

I play specific music to accompany the guided meditations that I conduct for my students in my mediumship training programs. I find that certain music works better for getting students into extremely deep altered states of consciousness. I also usually have my students sing songs and chant affirmations to raise the vibrations and build the power. The results are evident in the beautiful energy that is experienced throughout the premises. Repetitive, well-known songs work best. I typically use Christmas songs such as *Rudolph the Red-Nosed Reindeer* and children's numbers such as the *ABC Song*. Often I engage participants at group meetings before I work in singing, which always results in a powerful increase in the psychic force. People often attend public demonstrations of mediumship holding attitudes that are detrimental for the process of spirit communication such as negative skepticism, lethargy, apprehension, and wanting things done a certain way. The right music will positively transform such disharmonious mindsets and make the atmosphere much more conducive for spirit communication.

So often a medium will attempt to demonstrate in public and find that the audience is more dead than the people in the spirit world. I have worked in many venues around the world, and the easiest, most powerful places energetically to do mediumship in are those that include enthusiastic singing and music as part of the program. Years ago, I regularly served a Spiritualist church in the Boston, Massachusetts, area that did not include singing as part of their Sunday meeting. The reason was that the pastor disliked religious hymns as he was turned off by a Christian style worship service. The fact that the meetings were held in a Protestant style church with pews and other trapping of orthodox Christianity did not seem to matter to him. The use of sound to raise the vibrations for spirit communication is not done out of religious sentiment, but for scientific and practical reasons that work. Because the energy at the above church was low, I always engaged the congregation in a lively rendition of *You are My Sunshine,* which always succeeded in raising the vibration. Of course, some might argue that a medium does not need music or singing to work. However, the science of mediumship demonstrates that lively singing opens people up and creates a psychic atmosphere favorable for spirit communication.

Spirit Communication is like a Phone Call

The vocal response of the recipient of spirit messages strengthens the link with the spirit world. The process of mediumship communication is a two-way street with the medium merely functioning as an intermediary between the spirit communicators and the recipient. In a phone conversation, if an individual remains silent and does not respond, the other party will conclude that they are not there and will hang up. This same principle applies to spirit communication. Both the medium and the recipient should vocally speak to the spirit communicators as the use of sound vibration strengthens the telepathic and energetic connections between the two worlds. I have found that this is also accomplished when I speak loudly during my delivery of spirit messages.

Words That Heal

Sound healing is an approach that is sadly overlooked by most practicing mediums I know in the Spiritualist movement. On the other hand, many healing practitioners within the alternative healing community make use of sound for healing treatments. We know that everything is energy and vibrates at a different frequency. We have both negative and positive sounds. Loving, encouraging words bring about psychological healing, while negative words create mental disharmony, unhappiness and pain. The same is true for music or other frequencies of sound. Playing certain types of music, such as Classical, enhance the growth of plants, while playing ear-splitting Heavy Metal or Rap do the exact opposite.

The Physical Body is Mainly Water

The subtle body with its energetic chakra and meridian systems as detailed in Oriental and Ayurvedic medicine are a blueprint for the physical vehicle. According to medical science, about 65 percent of the physical body is comprised of water with individual organs sometimes containing even a greater composition. The brain, muscles and heart are made up of 75 percent water, the lungs 86 per cent, the liver 85 percent and the kidneys 83 percent. The Japanese researcher Masaru Emoto (1943-2014) authored a series of fascinating works detailing his experiments on the effects of thought and sound on the molecular structure of water. Emoto discovered the molecular structure of water varies depending upon its source and may be altered in a positive or negative manner by energy or sound directed toward it. Emoto documented his experiments with photographs showing the often dynamic changes that take place within the formations of crystallized water.[1] With this in mind, it makes sense that certain sounds may be extremely healing, not only psychologically but on a physiological level as well. Although mainstream scientists consider Emoto's research to be pseudoscience, the results of his work are consistent with my understanding of the subtle energies involved in mediumistic healing.

Sarah Benson Master Soul Musician

The late Sarah Benson (1935-2007) was one of the most powerful mediumistic healers I have met. She lived off the Mohawk Trial in Massachusetts, a half-hour drive from my home at the time. As a working medium, I noticed Sarah's name for years as she served many of the New England Spiritualist churches and camps as a guest speaker and workshop facilitator. Sarah was best known as a leading pioneer of the sound healing movement in the late 1970s and early 1980s. Sarah mastered the art and science of sound healing, and for decades taught programs throughout the United States and internationally. The majority of prominent teachers of sound healing in the USA studied with her.

---

[1] Emoto, Masaru, *The Hidden Messages in Water*, Atria Publishing, New York, New York, USA, 2005.

Sarah recorded many tapes and CDs of her work, both solo projects and collaborations with other prominent sound healer musicians that are amazingly effective as vehicles for higher levels of healing to take place.

When I finally met Sarah at a Spiritualist church and found out that she lived close to me, I immediately invited her to attend one of my weekly mediumship development groups. I loved her energy instantly and for the next few years Sarah attended my Tuesday morning circle. At the time I was teaching four or five development classes weekly as well as holding an open healing sanctuary for the community on Monday evenings. As a sound healer, Sarah utilized every type of musical instrument imaginable. String, woodwind, brass, and percussion-all were used by Sarah in her workshops and public healing performances.

Sarah and I facilitated several Spiritualist church services together. At one memorable meeting, Sarah performed the healing portion of the service while I delivered the inspirational address and spirit messages. The church had been used for spirit communication since it was purchased by the Spiritualists in 1918, and the energies inside the building were extremely powerful. During the healing portion of the service, I performed hands-on treatments with other church healers for members of the congregation. Sarah stayed on the platform, sitting cross-legged. She began to play various exotic musical instruments and vocalize sacred tones and prayers. Although my back was turned away from her, facing the congregation, as I channeled healing and worked with my spirit doctors, the energy that I felt was incredible. Physically, Sarah was petite, but the size and intensity of her energy field was unbelievably powerful. I could mentally sense the spirit healers who were influencing her from her position on the church platform behind me. The energy of the spirit healers directing the healing through her was exceptionally strong. As she loudly vocalized prayers and chanted, you could feel the vibrations within the church intensify with each passing moment. Sarah undoubtedly was one of the greatest, most influential teachers of sound healing in the world. Her recordings are exceptionally potent tools for spiritual healing. Sarah and I collaborated on a healing meditation CD comprised of two guided meditations led by me and accompanied by her music

Experiment and Expand

Not all mediums possess musical ability or are able to sing well. However, mediums should utilize sound as much as possible for their personal spiritual growth as well as for the application of mediumship and healing. With toning and healing through the voice, the intention of the healer is far more important than the quality of the voice. Crystal or brass singing bowls, tuning forks, rattles, and gongs are musical instruments that easily can be played by a musically unskilled individual for sound healing. Traditional indigenous drums are used in Shamanic practice for journeying to connect with spirit teachers and guides. Learn more about the indigenous approaches and, if practical, integrate them with conventional Spiritualist practices. Mediumship development is progressive. Expand your approach to working with the spirit world through studying unorthodox and unfamiliar methods. Experiment with your voice. Learn about mantras from the Vedic, Buddhist and other traditions. Circle leaders should actively encourage sitters to sing and encourage participants to bring musical instruments such as guitars to play at mediumship meetings.

Transcendental Sound Bath

The use of sacred sounds purifies our consciousness. Sacred sound provides the means of direct communication and association with God as sound vibration. On a more mundane level, sound may be effectively utilized for the cultivation of mediumistic and healing abilities. As previously mentioned, sound may be used in mediumship to achieve deeper levels of trance, dissociation, and attunement with the spirit operators.

The effectiveness of using sound for healing oneself and others mentally and physically also cannot be over emphasized. God is light, but God is also sound. Spiritually we are all parts and parcels of the Supreme Spirit and we possess the same qualities as God. Although we are eternally individuals through the medium of sound, the barriers that exist between ourselves and others can be eradicated, and the material imperfections within our hearts that separate us from God may be cleansed. The energetic and telepathic exchanges between the spirit world and the material world are intensified by the use of sound vibration.

Sound Vibration Exercises

EXERCISE 107

Sound Spirits

Participants take turns standing up in front of the group and delivering spirit messages to three of those present. After everyone has worked, the process repeats itself, but with the group loudly singing a variety of upbeat songs for five to ten minutes before each participant works.

Compare and contrast the difference between delivering spirit communications without singing and after singing has taken place. Note the effect singing has upon raising the vibrations and the process of mediumistic attunement and the delivery of spirit messages.

EXERCISE 108

Om Vibration Overshadowing

The group surrounds the medium, who sits in a chair or stands behind a chair with his or her hands resting gently on its back for support. The group loudly chants the mantra Om for ten minutes, while the medium goes into a deep, meditative state and invites a spirit helper to step forward and mentally blend with his or her energies. The medium shares space with the spirit, allowing overshadowing and a deeper level of control to take place. At the completion of the chanting, the medium can gradually return to regular consciousness. Members of the group can take turns participating.

Note, the effect of the sound vibration in assisting the process of deepening the trance state and overshadowing with the spirit.

EXERCISE 109

Singing Bowl Trance

The medium sits in a chair or stands behind a chair with his or her hands resting gently on its back for support. Loudly play a singing bowl for ten minutes within the medium's energy field. While the medium goes into a deep, meditative state and invites a spirit helper to step forward and mentally blend with his or her energies. The medium shares space with the spirit, allowing overshadowing and a deeper level of control to take place. At the completion of the sound bath, the medium can gradually return to regular consciousness. Members of the group can take turns participating.

Participants should note the effect of the sound vibrations upon deepening the trance state and assisting the process of overshadowing. This exercise should be done with an actual musical instrument and not a music recording. Bowls made of crystal or metal are ideal. However, a gong or tuning forks can also be effectively used.

EXERCISE 110

Singing Bowl Spirits

Participants pair up, facing each other in two lines of chairs and holding hands, take turns delivering spirit messages for each other. The group leader should allow five minutes for each participant to work before switching roles. After both partners have worked, the participants should move to the right and repeat the process with a new partner. This process should be repeated until the participants are paired with the individual they started the exercise with. The length of time spent participants spend working with each other can be adjusted by the circle leader depending upon the size of the group.

Next, the process repeats itself with the participants delivering spirit messages for each other and changing partners in the exact same manner. However, in this case, a singing bowl is loudly played for several minutes prior to the participants working with each partner.

CHAPTER 15

Spirit Narratives

Evidential mediumship is all about storytelling. Everyone loves an interesting story. Everyone's life is a story from birth until physical death and beyond. A medium who is adept at storytelling will be extremely proficient at delivering the stories of individuals in the spirit world. In the same way that a talented storyteller captivates an audience and keeps them listening to every detail with rapt attention, a good medium also accurately delivers the spirit messages engaging the recipient and others.

A story always features a protagonist and often includes other supporting characters as part of the plot. A good narrative infuses audience interest in a focused, well-structured way. In addition, a story appeals to the emotions of an audience with unexpected twists and drama. Ultimately, a classic narrative imparts a higher message that enhances the audience's lives spiritually and materially.

An evidential spirit communication, whether a shorter spirit greeting or longer in-depth session, focuses on the story of the spirit communicator, who describes the events in his or her former physical life. Often novice mediums will initially focus on receiving information about spirit communicators that is factual and detailed, such as names, dates, descriptions of physical objects, manners of passing, and other recognizable attributes. Many developing mediums provide one or more generalized pieces of information that could apply to many individuals, such as a tall elderly man wearing a business suit who passed over with a heart attack or a grandmotherly woman with white hair and glasses with an apron who liked to bake chocolate chip cookies. A less experienced medium typically receives such vague descriptions mainly because of the mechanics involved in telepathic communication and his or her stage of unfoldment. A novice medium also generally lacks sufficient discipline and strength in his or her mediumship to maintain a link with a spirit communicator for more than a short time without getting his or her analytical mind in the way. Messages received through such a medium often will be fragmented and the story incomplete.

As a medium gains experience and strengthens his or her attunement with the spirit world, the generalities received as a novice are replaced by specific messages including such details as license plate numbers, street addresses, and other factual information. However, a spirit message containing precise details alone is insufficient without the including deeper attributes and memories from the spirit's former physical life. For example, a medium may accurately describe the diamond wedding ring of a spirit grandmother and even provide its engraved inscription. Although this message is highly evidential, a medium must learn to take the evidence further by relating the story of the wedding ring and the memories associated with it from the life of the beloved grandmother who wore it. A medium may bring through a spirit who committed suicide because of chronic depression. The message may be highly evidential as it contains an accurate description of the spirit, his or her manner of passing, and other recognizable attributes. However, the message's impact will be significantly greater if the spirit provides memories from his or her former physical life of events that negatively affected his or her mental health and contributed to his or her suicide.

A medium should use all of his or her psychic senses in the process-seeing, hearing, sensing, smelling, tasting, and knowing. A medium will feel as though he or she is reliving the memory of the spirit through all of his or her psychic senses. In addition, the medium will sense the spirit's emotions in the present in regard to the memories of his or her former physical life. After physical death, the individual realizes the necessity for further soul progression and personal healing. Many spirits often relate painful incidents from their former physical lives, their attitudes, how they have grown spiritually and what obstacles they overcame in the process. In addition, many spirits explain their present realizations in terms of the life lessons that they have learned. Soul evolution and healing are readily made available for those who make the transition to the spirit world. The life story of the individual does not end with the destruction of the physical body. Physical death results in the individual having to take complete responsibility for his or her conduct and past misdeeds. Invaluable spiritual and moral lessons are imparted in the stories of individuals who neglected to live in harmony with God's law and work on their soul growth.

Public Storytelling

How many times have you watched a medium demonstrate from the platform and been completely bored by his or her presentation? Not all mediums possess the qualities necessary for public work. In fact, many mediums are better suited for individual sessions. A medium delivering spirit communications in public must know how to involve the entire audience and accomplish much more than merely stating evidential facts and details. My ex-step-grandfather-in-law Ken Pretty (1931-2018) from the UK was a prominent medium who in 1960 enthralled an audience of 300 for several hours at Speakers Corner in Hyde Park, London. Ken was a dynamic, charismatic performer who articulated evidential messages in a way that captivated his audiences. Ken was a master medium who invoked strong emotional responses from both the recipient and others present as he told the stories of the spirits who communicated through him.

A medium's words make the memories of the spirits become alive in the minds of the listeners. A recipient will generally recognize the information about the former physical life of the spirit, and at the same time other listeners will be able to relive the narrative within their minds. The spirit recollects his or her former physical life through the medium, and the audience feels as though they are sharing the experience. A medium who blends his or her mind and energies with the spirits can convey the intimacy of the spirit's life through both the details and emotions. The recipient and others present will strongly experience the presence of the spirit as he or she works through the energy field of the medium.

A spirit's narrative delivered publicly, besides documenting the individual's former physical life, often transmits ethics, values, and guidance that applies to the recipient as well as other parties present. This is an expedient way for the higher spirits to impart wisdom and assistance to those in need in this physical world. A spirit who in his or her former physical life lived contrary to the laws of God will relate such details and the lessons learned. Most spirit messages are carefully planned out by the higher personalities with a major theme or lesson to impart. The spirits will deliver the story from the view of the protagonist to the recipient at the right time. This will take place even if the recipient does not want to hear it.

Allow the Spirits to Dramatize Their Stories

The most effective messages start with a hook and emphasize key points, which often contain evidence of survival as well as provide practical guidance for the recipient. Mediums should allow the spirits to dramatize their stories and express their personalities and attributes. This can be done without unnecessary exaggeration. Mediums should not hold back and allow their body language and mannerisms to respond to the intensity of the spirit communicators. The spirit narrative should not only be told in words, but should also be expressed in the movements and energy of the medium.

How to Develop Good Storytelling skills

Are you good with words? Do you know how to emphasize portions of your spoken words to make important points? Even if you are not good with your use of words through regular practice, such skills can be cultivated. How can a medium develop his or her ability to tell the stories? A medium should ask the higher spirits for help in cultivating proficiency as a storyteller with his or her mediumship. In addition, he or she should as much as possible practice telling stories and listening and reading the stories of others. The medium's spirit team will accommodate his or her request by gradually introducing such information within the structure of the spirit message.

Secret Stories

An individual mediumship session has a very different dynamic compared to a public demonstration of spirit communication. The spirits will refrain from conveying personal details about themselves or recipients that should not be revealed in front of others. Although most mediums are generally not trained in the mental health field and such a focus is beyond the scope of their practice. A mediumship session often goes deeper in providing healing and insight into a recipient's life than traditional psychotherapy or counseling does. A mediumship session is often more for the communicating spirits than for the recipient. However, in most cases, the healing received during the session goes both ways. A spirit who shares his or her story reveals aspects of his or her life that often have never been told. In many cases, the recipient and spirit communicator equally benefit from the exchange.

Family secrets can be openly disclosed and discussed during a private mediumship session.

One of my students from Vermont attended my annual psychic mediumship retreat that is held every October in Massachusetts. She scheduled a private mediumship session with me hoping to contact a significant family member who shared an anniversary on the same date as my retreat. My student had felt the presence of this family member for the entire weekend and eagerly sought out the session with me as she wanted the loved one to come through. I did not know any of this when I worked with her.

A male spirit strongly communicated during the session and shared memories of his former physical life. Although she could not recollect his name, she recognized the spirit as a man from her childhood who lived in her neighborhood. The story he conveyed was extremely evidential. The man had sexually molested many children in the neighborhood and had been sentenced to prison. She had not been one of his victims, but she remembered him clearly from her childhood. I do not know why the loved one she desperately wanted to connect with failed to come through. However, the higher spirits clearly prioritized the pedophile as the communicator for the session for his healing and retribution. The doorway for reformation is never closed, even for the greatest sinner.

The Serial Killer

I served as a guest speaker and medium at a Spiritualist church in Hartford, Connecticut. During the spirit message portion of the service, I felt drawn to one of the church mediums sitting in the back. I felt a Native American guide with her who was bringing through a male spirit. All I could see in my mind's eye were human body parts. I did not see the spirit, but instead sensed much of the information. I felt that during his former life he had taken many human lives. In addition, I sensed that the spirit was psychologically diseased, and he now realized what he had done was wrong and had much work to do for retribution. The medium shared with me after the service. "I know that man. He was a famous serial killer. He used to rent out a house from my family for eleven years..."

The former serial killer did not speak as directly about his life as some communicators do, but was assisted by the helpers. The story he related was incomplete and more of an overview of his past. However, the information provided along with the memories was instantly recognized by the recipient and accomplished its objective in letting her know of his present status in the spirit world. Many spirits who communicate have happy and uplifting stories about their former physical lives to share. But many other spirits have issues and imbalances that also need to be expressed. In most cases, the spirits have ascended in consciousness and worked through their dysfunctions by the time they communicate through a medium. In other cases, they are still working on themselves and have taken responsibility for their transgressions and imperfections. Such spirits as the pedophile and serial killer need our prayers and healing light. Mediums are a voice for the higher spirits to speak through and for lower and ignorant spirits to convey their realizations and histories.

The Cheerleader

A young woman in my development classes in Massachusetts came to me for a private mediumship session. A pimply faced girl, fourteen years old, wearing a cheerleading uniform presented herself, who I felt was an acquaintance to the recipient. My student did not recognize the spirit who emphasized her eating disorders, emotional insecurities, and neediness. I asked the girl to provide further evidence. She responded with a memory from her former physical life, which I related to my student. "She got into the car with the wrong guys, and that was it." My student instantly remembered the spirit as her former classmate who had accepted a ride from some men who raped and murdered her. She could now recognize all the details and attributes about the girl as being correct.

My student did not know the girl well, but they had attended the same classes together when they were fourteen. The spirit emphasized her emotional issues and explained that she would help my student work with teenage girls with similar issues to herself. My student understood this information completely as she worked as a counselor for early adolescent girls with eating disorders. Although this spirit's story was tragic, she was clearly using the wisdom gained from her experience to assist others in going through similar situations.

The Vulcan Salutation

A well-known animal communicator and healer attended a group mediumship session that I did in California. After the meeting, she scheduled a private mediumship session for her husband with me for the next day. The session with her husband went well with many spirit loved ones and much practical guidance coming through for him. A seventeen-year-old boy stepped-in toward the end of the session. I felt that he had been extremely depressed and taken his own life. My client could not identify the spirit, so I asked the communicator to provide further information for recognition.

The spirit kept talking about *Star Trek* and science fiction. I felt like I wanted to do the *Star Trek* hand sign made popular by the actor Leonard Nimoy, who played Spock on the famous television series. As I spoke, I raised my hand forward with my thumb extended and my middle and ring fingers parted. My client still could not recognize the spirit coming through. I again asked for further details. The young man in the spirit world showed himself wearing a yarmulke or Jewish skullcap. "I see him wearing a yarmulke on his head; he was Jewish." Immediately, my client remembered the young man from when he was seventeen, when he had traveled with my client and his father to a *Star Trek* convention for the weekend. Although my client could not recollect the young man's name, he remembered the weekend they spent together distinctly. It is interesting to note that the young man emphasized his religious background with the Jewish headpiece and also his mention of the *Star Trek* hand sign, which is a physical representation of the Hebrew letter *shin* and comes from a Jewish prayer ceremony.

Many times, a spirit is not immediately identified by the recipient. Often, the individuals who come through from the spirit world are not who we would expect to communicate. Sometimes, it only takes one evidential detail from the communicating spirit for identification to take place. Here, the young man's story focused on the shared memory of the *Star Trek* convention. The intelligence and planning in the spirit world that goes into mediumistic communication is incredible. Unfortunately, the messages conveyed are often incomplete or easily mistranslated by the medium. A medium's proficiency to tell the spirit narrative as he or she receives it will result in accurate delivery of the spirit message. Storytelling as an art should be mastered by all mediums.

Ask the Spirits to Share

Mediums need to actively work with their spirit team as well as the various spirits who come through. A story contains characters, a setting, a plot, a conflict, and the resolution. Ask the spirits to share what happened in their lives and what they learned from the experience.

What spiritual and practical lessons do they wish to impart that are demonstrated in their stories? What is the relevance of a spirit's story to the situation of the recipient? Is it a similar situation or pattern? What advice or guidance is the spirit able to share, based on his or her experiences in his or her former physical life? How did such experiences affect his or her condition and spiritual outlook once he or she transitioned into the spirit world? What moral lessons or wisdom can the spirit impart? How have they evolved on a personal level since their physical death? A medium who gains proficiency in the art of spirit narrative will enhance the effectiveness and evidentiality of his or her mediumship.

Platform Exercises

EXERCISE 111

Connect the Dots

In a group or platform situation, the medium connects with a spirit communicator for the recipient. The medium has the spirit provide evidence for recognition, followed by details about his or her relationship with the recipient. Next, the medium has the spirit go to another individual in the audience and share details about this other connection. Finally, the spirit explains how both recipients are connected and share the spirit in common between them. This exercise can be done by either the indirect or direct method. If the exercise is done using the indirect method, the second recipient will also likely be able to initially identify the spirit.

EXERCISE 112

Platform With Back Turned Restricted

The medium stands up in front of the group with his or her back turned and links with the spirit world. The focus of this exercise is to receive evidential details from a recognizable individual. The medium works indirectly for three five-minute segments using only one phase of mediumship in each inclement. The mediumship teacher times each inclement and states to the medium which phase of mediumship he or she will use.-Clairvoyance, clairaudience and clairsentience. The medium must be disciplined and receive information only in the phase of mediumship selected. The medium shares evidential details but receives no verbal feedback from the recipients who remain absolutely quiet. The recipients silently indicate by nodding their heads to the teacher when the medium is correct or moving their heads side-to-side if incorrect. The recipients can motion with their hands if they are uncertain if the information is correct or incorrect. The teacher shares the responses with the medium as he or she is bringing through the communication. Members of a group can take turns working.

EXERCISE 113

Platform With Back Turned Two Connected

The medium stands up in front of the group with his or her back turned and links with the spirit world. The focus of this exercise is to receive evidential details from a recognizable individual who is connected to two individuals in the audience. The medium works indirectly for about ten minutes. The medium first brings a spirit communicator to a recipient in the group who is able to identify the individual coming through. Next, the medium connects the same spirit to another recipient in the audience who also recognizes the individual. The medium allows the spirit to explain his or her relationship with both recipients and also any connection between the two of them. The medium shares evidential details but receives no verbal feedback from the recipients who remain absolutely quiet. The recipients silently indicate by nodding their heads to the teacher when the medium is correct or moving their heads side-to-side if incorrect. The recipients can motion with their hands if they are uncertain if the information is correct or incorrect. The teacher shares the responses with the medium as he or she is bringing through the communication. Members of a group can take turns working.

EXERCISE 114

Two Unconnected One Link

The medium stands up in front of the group with his or her back turned and connects with two spirit people, unconnected to each other, who share nearly identical attributes and life stories and come through on the same link. All of the evidential details should be recognized by two unconnected recipients in the audience. The medium works indirectly for about ten minutes and receives no verbal feedback from the recipients who remain absolutely quiet. The recipients silently indicate by nodding their heads to the teacher when the medium is correct or moving their heads side- to-side if incorrect. The recipients can motion with their hands if they are uncertain if the information is correct or incorrect. The teacher shares the responses with the medium as he or she is bringing through the communication. Members of a group can take turns working.

Spirit Memory Exercises

EXERCISE 115

Grave Details

Participants pair up, hold each other's hands, and connect with the spirit world. Allow a spirit linked with the recipient to show his or her headstone, memorial or grave marker. Observe the headstone, memorial or grave marker and describe it in detail, including its location and surroundings. Read any inscriptions to the recipient, especially noting specific names, dates, places, poems, quotes or other details. Describe also any markings present. In some cases, the spirit's physical body was cremated and placed in a cremation urn or scattered. If so, describe the urn or container for the ashes and its location or the location of where the ashes were scattered. Take turns working.

EXERCISE 116

Spirit History

Participants pair up, hold each other's hands, and connect with the spirit world. Allow a spirit linked with the recipient to present a location in his or her former life in the physical world that is of regional or national historic significance. Feel as though you are there in the shoes of the spirit. Allow the spirit to share the history of the place and include as many unknown details that will require research for validation. Take turns working.

EXERCISE 117

Past and Present

Participants pair up, hold each other's hands, and connect with the spirit world. Allow a spirit linked with the recipient to provide details from his or her former physical life about the living conditions and society, and contrast with the details of similar conditions in the present. For example, trains then, and trains now, or forms of entertainment from the past compared to the present era. The spirit includes unknown details about the subject that will require research for validation. Take turns working.

EXERCISE 118

Spirit Shopping

Participants pair up, hold each other's hands, and connect with the spirit world. Allow a spirit linked with the recipient to take you on a memory from his or her former physical life of shopping for food at the market or grocery store. What are the foods, and how are they packaged? Allow the spirit to zoom into close-ups of product packaging and describe a typical shopping excursion. Take turns working.

EXERCISE 119

Spirit Meal

Participants pair up, hold each other's hands, and connect with the spirit world. Allow a spirit linked with the recipient to show his or her favorite meal. Name all the different foods. Notice how the meal is prepared and served. Feel the memory of the meal. Feel the surroundings and others present. What is the atmosphere and time of year? Smell and taste the food. Feel the satisfaction in the stomach experienced by the spirit. Take turns working.

EXERCISE 120

Spirit Cooking Lesson.

Participants pair up, hold each other's hands, and connect with the spirit world. Allow a spirit linked with the recipient to show his or her favorite food and provide the ingredients involved with the details for preparation. Smell and taste the food. Feel the satisfaction in the stomach experienced by the spirit. Take turns working.

EXERCISE 121

Spirit Handwriting.

Participants pair up, hold each other's hands, and connect with the spirit world. Allow a spirit linked with the recipient to show his or her handwriting. Is the writing cursive or block letters? Is it neat or messy? What language are the words in? What are the words written on? Read exactly what is written and share with the recipient. Take turns working.

EXERCISE 122

More Spirit Writing

Participants pair up, hold each other's hands, and connect with the spirit world. Allow a spirit linked with the recipient to show his or her handwriting. Feel the spirit blend his or her energies with you. Feel as though the hands of the spirit are sharing the same space as your hands. The spirit writes his or her name and a date, month, day and year. What is the significance of the date? Is the writing cursive or block letters? Is it neat or messy? What language are the words in? What are the words written on? Note also details about the hand. Is the spirit left or right handed? Are there missing fingers, age spots, or rings, etc.? What type of writing instrument is he or she using? Feel how the spirit used his or her hands, arthritic conditions, etc. Take turns working.

EXERCISE 123

A Personal Note

Participants pair up, hold each other's hands, and connect with the spirit world. Allow a spirit linked with the recipient to show his or her handwriting. The spirit writes out a personal message for the recipient about the current situation of the recipient. Is the writing cursive or block letters? Is it neat or messy? What language are the words in? Read exactly what is written and share with the recipient. The message should demonstrate the spirit's awareness of the recipient's present life. Take turns working.

Traveling Clairvoyance-Zoom In Exercises

EXERCISE 124

License Plate

Participants pair up, hold each other's hands, and connect with the spirit world. Allow a spirit linked to the recipient to present a vehicle connected with his or her life in the physical world. Zoom into the license plate or similar specific markings. Describe the license plate's features, color, region, words, etc. Take turns working.

EXERCISE 125

Spirit Vehicle

Participants pair up, hold each other's hands, and connect with the spirit world. Allow a spirit linked to the recipient to present a vehicle connected with his or her life in the physical world. Describe the outside of the vehicle. Go inside the vehicle and feel the interior from the viewpoint of the spirit. Observe and describe the details. What does this indicate about its owner? Take turns working.

EXERCISE 126

Outside the House

Participants pair up, hold each other's hands, and connect with the spirit world. Allow a spirit linked to the recipient to present the outside of a former residence from his or her life in the physical world. Feel and observe the location of the residence. Describe its features, nearby landmarks, etc. What does this indicate in terms of its owner? Take turns working.

EXERCISE 127

House Tour

Participants pair up, hold each other's hands, and connect with the spirit world. Allow a spirit linked with the recipient to show his or her former residence in the physical world. Feel as though you are in shoes of the spirit. In the manner of a real-estate tour, allow the spirit to start at the outside of the house and go inside. Tour the entire house: all the rooms, upstairs and downstairs. Feel the memory of the spirit. Observe the details and describe. What does this indicate about the spirit? Note the surroundings of the house. Take turns working.

EXERCISE 128

Street Address

Participants pair up, hold each other's hands, and connect with the spirit world. Allow a spirit linked to the recipient to present the outside of a former residence from his or her life in the physical world. Zoom into the number of the residence or similar specific marking. Take turns working.

EXERCISE 129

Object Inside House

Participants pair up, hold each other's hands, and connect with the spirit world. Allow a spirit linked to the recipient to present the outside of a former residence from his or her life in the physical world. Go inside the residence. Feel the memory of the spirit. Find an easily noticeable object, in the surroundings, connected to the spirit, and still possessed within the family. Feel the object. Describe its energy and history, and how it relates to the spirit. Take turns working.

EXERCISE 130

Buried Treasures

Participants pair up, hold each other's hands, and connect with the spirit world. Allow a spirit linked to the recipient to present the outside of a former residence from his or her life in the physical world. Go inside the residence. Feel the memory of the spirit. Go inside boxes, bookcases, drawers, etc. Take out an object. Feel its energy and history, and how it relates to the spirit. Take turns working.

EXERCISE 131

Worn Item

Participants pair up, hold each other's hands, and connect with the spirit world. Allow a spirit linked with the recipient to show a small personal item such as a piece of jewelry or cufflink that he or she wore in his or her former physical life. Feel the object, its history, and how it relates to the spirit's life. Describe in detail. Take turns working.

EXERCISE 132

Reading Material

Participants pair up, hold each other's hands, and connect with the spirit world. Allow a spirit linked to the recipient to show a bookcase, or individual books and other reading material, such as magazines, publications, etc. connected to his or her former physical life. Describe the type of books or reading material that is presented. Take turns working.

EXERCISE 133

Spirit Book

Participants pair up, hold each other's hands, and connect with the spirit world. Allow a spirit linked to the recipient to show a bookcase, or individual books and other reading material, such as magazines, publications, etc. connected to his or her former physical life. Take a single book out of the bookcase. What is its title? What is the name of the author? Feel the energy and history of the book and how it relates to the spirit. Open it up and look inside. Are there signatures, notes, damage, or library stamps? Take turns working.

EXERCISE 134

Old Photos

Participants pair up, hold each other's hands, and attune to the spirit world. The medium connects with a recognizable spirit, who presents an old, framed or unframed photograph. The photograph should be known to the recipient and identifiable, but not necessarily in his or her possession. Allow the spirit to tell the story of the event or incident captured in the photograph. The medium observes and feels both sides of the photograph noting details about the image on one side and any specifics of writing on the rear side. Take turns working.

EXERCISE 135

Spirit Letters

Participants pair up, hold each other's hands, and connect with the spirit world. Allow a spirit linked with the recipient to present a letter or document connected with his or her former physical life. Feel the paper and its history. Describe any details such as names, addresses, letterhead or other markings present and how this information relates to the spirit. Take turns working.

EXERCISE 136

Spirit Trip

Participants pair up, hold each other's hands, and attune to the spirit world. The medium makes a link with a spirit connected to the recipient, who impresses the mind of the medium with the memories of a physical journey he or she took in his or her former physical life. The entire memory of the route is experienced by the medium as though he or she is the spirit. The medium should observe the details and surrounding of the trip, and feel through all the senses the memory impressed by the spirit. Take turns working.

EXERCISE 137

Stamps

Participants pair up, hold each other's hands, and attune to the spirit world. The medium connects with a spirit, who presents old mail. The medium mentally feels and describes the memories associated with the envelope and looks close up at its details. The medium observes and describes the stamp, post mark, location and dates, and the addresses of the sender and the recipient. The medium mentally pulls the contents of the envelope out and feels the paper and describes the writing. Carefully note, any signatures, names, addresses, letterhead, art or photographs contained within the envelope, or on its contents. Take turns working.

EXERCISE 138

Old Postcard

Participants pair up, hold each other's hands, and attune to the spirit world. The medium connects with a spirit, who presents an old postcard. The medium holds the postcard and feels and describes the memories associated with it. The medium observes and feels both sides of the postcard noting the photograph or image on one side, and such details as the postmark, dates, places, names and writing. Take turns working.

EXERCISE 139

Old Newspaper

Participants pair up, hold each other's hands, and attune to the spirit world. Allow a spirit connected with the recipient to present a newspaper from the time of his or her former physical life. After viewing the front page, allow the spirit to present additional pages.

What is the name of the newspaper? Where was it published? In what language are its contents? What is the date of publication? Note the headlines on the front page and the headers for other articles throughout the publication. In addition, describe the newspaper's content including photographs, illustrations and advertisements that are present. What does this information tell you about the time period and the former physical life of the spirit communicator? Take turns working.

EXERCISE 140

Seasons of Spirit

Participants pair up, hold each other's hands, and connect with the spirit world. Bring in a spirit connected to the recipient who presents memories of his or her former physical life in a winter environment. Pay particular attention to the story presented with this memory and the evidential details related to the season of winter. Next, bring in another spirit connected to the recipient who presents memories of his or her former physical life in a summer environment. Pay particular attention to the story presented with this memory and the evidential details related to the season of summer. Feel the contrast between the two spirits and especially the two seasons. Take turns working.

CHAPTER 16

Conditions of Passing

W hat is the manner in which you would like to physically die? Sometimes people say *old age*, but there are many causes of death that affect the elderly as their physical bodies gradually weaken in the last stage of physical life. The process of death affects everyone as the physical body we temporarily inhabit during our present incarnation eventually ceases to function properly and then we have to leave it. Mediumship demonstrates the reality of life after death and that the personality is eternal and continues to exist in the spirit world.

Many mediums work indirectly when doing public demonstrations of mediumship. They connect to the spirit world and share evidential information until an individual in the audience can identify the communicating spirit. As previously noted, the problem with the indirect approach to delivering spirit communications is that it encourages mediums to ask many questions and gives the impression that they are uncertain in their abilities as instruments for the spirit world. In some cases, mediums will throw out the cause of death for the spirit they are connecting with. "I have a man here in the spirit world who passed over due to a lung condition." "Does anyone here know someone who passed over because of a stroke? " "Do you know a man or woman who passed over due to a heart attack?" There is nothing wrong with a medium receiving the spirit's manner of passing as part of the evidence. However, throwing out generic information that could apply to many is not convincing as evidential mediumship. In a large assembly, many audience members would know individuals who passed over due to any of the major causes of death.

As a medium, I prefer the direct approach to delivering spirit messages. I consider the indirect approach unnecessary and time-consuming. A medium who makes direct statements, in general, comes across as confident with his or her mediumistic abilities and not as though he or she is eliciting information from recipients. Of course, mediums should ideally avoid giving out generic messages with any presentation approach. Mediums should be as specific as possible, especially when relating the manner of physical death for the communicating spirits.

What are some leading causes of physical death? They include heart disease, cancer, accidents (unintentional injuries), chronic lower respiratory diseases, stroke (cerebrovascular diseases), Alzheimer's disease, diabetes, influenza, pneumonia, nephritis, nephrotic syndrome and nephrosis, and intentional self-harm (suicide). Millions of people worldwide pass over annually because of these conditions. Mediums should be familiar with these common causes of death, as such information is likely to be regularly included in the spirit messages they deliver.

A medium should always receive, if relevant, the manner in which a spirit communicator passed over to the spirit world. A medium can receive information about how the spirit physically died through any or his or her psychic senses. Mediums should avoid surface level descriptions of the common causes of physical death. Instead, mediums should as much as possible focus on bringing through manners of physical death that are unusual and stand out. For example, a man who passed over due to a heart attack while engaging in sexual intercourse with his wife would be a form of physical death that took place in a memorable situation. A woman losing her physical life through a shark attack would certainly stand out as a unique manner of death. Mediums who receive messages from spirits that include common causes of physical death such as heart attacks, strokes, or respiratory conditions should focus on the distinct circumstances of each situation. Unusual causes and circumstances of physical death make for the best evidence, as such details are easily remembered.

Many mediums feel uncomfortable receiving information about the cause of the spirit's physical death. In some cases, a medium may not even want to deliver such details as part of a spirit message, because of his or her belief that such information might upset the recipient. At a Spiritualist church in San Francisco, I brought through a spirit who had passed over due to accidental decapitation. "I feel like I don't have a head," I stated to the recipient. I heard later that a medium involved in running the church felt that such information was inappropriate and should not be part of a spirit message. The reaction of this medium clearly had to do with his own issues. The content of a spirit message, including the manner of the spirit's physical death, is given for a reason and should be delivered to the recipient. Mediums generally should not edit messages or allow their prejudices or inhibitions to get in the way.

A spirit communicator often presents the manner in which he or she died to the medium visually. Some mediums hesitate to receive causes of physical death, as they do not want to see anything gruesome or disturbing. In such cases, the clairvoyant pictures presented are never bloody or upsetting. I have worked as a medium for decades and brought through thousands of spirits. I have never once received a communication that contained scary or unpleasant imagery or information. Many people are unnecessarily uncomfortable with the subject of death and naturally shy away from it in conversation. Many mediums similarly feel that spirit messages should not contain precise details about the manner that the spirits vacated their bodies.

In most cases, the spirits use clairsentience to convey the cause of physical death. I typically feel the manner in which an individual physically died in my own body along with his or her personality, character, emotions, and other attributes. I have experienced numerous ways in which spirits have passed over such as the sensation of being hung with a noose around my neck, the anxiety and falling feeling experienced prior to a plane crash, my lungs filling with water through drowning, the awareness of stepping off a high surface and plunging to my death, the intense fear and compression of being trapped in a tight space, and many more. The sensations of physical death can be as intense as the physical occurrence. However, in most cases the feeling will be a subdued mental impression that is registered within the medium's body. I knew a medium who felt overwhelmed by the feeling of a spirit communicator's head being crushed inside a motorcycle helmet. A medium can always request that his or her spirit team tone things down should a sensation be too intense.

In the past, many spirits commonly entranced their mediums and dramatically reenacted their physical deaths as an evidential test. This phase of mediumship is known as personation and involves the medium taking on the conditions and mannerisms of the spirit.

I delivered an interesting spirit message to an elderly medium during a worship service at Temple Heights Spiritualist Camp in Maine. As I connected with a spirit communicator, I instantly felt as though I did not have a head and that the individual who I was bringing through physically died as a result of decapitation. I also was shown a forklift truck and the inside of a warehouse. The recipient told me after the service that the spirit coming through had been a good friend of her granddaughter. At the time of his physical death, he had been driving a forklift truck with his young son riding on the back. Because he had been playing around and not paying attention to where he was going, he accidentally decapitated himself.

Many mediums limit the types of physical deaths that they describe in spirit messages to only a few conditions. This is because they lack sufficient knowledge of the many causes of physical death. In other cases, they only feel comfortable including certain types of physical deaths in the spirit messages they deliver. For example, I knew a medium who in all of his public mediumship demonstrations brought through at least one spirit who died in an explosion. Mediums should learn as much as possible about the leading causes of physical death and ask their spirit teams to focus on providing this type of information in the messages they receive. While not the only type of evidence that mediums can receive, a medium should not hesitate to include the spirit's manner of physical death in the messages he or she delivers.

Causes of Death Exercises

EXERCISE 141

Manner of Death

Study the major natural causes of physical death and the percentages for various demographics. Learn the physical symptoms associated with various manners of death.

EXERCISE 142

Feel How I Died

Participants pair up, hold each other's hands, and connect with the spirit world. The medium brings in a spirit communicator connected with the recipient who provides his or her manner of physical death along with a basic description. The medium should feel through clairsentience the cause of physical death in his or her own body. The medium should allow the spirit to step back and link with another spirit connected to the recipient, who also provides his manner of physical death along with a basic description. The medium again should feel through clairsentience the spirit's conditions of passing over in his or her own body. The medium should mentally note and contrast the sensations experienced with both spirit communicators and how they passed over. Take turns working.

CHAPTER 17

Fake Mediumship

I t is easy to fake mediumship, as many people are incredibly gullible.
The desire to believe often supersedes skeptical inquiry. Attend a fake
séance and compare the experience with genuine spirit communication. Are you able to distinguish between fraudulent mediumship and
the real thing? Fake physical phenomena imitate genuine mediumistic
manifestations. Many of the nineteenth-century mediums, pioneers of
the modern Spiritualist movement, engaged in trickery part of the time
and, in some cases, all the time. There are many sincere testimonials of
physical mediumship that occurred in this period, few of which took
place under strict test conditions.

Harry Houdini (1874-1926), the brilliant Hungarian-born American
magician and escape artist, delighted in exposing fake mediums, and
disrupting fraudulent seances during the 1920s. Interest in mediumship
accelerated considerably following the First World War, due to the massive
numbers of individuals who had suffered the loss of loved ones in the
conflict and the 1918 influenza pandemic. Houdini initially attended
seances hoping to contact his deceased mother. It was an unsuccessful
and disappointing endeavor, in which he experienced firsthand the tricks
and sleight of hand practiced by many so-called mediums.

Physical mediumship is easily duplicated through stage magic tricks
and mentalist techniques of deception. However, imitation phenomena

are insufficient in duplicating the incredible power demonstrated through authentic physical manifestations. One of the best books on fake mediumship is M. Lamar Keene's *The Psychic Mafia,* which details his practice as a fraudulent medium within the Spiritualist movement. I recommend all students of mediumship read Keene's classic book. Keene (1936-1996) co-pastored a Spiritualist church in Tampa, Florida, and served for many years as a staff medium at Chesterfield Spiritualist Camp in Anderson, Indiana.[1]

Keene thoroughly describes the extensive files, maintained and shared among mediums, containing personal information about their clients. Keene also explains how he and other phony mediums produced bogus spirit phenomena for sitters in the darkness of the séance room. Although I remember seeing Keene's newly released book, as a child at a bookstore in the local shopping mall, I did not hear about it again until my teacher, Sylvia, talked about it at her home development circle.

As a teacher, Sylvia emphasized honesty within the practice of mediumship. She was disgusted that anyone could resort to trickery in regard to spirit communication. At one point, she attended a worship service at a local Spiritualist church, run by a dishonest medium mentioned in Keene's book. Sylvia described her experience at the evening service, which included a demonstration of phony blindfold billets. A billet is a small card or piece of paper, on which the sitter writes questions, names of departed spirits, or other information. The billet is folded, with the front marked by the recipient for identification. Billet reading is an authentic approach for receiving spirit communications, and works in the same manner as psychometry, or object reading. The medium uses the vibrations of the billet to connect with the spirit world. It is unnecessary for a medium to read the information contained within the billet. It is also unnecessary for the recipient to write any personal information or details. All that matters is that the recipient's energy is on the billet.

---

1 Keene, M. Lamar, *The Psychic Mafia,* Dell Publishing, New York, 1976.

Blindfold Billets

At this church service, the completed billets from the members of the congregation were collected in a basket and brought to the rostrum for the medium to work with during the spirit message portion of the service. The entire process was made into a big show with the medium's eyes taped over and blindfolded. The medium held one billet to his forehead, with his other hand in the basket, and read the personal information provided by the recipient, while pretending to bring through the named spirits, and answering the questions asked on the billet. A small light on the lectern assured that the medium could clearly view the details of the billet through the blindfold. Another medium, I knew, attended services at that church another evening, and the lectern light malfunctioned. Until the light was fixed, the medium could not deliver spirit messages with the billets.

I knew several individuals, unable to see through the trickery, who believed the mediums at this church were amazingly accurate. They did not realize that the discarded billets, collected from years of church services, were filed away as sources for future fraudulent spirit communications. Occasionally, I attended services at this church and deliberately wrote fictitious spirit names and questions on my billet, only to have the information later fed back to me as a spirit message.

There are many ways to do fake billets. A medium at Cassadaga Spiritualist Camp in Florida, explained to me how one of his relatives read information written on billets by reading their reflection in a mug of coffee kept on the lectern. Genuine billet mediumship does not require the sitter to provide personal information. As long as the sitter's vibrations are on the billet, an authentic medium can work, either by psychically reading the energy, or making a link with spirits connected to the sitter. Billets are always a fun exercise for mediumship development circles to do.

Camp Silver Belle

Silver Belle Spiritualist Camp, in Ephrata, Pennsylvania (1932-1991), was another establishment, in which phony physical mediumship regularly took place. Ethel Post Parrish (1885?-1958), the founder of Silver Belle, named the camp after her Native American guide. Although authentic mediumship undoubtedly took place at Silver Belle, the rampant fakery practiced by many of its mediums is well-documented. As a student medium, I first heard about Silver Belle Spiritualist Camp from many of the mediums and congregants at the Church of Two Worlds in Washington, DC, who described their wonderful experiences attending the physical seances held there.

My friend Fern, the elderly church organist, was especially impressed by the materialization seances, in which the spirits used ectoplasm to materialize and converse with the séance participants. One evening, Fern drove with me to Sylvia's home circle and described to the group how the inventor Thomas Edison materialized at a Silver Belle séance. Immediately, Sylvia challenged Fern, asking her; "Why would Thomas Edison want to materialize at a séance?" She bluntly explained to Fern that the physical phenomena at Silver Belle were tricks performed by fraudulent mediums.

At the time, two separate Spiritualist groups operated in Ephrata, both engaging in fraudulence and trickery.

In 1976 a split took place between members of the board of the camp, with one group maintaining meetings at the Mountain Springs Hotel under the name *Temple of Truth,* and the other group, using the name *Silver Belle,* operating at another location in Ephrata. I wanted to visit both establishments. I did not care whether the phenomena were genuine or trickery. My main interest was experiencing Spiritualism in all its forms, and as a student of mediumship, even fake mediumship would be educational for me.

A Memorable Visit

In June 1988, I drove with Fern and several of her friends to the Temple of Truth. We arrived Saturday morning, right after the healing class finished, and in time for the 11 AM philosophy class. At the Temple of Truth, there were activities scheduled all day that were mainly held in the large chapel on the grounds. At the time of my visit, the entire camp was extremely dead, with only twenty visitors for the weekend, most of who were registered to attend a week-long series of seminary classes. Besides myself, there was only one other person, a woman from Manhattan, who was under the age of fifty-five. Most of the attendees were well over eighty years of age.

At 1 PM, I attended the worship service in the camp chapel. During the spirit message portion of the service, the medium told me that I needed to meditate more, which seemed odd because I meditated diligently for several hours a day. At 4 PM, I attended a development class on physical mediumship conducted in one of the séance rooms. I will never forget this class for as long as I live. After an opening prayer, the medium proceeded to go into trance and speak in a high-pitched squeaky voice: "My mommy, she is asleep now". Thank God that I had never been exposed to anyone pretending to channel *Joy Guides* before this, as I would have been completely turned off by Spiritualism. A Joy Guide is a child guide who appears at séances to raise the vibrations through jokes and juvenile antics. For example, the spirit control of Mary Pepper Vanderbilt (1867-1919), a prominent American medium from Brooklyn, New York, who held seances for the Czar of Russia in 1906, was a Native American girl named Bright Eyes. Little Bright Eyes was known by séance attendees for her laughter and sense of humor. [2]

---

[2] Cadwallader, M. E., Mary S. Vanderbilt, A Twentieth Century Seer, The Progressive Thinker Publisher House, Chicago, 1921. p. 5.

Insane Séance Room Antics

The medium continued to speak in the same silly, childish voice, as she taught class for the next two-and-a-half hours. Although I was deeply eager to learn, I found the experience extremely boring, and a waste of time. I would have preferred that the medium skip the phony theatrics and teach the class as herself, but I assume she wanted to please the other participants. The attendees appeared mainly interested in experiencing sensationalistic spirit manifestations.

Several different sized spirit trumpets were positioned on a table in the center of the room, and she instructed the participants to get up and sense the vibrations around them. "Do you feel the energy around the trumpet?" she asked. I cannot express the happiness I felt when the class finally ended and the medium pretended to come out of trance. When the medium was asked by a woman what she experienced while in deep trance, she explained, "I went out of my body to the spirit world and took a walk around..."

Sunday morning, a worship service in the chapel took place that involved billets. A woman at the door handed me a slip of paper, on which I was to write a question and on the other side my initials for identification. During the service, the medium took each billet and allegedly brought through deceased loved ones for the recipients.

At the end of the message portion of the service, the medium's assistant returned the billets to the recipients. Several of the elderly participants received their billets back, on which were written in ballpoint pen messages from the spirit world. One elderly medium in his 90s stood up, and exclaimed to all present the marvelous message that he received. "We are with you always." Of course, in his excitement, he never considered the fact that the woman, who distributed and collected the billets, wrote the purported spirit messages.

None of the mental mediumship I observed at the services and programs that weekend was genuine. The mediums provided the others, all regular attendees at the camp, with names and details about their deceased loved ones. However, I received the most generic, vague messages possible. A novice, not knowing any better, would not recognize the difference as their use of language and presentation expertly duplicated that of genuine mediums. As I observed the camp mediums work throughout the weekend, their lack of attunement with the spirit world was obvious. On Saturday night, they would not let me attend any of the physical materialization seances held. They explained, "If someone touches the ectoplasm, it could kill the medium." True, a sitter unexpectedly touching ectoplasm during a séance could harm an authentic physical medium, but the real reason that they did not allow me to attend is they did not want to risk the possibility that I might disrupt their bogus séance.

The next morning, Fern remarked how wonderful the seance she had attended had been, and proceeded to name off the famous historic and Biblical personalities who had appeared. She remarked to me that she could not understand why George Washington, who had materialized in the seance room, needed to tell such dirty jokes to the seance participants. The Temple of Truth's final season was the summer of 1988. It did not reopen the following year, and the property was put up for sale. I also visited Camp Silver Belle in Ephrata in June 1990. The mediumship exhibited there too was also highly questionable. The camp closed its doors for good the following year.

Phony Spirit Photography

Many individuals showed me alleged spirit photographs obtained at Silver Belle, depicting their portrait surrounded by the faces of spirit guides. When the contents of the Mountain Springs Hotel were publicly auctioned off in 1989, the local historical society managed to purchase many of the items on sale, including several boxes of such photographs, along with an extensive collection of various cut out heads used to produce the fake spirit extras when producing the phony spirit photography.[3]

[3] Spohn, Clarence Edwin, *The Ephrata Mountain Springs Volume II: The Later Years, 1882-2004, Including the Von Nieda Years, Camp Silver Belle and the Temple of Truth, and Ephrata's First Hospitals,* Historical Society of the Cocalico Valley, Ephrata, Pennsylvania, 2010. pp. 305-306.

Spirit Gifts Made in China

An apport is a physical object that is dematerialized by the spirit chemists and transported to the séance room where it is rematerialized. Apportation is an amazing and genuine phase of physical mediumship. The apports manifested at phony physical seances are usually inexpensive objects easily purchased online or at discount outlets. One phony medium dramatically regurgitates small stones all over the floor at his seances which he presents to séance attendees as gifts from various Ascended Masters and other advanced spirits.

A Fake Materialization

A Spiritualist medium I know told me an account of a noted physical medium's materialization séance attended by his wife. As the medium sat in trance within the cabinet, the cabinet curtain parted as a child spirit appeared. Suddenly, the cabinet tipped over, smashing onto the floor. The child spirit was the medium on her knees, who accidentally bumped into the cabinet. The medium's wife demanded her money back.

The Return of Martin Luther King Jr.

In Washington, DC, I attended a trance circle held at a Spiritualist church. An elderly former Silver Belle medium and a student in his twenties, served as the mediums. Child guides controlled both mediums simultaneously and engaged in a conversation with each other in squeaky voices. A variety of exalted spirits, including Biblical prophets, communicated to the circle participants. Martin Luther King. Jr. highlighted the session with an off-key rendition of the song *We Shall Overcome*. After the session I chatted with the younger medium, who was around the same age as myself. It was amusing to watch his reaction when I told him that I was a medium. The unease registered on his face was priceless.

The Ideal Fake Physical Séance

Require all attendees to fill out a detailed application form providing personal details, questions they want to ask the higher spirits, and the names of deceased personalities they wish to contact.

Make it mandatory for the sitters to include copies of their ID cards or passports with the application. This way you know their genuine identity, and can plan accordingly.

Require all attendees to remove their shoes and empty their pockets. Use a metal detector to make sure they have no hidden flashlights, cameras or other devices on their persons.

Make a great show of having someone present search the cabinet. But don't allow anyone to search you. Control the proceedings.

Use zip tie elastic handcuffs to secure yourself to your seat. Never use metal handcuffs or anything that might actually restrict you.

Control where the participants sit. In a genuine séance, it is good to alternate sitters by gender and position those who are good batteries in key positions to provide power. But on the flip side, -when a phony medium positions sitters, it enables him or her to know where everyone is seated for the phony mediumship that will take place in the session.

Play really loud, ear-splitting music at the beginning of the session and in-between phenomena. Forget boring religious hymns; upbeat contemporary music is best. Sitters can sing along and, best of all, the music effectively masks the sound of your movement.

Require everyone to hold hands. While this is genuinely useful for building the power in an authentic séance, it also allows you to control the movements of those involved and prevent interference.

Repeat the same performance or variations of it, multiple times in multiple locations.

Channel deceased celebrities. Pop stars are the best. Talk in a funny foreign accent. Make sure you get your facts straight, make sure that you don't channel Abraham Lincoln with a phony Southern accent.

Student Discernment Exercises

EXERCISE 143

Fake Blindfold Billets.

Bring an individual to the group who is unfamiliar to the participants. Tell students that he or she is a medium and will demonstrate spirit communication via blindfold billets.

Hand out blank billets to members of the group, who write the names of deceased loved ones on the billets along with a personal question. The students fold the billets, and on one side write their initials for identification. The billets are placed in a basket.

Place the basket on a lectern or table with a light that can be turned on. Blindfold the medium securely with a fabric that can be seen through easily, especially under a strong light.

Next, the medium pretends to connect with the spirit world. He or she brings through all the spirits written on each billet and answers the question asked. Impress your students.

At the end of the guest medium's amazing demonstration of mediumship, tell your students that he or she was faking it and explain in detail, how the trick was accomplished. Contrast the fake mediumship exhibited with real mediumship, by using the same billets to demonstrate genuine spirit communication.

Anne Gehman, a prominent American medium, told me her experiences doing a variation of this exercise with her mediumship development class to teach them discernment.

EXERCISE 144

Fake Channeling

Bring an individual to the group, who is unknown to the participants. Tell students that he or she is a trance medium and will demonstrate trance channeling. Instruct the students to tune into the vibration of the medium, while he or she is bringing through spirits.

The medium sits in front of the group and pretends that he or she is entranced by a spirit teacher, who proceeds to deliver a short address to those present.

Afterwards, ask the students to share their feelings about the talk. Explain to students that the medium was not genuinely entranced and was pretending to channel a spirit teacher. Emphasize how to ascertain authentic entrancement and spirit communication.

CHAPTER 18

Ethical Considerations

A friend of mine, who practices mediumship in the UK, told me about an experience she had as a novice studying with an extremely well-known international medium at the Arthur Findlay College of Psychical Science in Stanstead, England. At the time, my friend regularly attended courses facilitated by various instructors at the college. During an exercise, she brought through a young male spirit, who passed over into the spirit world suffering from Auto Immune Deficiency Syndrome (AIDS). While in the middle of delivering the message to the recipient, the instructor slammed her notebook onto the floor, loudly cut my friend off from completing the communication, and stormed out of the room. The instructor exclaimed in front of the entire class how the information in the spirit message was inappropriate. "It is emotionally insensitive to convey such a message to the recipient."

My friend felt disturbed by this teacher's response. The spirit message was articulated correctly and understood by the recipient who did not have any problem with its content. The instructor, however, continued to voice her disapproval "What if the mother of the recipient was present and did not know that her son was homosexual?" Should mediums censor information they receive from the spirit world? Are there messages that could harm the recipient and therefore should be blocked by the medium? If so, what are they?

First, the process of spirit communication is carefully orchestrated by the higher spirits, who set the agenda for the content of the session in terms of both the spirit communicators and messages. Any spirit communicating through a trained medium not only wants to come through, but is permitted by higher spirits in charge of the session. Spirits attend classes in the spirit world to learn the process and even observe spirits coming through mediums as part of their training.

In addition, the spirit team of the medium functions as intermediaries between the spirit communicators and their medium. Spirit communicators are carefully vetted by the spirit team. Information given during a session is prioritized in terms of importance for both the recipient and spirit communicators. Although a medium bringing through spirits often seems to be spontaneously working, a great amount of planning and effort goes into any mediumship session.

It is important that teachers of mediumship emphasize to their students the need for their students to exude compassion, respect, and sensitivity to the emotions and situation of a spirit message's recipient. In public demonstrations of mediumship, it is always proper etiquette to ask permission to deliver the communication before bringing the message through.

In all the decades that I have demonstrated mediumship from the platform, there have only been a few times when someone has not wanted to receive a spirit message. However, a medium should never assume that everyone in attendance at a mediumship demonstration wants to receive a personal message.

The Five Stages of Grief

It is common for individuals to consult a medium to connect with their deceased loved ones. The Swiss psychiatrist Elizabeth Kubler-Ross

(1926-2004) originated the concept of the Five Stages of Grief that individuals suffering a loss typically experience. These stages are Denial, Anger, Bargaining, Depression, and Acceptance. These stages occur for most bereft individuals, although not necessarily in the above order. An individual going to a medium may be experiencing any of these stages. Similarly, individuals suffering psychological turmoil also consult mediums. The typical student of mediumship lacks an in-depth understanding of psychology, and how to effectively deal with mentally ill individuals. How a medium delivers a spirit message greatly impacts the recipient. The words of a medium can potentially heal or damage the recipient.

A medium is responsible for what he or she says. He or she holds great power over his or her clients, who often are afflicted with emotional imbalances. A medium needs to know when to refer clients to other practitioners and not attempt to work beyond the scope of his or her practice. It is good for a practicing medium to have such contact information available for clients, should the need to make a referral come up. A medium's responsibility is to serve God and the spirit world as an instrument for the higher spirits to work through. Often, within the Spiritualist movement restrictions are placed upon mediums as to what type of information a medium should receive, and how it should be delivered. For example, some teachers of mediumship dogmatically assert that a spirit message that does not contain evidence of survival is inferior and insufficient. Often, a nonevidential message is classified as a psychic message.

In many Spiritualist churches mediums are restricted from delivering messages containing descriptions of spirit guides, past lives, practical guidance, and predictions. Mediumship is not about fortune telling or superficial psychic information. It is soul-to-soul communication from the heart to the heart. Mediumship is the expression of the communicating spirits and should never be unnecessarily restricted. Evidential mediumship serves an important purpose in assisting individuals in their soul journey.

However, the emphasis placed on this approach to mediumship neglects the fact that the information the higher spirits may want to communicate to an individual may not be very evidential at all.

Past life information, practical guidance and even predictions, at times, all serve a purpose in enlightening, healing, and uplifting those in need. Mediums generally should not restrict the type of information they receive. The higher spirits know what the recipient needs to hear for their highest good and greatest growth. A medium should avoid diagnosing and prescribing unless he or she is a licensed medical practitioner. A medium working as a traditional healer in indigenous cultures is expected to provide information relating to health conditions. However, in most countries there are laws to protect patients from unqualified medical practitioners. A medium is responsible for the advice that he or she gives to the recipient. It is better ethically and legally for mediums to not provide such information. My spirit helpers do not diagnose health conditions, nor do they prescribe treatments. Similarly, mediums should not provide legal advice, unless they are licensed to practice law.

A medium should also be careful when bringing through guidance from the spirit world. The higher spirits provide constructive suggestions and input, but they never tell individuals what to do or interfere with their freewill. Some individuals who lack maturity or emotional balance will blindly follow anything a medium says without applying their commonsense and intelligence. Spirit messages can also easily be misconstrued or misunderstood by recipients in a way that is detrimental. A medium cannot completely prevent this from happening, but he or she can minimize it by maintaining a high standard of mediumship.

As a medium, my spirit team edit the messages beforehand. The higher guides connected to the recipient know what information he or she is ready for and capable of receiving. They understand the psychology and soul history of the recipient. The higher spirits always provide encouragement and support. Criticism is always delivered in a positive, constructive way. In a public situation, the higher spirits know the effect a message will have upon a recipient. All messages are conveyed by the higher spirits for a reason. It is not the responsibility of the medium to understand the context of the message or how it relates to the recipient's life. Never edit a spirit message. Give out what you receive exactly as you get it. Don't assume that a message will embarrass or upset a recipient in public. The higher spirits know where individuals are at and how they will react. Never project personal sensitivities or issues into the delivery of spirit communications. Trust the higher spirits and the healing they impart.

A teaching medium stated how inappropriate and horrible it was for another medium to deliver a spirit message to a grieving mother that contained the grisly details of the recipient's daughter's murder. The teacher felt that such information would only further traumatize the fragile emotions of the distraught mother. It is understandable that a medium might feel uncomfortable delivering such information. However, the higher guides in charge of the session will never provide information that distresses a recipient.

A spirit grandfather related his physical health conditions to a medium and how he lost control of his bowels, soiled his clothes and smelled. Is it appropriate for a medium to share this message during a public mediumship demonstration? Should a medium omit the parts of this message that he or she deems unpleasant?

A medium has freewill to edit or censor all or part of the message he or she receives. However, when this takes place, it generally has to do with the medium feeling uncomfortable. The spirit grandfather presented his loss of bowel control as part of the message for a reason. It is wrong for mediums to interfere with a message's content and disrespectful to the spirit communicators. The higher spirits know what the recipient can handle. They will never convey information that harms, embarrasses, or contributes to the anxiety of the recipient.

Don't limit your mediumship. A good therapy session involves identifying and recognizing issues that need work. Sometimes healing is difficult and painful.

Evidence of survival does not always focus on the positive attributes of the spirit communicator. Spirit communicators are real people with defects and dysfunctional issues. There are times during a mediumship demonstration in which a medium receives a message that is best shared privately. In such a situation, the medium is told by the spirit team that this is the case, and not because he or she feels uncomfortable about the content of the message. The medium will be directed to request the recipient to see them privately at the conclusion of the demonstration.

Deliver messages in a straightforward, compassionate manner, without deliberately altering or leaving out any of the information. Always exercise common sense, but realize the spirit team vets the spirit communicators, and the higher guides set the agenda in terms of the content. I knew a medium whose spirit team messed up in vetting a spirit communicator. The spirit ex-husband came through during a public demonstration and in foul language expressed his disdain for his former wife. In this situation, the spirit team clearly did not do their job properly and somehow this spirit slipped through. The medium rightfully did not convey the message. This sort of situation is rare and should never occur if a medium works properly. Undisciplined mediumship results potentially in dishonest, rude, and disruptive spirits coming through.

Sensitive information comes through from the spirit world for a reason. A message that could adversely affect a recipient is always transmitted by the spirits in a loving manner. Sexual predators and abusers often communicate from the spirit world to their victims and members of their families. It is the medium's responsibility to deliver such facts about communicators with kindness and love.

The content that is presented in a spirit message is well thought out and serves a higher purpose. Faults and shortcomings are emphasized for a reason. For example, a spirit uncle who passed over from liver damage due to alcoholism may emphasize how this addiction destroyed his life. The evidential details about this aspect of his former physical life could be portrayed in numerous ways depending upon the points needing to be made. An incident in which the intoxicated uncle crawled on the floor through his own vomit or similar memories could be presented. In this case, such heavy information might be given for the highest good of the message's recipient, who also suffers from alcoholism. The spirit uncle's message is both evidential and also provides soul guidance for the recipient.

Many mediums feel uncomfortable describing the manner in which an individual passed over to the spirit world. While a graphic description of an individual's physical death is potentially upsetting for those in mourning to hear, the higher spirits know what messages recipients can handle. They do not want to traumatize or upset anyone. Mediums do not see the bigger picture or implications of a spirit message for the recipient. A medium's responsibility is to give out exactly what is received. A medium at a Spiritualist church brought through a young man who sexually abused children. The message was delivered in a supportive and loving manner. The secretary of the church, however, was disturbed by the message and banned the medium from working at the church.

During a private mediumship session, it is perfectly fine for a spirit communicator to swear or use foul language, if such language is evidential or serves to make an important point. This would never happen if such language offended or upset the recipient. Foul language will also never come through during a public demonstration, as this would be inappropriate. In public situations, with my mediumship, I am shown cartoon word balloons with black clouds that symbolically convey the foul language spoken by the spirit. I also feel the idea of the spirit saying off color words-without hearing the specifics.

The Witch Doctor

My teacher Pauline, as part of her examination for mediumship certification, was required to do a complete service as a guest speaker and medium at a Spiritualist church other than her home church. As Pauline delivered spirit messages, she was drawn to a young, stern looking black man sitting in the congregation of the mainly white church. Pauline felt the spirit presence of an African witch doctor, who showed her a small pouch filled with bones and other items related to his healing work. Pauline hesitated to give the message. This happened during the 1960s, when the civil rights movement was in full swing with riots and civil disturbance taking place throughout the USA, including the city in which the church was located. Pauline did not want to say anything that could be perceived as racially insensitive or insulting to the recipient.

Pauline went ahead and conveyed the message to the recipient, who sat stone-faced as she described the witch doctor and the contents of the pouch in detail. Pauline concluded the message and quickly moved on to deliver a message to another individual in the congregation. Out of the corner of her eye Pauline saw the recipient of her last message stand up. "Oh no, now I am in for it," Pauline thought. The young man faced the congregation and stated: "I want everyone in this church to know the pouch that she described belonged to my grandfather. He was his tribe's witch doctor, and I have his pouch at my home." A medium should trust the information that he or she receives from the spirit world, and convey messages without hesitation, knowing that the higher spirits always have the best interest of the recipient at heart.

Spirit Warnings

Make sure that spirit messages are properly worded. Often, a seemingly negative prediction is a warning given by the higher spirits to prevent a potential mishap from taking place. For example, a medium sees an image of the recipient driving on an ocean-side mountain road excessively fast. The car veers off the side of a cliff into the ocean, breaking into pieces and exploding. A novice medium might tell the recipient that he or she was going to drive off the side of a cliff and die. This clearly would be an inappropriate, negative message, as it would adversely affect the recipient. It also would be an incorrect translation of the information given by the spirit world. Perhaps the recipient regularly drives fast on such an ocean-side road and does not exercise much caution. While the clairvoyant imagery accurately describes the recipient's situation, the real message is that the recipient needs to slow down and exercise caution to avoid a potential accident.

Years ago, at a Spiritualist church in Vermont, I delivered a spirit message to an elderly couple. I was shown the top shelf of a closet, packed full of boxes and other items. The spirits told me that the recipient needed to be careful when opening the closet as items could fall from the top shelf and cause injury. An inexperienced or poorly trained medium could easily misinterpret such a warning and state the information as an unavoidable prediction.

Channeling Living People

In some circumstances, a medium may receive communications from individuals who have not physically passed over, such as those in a coma or suffering from dementia. If the recipient recognizes that the individual coming through is someone he or she knows to be still alive, it is important for mediums to state that they are not sure if the individual is positively physically dead yet, but they are bringing through the information. In others cases, a medium may receive information about individuals physically alive. A student medium must learn to differentiate between information about physically incarnate individuals and spirit personalities coming through. I have seen too many inexperienced and poorly trained mediums, after describing information about an individual, ask the recipient, "Is this person here in the physical world or in the spirit world?"

Honesty

A British medium I knew did a private session for an affluent Italian American woman on Long Island, New York. During the session, the woman's spirit father, a former Italian Mafioso, communicated. The woman had one major question that she wanted the spirit world to answer. She had two options to choose from, and she wanted the spirits to tell her the best choice. The woman was extremely pushy and insistent. She reacted strongly when the medium relayed that her spirit father said that he did not feel what she was planning was a good idea. The woman continued to pressure the medium for a definitive answer. This medium, to shut her up, could easily have told the woman that either of her choices was favorable, but, as an ethical medium with good training, he refused to accommodate her by changing the information and lying to her. The medium later found out that the woman wanted to hire a hitman to murder someone and wanted the spirits to pick the best possible candidate.

Picking Up Clients

I knew a very prominent medium who attempted to pick up many of his attractive male clients. This led to formal complaints from some of his clients, who were disturbed by his inappropriate advances and his dismissal as a staff medium at a prestigious Spiritualist center. Another medium I knew sexually abused the young men who came to him for mediumship sessions and healings. Once at the Lily Dale Assembly in New York, I watched him demonstrate mediumship at an outdoor spirit message service in front of a standing room only audience of several hundred people. He stood on the concrete covered stump and addressed a large breasted woman sitting in the front row while making grabbing motions toward her chest with both his hands "Can I read for you? I can read Braille..."

The teenage son of a medium, I knew, almost committed suicide as a result of the abuse that took place. A resident medium at Lily Dale in the summers and Cassadaga Spiritualist Camp in Florida in the winters, the abusive medium's predatory behavior was largely ignored by others within the Spiritualist movement. He finally was formally removed as a registered medium at Lily Dale after a victim threatened legal action against the association. His removal did not prevent him from continuing to work out of his residence on the grounds. However, he ended up switching the focus of his operations to Cassadaga Spiritualist Camp. For every action there is a reaction, such is the Law of Cause and Effect. The following year he was bludgeoned to death and robbed by a man he brought home, after meeting in a bar. As a medium, it is important to keep your personal life separate from the people you are working with.

Things Not to Do as a Medium

- Predict death, disasters, or divorce.
- Diagnose or prescribe.
- Extort money.
- Steal.
- Lie.
- Engage in sex with sitters.

Some Points to Consider for Message Delivery

- Be delicate.
- Be polite to sitter and spirit.
- Be compassionate and understanding.
- Be tactful.
- Don't edit give what you get-Express the spirit.
- Don't let your own inhibitions or issues get in the way of the message.
- Exercise common sense, but don't sugar coat the information.
- If the spirits give information, there is a reason.
- Be honest at all times.

When am I ready to Do Sessions?

A good mediumship program facilitated by a competent teacher always includes opportunities for students to work with the public. This is true for any educational program of study. Many years ago, I attended school for massage therapy, which involved hundreds of hours of training for over a year and a half. In the final semester, students were required to perform instructor supervised full body massage sessions, with paying members of the public. As a student medium at the Church of Two Worlds in Washington, DC, I did private mediumship sessions, delivered spirit messages from the platform, and learned to moderate all aspects of a Spiritualist worship service, including delivering an inspirational address.

Patience and Persistence

Students understandably want to work publicly as quickly as possible. The enthusiasm and the desire to work with the spirit world are good things. In the past, many teachers required their students to only practice mediumship within the confines of the development circle. While this might sound unnecessarily restrictive, this approach produced incredibly strong instruments for the spirit world. You cannot cut corners with mediumship development. Patience and persistence over a period of many years result in a high standard of mediumship.

A young woman attended a mediumship development workshop that I facilitated in Texas. She had never taken part in anything having to do with mediumship before. As part of the training, I worked with her so that she could link with a spirit communicator for another workshop attendee. Through my prompting, she accurately brought through the spirit personality's former street address, and first and last names. Anyone can learn to receive spirit messages and accurately deliver them. A total novice is capable of this under the right conditions. Many individuals participate in online mediumship groups, or attend a few workshops, and afterwards set themselves up as professional mediums.

Certified by God

Many years ago, at Cassadaga Spiritualist Camp in Florida, a man attended several of my workshops. As a student, his abilities were typical for someone with his amount of experience. A year later, when I returned for more teaching work, he contacted me and explained that he was now a certified medium and had set himself up professionally doing readings across the street from the camp. As a teacher, I could tell that there was absolutely no way that this individual was ready to work professionally with the public. I asked him where he had received his certification, and he explained that he had been certified by God.

Mediumship and Spirits

Alcohol, cannabis, and other intoxicants do not mix with mediumship. Mental mediumship requires a clean mind, clear of analytical clutter and delusion. Many mediums are imbalanced emotionally and turn to alcohol as a means of escape. Indeed, many great mediums of the past, including the Fox Sisters, Katie (1841-1892) and Margaret (1838-1893), founders of the Spiritualist movement, suffered from alcohol addiction. So did two outstanding platform mediums, John Slater (1861-1932) and Arthur Ford (1896-1971), physical mediums Charles Foster (1838-1888), Helen Duncan (1897-1936) and Margery Crandon (1888-1941) and many others.

At my teacher Pauline's Friday evening open development circle, a regular attendee showed up to class completely drunk, after attending the happy hour at a nearby bar. Nobody, including Pauline, realized that he was drunk, until after the meditation had started, when he repeatedly left his seat to urinate and get water to drink. At the completion of the circle, Pauline severely chastised him and warned him never to come to class drunk again. As a depressant, alcohol enables individuals to disassociate with no inhibitions. Spirit messages are easily received in this condition. Cannabis, a stimulant, similarly helps get the analytical mind out of the way. However, it is best for mediums to open up to the spirit world in a holistic manner. A medium's mind should always be clear and in control of the process.

Intoxication clouds the mind and pollutes the energy fields. A medium's mind and energy fields should be spiritually clear for the higher spirits to work through. Like attracts like, and the lower vibrations produced through intoxication create the wrong energies for spiritual work. Some uneducated individuals degrade the act of mediumship by demonstrating spirit communication in liquor shops, wineries, restaurants and other venues with alcohol served as part of the function. The act of mediumship is sacred, and there should always be reverence for the process. Mediumship is not superficial or cheap entertainment.

EXERCISE

EXERCISE 145

Reformed Souls

Participants pair up, hold each other's hands, and connect with the spirit world. The medium allows a spirit linked with the recipient to come through, who engaged in unethical or criminal behavior in his or her former physical life. The spirit shares memories about his or her behavior and how such actions impacted his or her life and the lives of others. In addition, the spirit describes how he or she has progressed in the spirit world and his or her present activities there. Take turns working.

CHAPTER 19

The Multi-faceted Medium

I attended a mediumship workshop many years ago facilitated by a prominent UK teaching medium who emphasized the importance of evidential communications from the spirit world. During the workshop, she selected a participant to stand up in front of the class and bring through communications for another member of the group. The student connected with the spirit world and delivered information to the recipient. The teacher presented two small handwritten signs to the class. On one piece of paper, she had written *Mediumship* and the other paper she had written *Psychic*. As the student worked; she alternated between holding up either of the signs depending upon what was coming through. She pointed to the sign *Mediumship* when the information described the communicating spirit and pointed to the sign *Psychic* when the student stated guidance or details about the recipient.

Many mediums from the UK teach that the purpose of mediumship is to prove survival, and any information about the recipient of the message is considered to be psychically received. Such mediums teach that advice or information about the recipient is obtained by reading the energy field of the recipient. I disagree with this view. As discussed in previous chapters, mediumship should never be restricted in terms of content.

Evidential mediumship is essential. However, practical guidance to assist with material and spiritual concerns is also important. Guidance from the spirit world, although not evidential, is still mediumship as the information is coming from individuals in the spirit world.

I remember the first complete mediumistic session that I did for someone. I had been sitting weekly in my teacher Pauline's Friday night development circle and several other circles for about six months. Mediumship felt completely natural for me, and I easily received accurate spirit messages for others in the group. Pauline selected me and two other students from her circle who she assessed as ready to do longer mediumship sessions for other members of the class. As a teacher, Pauline's goal was to prepare her students to work proficiently as mediums for both public platform work and private sessions.

My First Mediumship Session

Jan, an attractive young woman from the class, volunteered to be the recipient of my mediumship. Jan and I went to a secluded section of the church to work, while the rest of the class continued the evening's lesson. I held Jan's hands and prayed to God, asking the highest and best of my spirit guides to work with me and bring through information that would help Jan for her highest good and growth. As I prayed, I felt an overwhelming warm presence in the back of my head and neck. I simultaneously experienced intense heat in the center of my chest. I felt my heart chakra open wide and an incredible wave of love flow from my chest and surge throughout my body. At the same time, a flow of information about Jan entered my mind from the presence that I felt in the back of my head and neck. I could not stop speaking as images, feelings, and words describing situations in Jan's life were presented to me along with encouraging guidance to assist her with the various challenges and personal issues that she was dealing with in her life. I experienced the strong presence behind me and the flow of love from my heart chakra throughout the entire session. None of the information that I channeled during this session could have been considered evidential, as I did not bring through or describe any spirit communicators for Jan. However, Jan understood all the information and remarked to Pauline and the class how spiritually uplifting the session had been.

A medium working will feel the connection with the spirit world as I described above. The energy of the spirit world vibrates at a much faster frequency, affecting the medium's physiological systems. The medium's physical body goes into the Fight or Flight Response with the sympathetic nervous system activated because of the sudden release of hormones. In addition, the sympathetic nervous system stimulates the adrenal glands triggering the release of catecholamines, which include adrenaline and noradrenaline. The medium's heart rate and breathing are also considerably accelerated.

Pauline encouraged me as a student medium to deliver messages from the platform during the Sunday worship services at the Church of Two Worlds. After greeting the congregation, I would feel the intense vibrations as the spirits exerted partial control over me. A continuous flow of sensations would fill my mind, requiring instant interpretation and delivery. I simultaneously would see, hear, sense, know, smell, and taste the information and deliver the messages rapid fire like a machine gun.

Connect With the Power

A medium must learn to connect to the power, let go and allow the higher spirits and energies to flow. This solid connection will stay with the medium however long he or she is required to work. The idea that a medium always receives parts of content given in a session from spirits and other information from reading the energy fields of a recipient is false. A trained medium possesses the discipline to raise his or her vibration and connect with the spirit world and bring through communications. This discipline is gained through regularly sitting in the power alone as well as in the confines of a harmonious, properly facilitated development circle.

Psychic Information is Flat

A medium can certainly psychically read energy. However, the sensations associated with reading energy, whether from the aura of an individual, a material object, or the residue energy of a physical location, feel completely different than information channeled from the spirit world. Psychic information is flat and lacks the intensity of a mediumistic message. The source of a mediumistic communication is soul, and there is always an indication of the personality and intelligence behind the information coming through. A message containing guidance comes through for a reason. Mediumship is about serving as an instrument for the higher spirits, and what they feel is for the highest good for the recipient. The teaching that messages that are not evidential are psychic is false.

My teachers for mediumship development did not emphasize evidential communications. Instead, they placed more importance on connecting with higher spirits and bringing through guidance for recipients. A medium's responsibility is to receive and deliver spirit messages as accurately as possible. He or she should not judge the content of the message. In some cases, an evidential message may be necessary. Other situations may require advice or other information for the recipient to come through. The higher spirits are in charge and decide what information should come through.

I attended my first International Spiritualist Federation congress in 1994 on the Isle of Wight in the UK. I had not been exposed to many UK mediums before that week. I found that the approach to mediumship taught by most UK mediums differed completely from that of teaching mediums in the United States. In the UK, the emphasis for mediumship focused on establishing a solid link with a spirit communicator and receiving recognizable information that proved the identity of the spirit communicator. I have received many invaluable ideas from UK mediums over the years which have enhanced and expanded my mediumship and strengthened my ability to bring through evidential spirit messages.

Many UK mediums teach the indirect method for delivering spirit messages from the platform, which entails the medium first making a link with a spirit and throwing out information about the spirit to the audience to find the correct recipient. A UK teaching medium once explained to me that the indirect approach was essential because otherwise a medium could pick up the information psychically. She explained to me that going to a recipient directly was an emotional link. This is incorrect. While a medium might be drawn by the energy of someone sitting in the audience, the higher spirits will direct a medium to the correct recipient as they know who they want to connect with and where they are seated in public demonstration. It is foolish to suggest otherwise.

American Mediums are Inferior

A distinguished international medium from the UK told me that during her training at the Arthur Findlay College that many of her teachers emphasized how American mediums did not know what they were doing and that the UK approach to mediumship was superior. She felt that many Arthur Findlay College mediums were arrogant with their approach to teaching and actually believed that their mediumship was the best in the world. She explained to me that, because this is what she had been told, she had thought this way the first time she traveled to the United States to teach mediumship. I have met many mediums who buy into the idea that the approach to mediumship taught at the Arthur Findlay College is the highest standard of mediumship in the world. I remember a medium in the Boston, Massachusetts, area who ran a Spiritualist church and placed UK mediums on a pedestal. His church, almost monthly, sponsored leading mediums from the UK to serve throughout the year. The UK mediums, although prominent as exponents of Spiritualism, were not necessarily better than many of the well-trained local mediums. For this reason, many local, students of mediumship lost interest in attending the workshops offered by these visiting mediums, as the novelty of their approach wore off. As a medium, I have worked in many countries worldwide. While methods differ in various locations, outstanding mediumship is not limited to one geographic location or the result of one approach. Snobbery and elitism for any reason are signs of insecurity.

Many people similarly consider popular mediums who have achieved notoriety as media personalities or best-selling authors as superior in their skills. Fame is relatively easy to achieve with the right, well-paid publicist. Television appearances are not indicative of quality mediumship ability. Some of the best mediums in the world do not teach at Arthur Findlay College or star in their own reality television show. Such mediums tirelessly serve the spirit world and are not necessarily well known outside their sphere of influence. Such individuals are often the greatest exponents for the spirit world. Mediumship is not about achieving status or material gain.

Often mediums are jealous of other mediums. I remember at a Spiritualist camp where I served, other mediums would count the number of people coming to me for private mediumship sessions, because they were concerned that I might get more clients than them. Instead of working on their spiritual growth, many mediums exhibit insecurity and harbor jealous feelings toward other mediums. Mediums should make a point of overcoming any inclinations toward jealousy and try as much as possible to cultivate the qualities of humility and compassion.

I highly recommend the Arthur Findlay College for mediumship training for its quality instruction in all aspects of spirit communication. However, the curriculum at the school is extremely conservative in approach. Gordon Higginson (1918-1993), a strong personality and a brilliant medium, led the school for decades. His traditional Spiritualist approach to mediumship continued after his physical death with many of his leading students and their students teaching at the school. I watched Gordon Higginson demonstrate mediumship in a television documentary when I was five years old. His contributions to the Spiritualist movement are commendable. Mediumship should be broad-minded and progressive. A strong traditional foundation is absolutely necessary for quality mediumship. Students of mediumship should be exposed to as many approaches as possible and not unnecessarily restrict the manner in which the higher spirits work with them.

The American approach to receiving spirit messages within the Spiritualist movement generally involves greater emphasis on guidance for the recipient. In the UK, more emphasis is placed upon evidential information. American mediums tend to be stronger in bringing through practical advice and soul guidance and UK mediums excel in providing details and descriptions of recognizable spirits. In addition, American mediums, when doing public platform work, are influenced by their helpers to deliver messages directly to recipients in the audience, as opposed to indirectly throwing out evidential information about the communicators in order to find the correct recipient. The indirect approach is often time consuming and leads many mediums to ask unnecessary questions. I prefer the direct approach. However, what matters the most is the strength of the medium's connection with the spirit communicator, the accuracy of the information received, and its positive effect upon the recipient.

The Progressive Medium

A well-rounded medium is comfortable working directly or indirectly. He or she possesses the skill to deliver spirit messages using either approach. He or she is able to establish and maintain a strong connection with the spirit world in order to receive and accurately deliver evidential messages as well as guidance, higher philosophy, medical advice, and predictions. In addition, a strong medium can teach and assess others in the process of mediumistic development. He or she should be able to work under varying levels of spirit control from fully to semi-conscious. Proficiency in hands-on spiritual healing is also essential, as the practice of healing provides the right motivation for working with all the phases of mediumship. A strong medium is not limited in his or her approach to mediumship or with his or her ability to serve the spirit world in a multifaceted manner.

Mediums should be careful about feeling proud about their mediumship. They should never boast about their abilities or unfavorably comment about other mediums. Student mediums should always be wary of mediumship teachers who present their approach to mediumship as superior. Never be jealous of other mediums. Always look for the good in how other mediums are working and encourage them. Never criticize other mediums' approaches to working with the spirit world. Instead, share constructive input with other mediums in a loving manner, with a desire to see the best flourish in the expression of their spiritual gifts.

Assorted Enhancement Exercises

EXERCISE 146

Name Poems

Stand in the middle of a circle of participants. Attune to the spirit world and allow a higher guide to blend with your energy. Step behind each participant. Place your fingers lightly upon his or her temple and allow the guide to convey the recipient's spiritual name and three or four verses of poetry that describe as nearly as possible his or her character. In a group situation, participants can take turns working. Cora L. V. Richmond (1840-1923), the world famous trance medium and exponent for the Spiritualist movement, in this manner channeled thousands of such poems in the course of her ministry.[1]

EXERCISE 147

Spirit Sports

Participants pair up, hold each other's hands, and connect with the spirit world. The medium allows information about sports or references to athletic activities, either symbolic or literal, to be presented that relates to a recognizable spirit communicator. The medium should elaborate on the sport or sport references with evidential details about the spirit communicator. Take turns working.

EXERCISE 148

Spirit Vessels

Participants pair up, hold each other's hands, and connect with the spirit world. The medium allows information about a watercraft such as a boat, ship, hovercraft or submarine, either symbolic or literal, to be presented that relates to a recognizable spirit communicator. The medium should elaborate on the watercraft reference with evidential details about the spirit communicator. Take turns working.

EXERCISE 149

Channeling Ethnicity

Participants pair up, hold each other's hands, and attune to the spirit world. Bring in an individual connected to the recipient from a different ethnic background. Allow the spirit to emphasize his or her cultural identity in a manner that involves using all of the psychic senses. See, hear, sense, smell, taste, and know the information presented. Take turns working.

---

[1] Barrett, Harrison D., *Life Work of Mrs. Cora L. V. Richmond,* Hack & Anderson Printers, Chicago, 1895. pp. 340-341.

EXERCISE 150

Numbers

Participants pair up, hold each other's hands, and connect with the spirit world. The medium receives the entire message completely with numbers, which may have significance within his or her own life experience. The medium interprets and translates their relevance and meaning for the recipient in terms of guidance and the spirit communicators. Take turns working.

EXERCISE 151

A Significant Year

Participants pair up, hold each other's hands, and attune to the spirit world. The medium brings through a spirit connected to the recipient who presents numerically a year that was significant in his or her former life. Take turns working.

EXERCISE 152

An Important Date

Participants pair up, hold each other's hands, and attune to the spirit world. The medium brings through a spirit connected to the recipient who provides a date that was significant in his or her former physical life. The date should be presented numerically such as 9-11-2001 or 7-4-1976. Take turns working.

EXERCISE 153

Actors and Protagonists

Participants pair up, hold each other's hands, and attune to the spirit world. The medium brings through a spirit connected to the recipient, who emphasizes details and attributes that he or she shares with a nonfictional personality or fictional character from television or film. Take turns working.

EXERCISE 154

Spirit Shapes

Participants pair up, hold each other's hands, and connect with the spirit world. The medium receives the entire message completely with shapes, which may have significance within his or her life. The basic shapes are the circle, triangle, square, hexagon, oval, rectangle, rhombus, trapezoid, pentagon, and octagon. The medium interprets and translates their relevance and meaning for the recipient in terms of guidance and the spirit communicators. Take turns working.

EXERCISE 155

Spirit Tattoo

Participants pair up, hold each other's hands, and attune to the spirit world. The medium links with a spirit connected to the recipient who shows a tattoo that he or she had on his or her former physical body. Allow the spirit to show a close-up of the tattoo along with its bodily location and the story behind its creation. Take turns working.

EXERCISE 156

Spirit Sign Language

For this exercise, both the medium and the recipient must be fluent in sign language. The medium does a mediumship session for the recipient and communicates the information completely in sign language.

EXERCISE 157

More Spirit Sign Language

For this exercise, the medium should not know sign language. However, the recipient should possess fluency. The medium links with a spirit connected to the recipient who in his or her former physical life was deaf. The spirit communicates in sign language. The medium imitates the gestures visually presented by the spirit or allows the spirit to directly control his or her movements.

EXERCISE 158

Important Dates

Participants pair up, hold each other's hands, and attune to the spirit world. The medium allows a spirit connected to the recipient to come through. In order to convey a date significant to the spirit, the medium receives a date significant to an individual from his or her life that is shared with the spirit. Take turns working.

EXERCISE 159

Heavenly Instrument

Participants pair up, hold each other's hands, and connect with the spirit world. The medium allows a spirit linked with the recipient, who played a musical instrument in his or her former physical life, to come through. The medium sees the musical instrument and describes its appearance as he or she hears the music associated with it. In addition, the medium mentally blends with the spirit, so that he or she feels the spirit play the instrument. The medium imitates such actions with his or her physical movements. The medium allows the spirit to share memories from his or her former life about the musical instrument. Take turns working.

EXERCISE 160

Heart and Third Eye for Clairvoyance

The medium sits comfortably in a chair with his or her spine erect and his or her arms and legs uncrossed. The medium uses deep breathing to progressively relax his or her physical body and attain a deep meditative state. Next, the medium focuses his or her awareness on the heart chakra at the center of the chest, followed by shifting his or her awareness to the third eye at the forehead. The medium brings awareness back down to his or her heart chakra and then back up again to the third eye. The medium should repeat this pattern at least a dozen times, while dissociating from his or her physical body and energetically blending with his or her spirit control.

EXERCISE 161

Letters and Numbers

Participants pair up, hold each other's hands, and attune to the spirit world. The medium allows a spirit connected to the recipient to present a refrigerator from his or her former physical life with colored letter and number magnets on it. Next, the spirit writes the names of spirit communicators, places, dates, and personal messages using the magnets. In addition, the medium should interpret the colors of the magnets used for the writing. Take turns working.

EXERCISE 162

Refrigerator Magic

Participants pair up, hold each other's hands, and attune to the spirit world. The medium allows a spirit connected to the recipient to present the exterior of a refrigerator from his or her former physical life. Next, the spirit opens the refrigerator for the medium to observe its content. The medium describes the interior of the refrigerator and what it reveals about the spirit. Take turns working.

EXERCISE 163

Political Story

Participants pair up, hold each other's hands, and attune to the spirit world. The medium links with a spirit connected to the recipient, who provides memories of his or her political involvement, including historic political events, in his or her former physical life. The spirit can present political memorabilia from his or her former incarnate life that is still around in the physical world. Take turns working.

EXERCISE 164

Compare the Clairaudience

Participants pair up, hold each other's hands, and attune to the spirit world. Allow a spirit connected with his or her partner to step forward and communicate clairaudiently. Listen closely to the vocal qualities of the message. Note the volume, pitch, tone, inflection, articulation, rate of delivery and any accents in the clairaudient message. What do these qualities indicate about the spirit communicator?

Next, allow a second spirit linked with his or her partner to step forward and also communicate using clairaudience. Again, note the vocal qualities of the message and what they indicate about the spirit communicator.

Compare the vocal qualities of both spirits and note the distinctions and similarities between them. Take turns working.

EXERCISE 165

Clairaudient Direction

Sit comfortably and go into a deep meditative state. Focus your awareness on your throat. Feel as though you are sitting in the center of a large sphere. Sense the spirits positioned around you and open your clairaudience to hear their voices. First, focus your clairaudience in front of you and listen to the spirit voices. Next, shift your clairaudience to hear the spirits on your right-hand side. Repeat by clairaudiently hearing the spirits behind you as well as on your left-hand side. Next, clairaudiently hear the spirits positioned below you and lastly hear the spirits above you. If the initial clairaudience was indistinct, ask your helpers to increase the volume and repeat the exercise.

EXERCISE 166

Spooky Kids

Participants pair up, hold each other's hands, and attune to the spirit world. Allow a spirit connected with the recipient, who passed over as a child or infant (stillborn, miscarriage or abortion) to come through. Allow the spirit to provide evidential details about a material object, such as a toy connected with his or her former physical life. Take turns working.

EXERCISE 167

Smoking Spirits

Participants pair up, hold each other's hands, and connect with the spirit world. The medium allows a recognizable spirit communicator to convey details about a smoking habit in his or her former physical life.

Describe the specific substance consumed by the individual, including the particular strain, amount used, favorite commercial brand, and any devices used. Take turns working.

EXERCISE 168

Flower Messages

The medium delivers a spirit message for each individual within a group. Each message includes a flower brought in by the communicating spirit. The medium should describe the meaning of the flower along with evidential details about the communicator. Mediums in a group can take turns standing up to deliver messages.

EXERCISE 169

Gay Pride

Participants pair up, hold each other's hands, and attune to the spirit world. The medium brings through a spirit connected to the recipient, who was a homosexual man or lesbian in his or her former physical life. Allow the spirit to convey evidential information relating to his or her sexual orientation. Take turns working.

EXERCISE 170

Control Contrast

Participants pair up, hold each other's hands, and attune to the spirit world. First, the medium links with a spirit connected to the recipient and conveys the messages in third person. Next, the medium allows the spirit to overshadow his or her energy and directly speak in first person to the recipient. The evidential information provided should include the names of the spirit and a physical location.

Next, the medium allows the spirit to step back and invites his or her spirit control to step forward. The medium describes his or her spirit control and allows this individual to blend with his or her energy and directly speak in first person to the recipient. Compare the energies of the two spirits. Note, the differences in vibration, attributes and the roles of the two spirits. Take turns working.

CHAPTER 20

The Art of Teaching Mediumship

*F*or *where two or three are gathered together in my name, there am I in the midst of them. —Matthew* 18.20 *KJV*

Teaching mediumship is a phase of mediumship often overlooked and misunderstood compared to other, more dynamic expressions of spirit communication. Yet, as a phase of mediumship, it is powerfully used by the higher spirit personalities to assist incarnate persons in the cultivation of their mediumistic gifts. In mediumship development circles, the spirit chemists utilize the energies of teaching mediums to bring out similar mediumship abilities in their students.

When we sit in the power with others in a circle or development group, the individual energies of each participant blend with the others present to create a collective energy. The spirit chemists utilize the energies of the experienced participants to enhance the energies of those with less experience and bring out similar mediumistic qualities within them. In this way, it is common to acquire similar phases of mediumship as those we sit with. Thus, by regularly sitting for development with a clairvoyant medium, a student of mediumship can unfold similar abilities. This is true of clairvoyance or any phase of mediumship.

The advent of the modern Spiritualist movement in upstate New York, in 1848 popularized mediumship worldwide. In this period, millions of individuals from all walks of life became interested in experiencing spirit communication. The dynamic mediumship of the Fox sisters consisted primarily of raps, fully audible to those present. The Fox sisters, under strict test conditions, demonstrated the reality of life after physical death.

Despite the massive interest in spirit communication, formal teachers and structured educational programs for mediumship did not exist. In order to expedite the message of life after death, the higher spirits accessed individuals with mediumistic potential and did their best to awaken their natural abilities. It was not uncommon for the spirits to entrance suitable individuals unexpectedly, or produce physical manifestations in their presence. The practice of spirit communication over the next decade spread across the globe.

Many individuals, although lacking knowledge of the mechanics of the process, met regularly in halls and private residences to connect with the spirit world. Through trial and error this widespread experimentation often yielded incredible results. At these early meetings, adherents increasingly asked the spirits in charge for instructions on the most effective methods for developing mediumship and receiving accurate communication. In the present era, methods for training mediums have evolved substantially, because of greater comprehension of how mediumship works. In addition, the educational resources and instruction available for mediumship students is remarkable. Many people are not aware that schools exist in the spirit world with classes to prepare spirit helpers to work with incarnate mediums as part of their spirit team. The methods used for communication taught at such schools in the spirit world have also improved over the past century.

The process of spirit communication takes place according to the natural laws of the universe, and requires carefully orchestrated teamwork between the medium and his or her band of spirit helpers. The journey of mediumistic unfoldment, for the student medium, occurs long before attendance in a mediumship development circle. Often, a medium works with spirit communication, during his or her physical incarnation, as part of his or her soul journey. Spirit helpers devote considerable time to learn about any would be medium. Spirit specialists assess candidates to determine their true mediumistic potential, along with blocks, psychological and otherwise, that could hinder unfoldment. All aspects of an individual's life, in both present and past incarnations, are revealed. The higher spirits can read the soul history of any physically incarnate individual. In addition, the medium's memory banks, deep within the unconscious mind, contain valuable information that the helpers utilize as frames of reference for the mediumistic communications.

As a medium, I find it quite common for the spirit teams of other mediums to include spirits, who worked formerly as mediums in their physical lives. Indeed, these spirits frequently come through for other mediums. This makes perfect sense, as such spirits possess considerable knowledge and proficiency, and as such make excellent helpers. Mental mediumship requires harmonious compatibility between mediums and their spirit team. The consciousness of the medium attracts similarly minded individuals in the spirit world and determines the nature of the messages communicated. Therefore, it is essential for mediums to work on themselves as much as possible. The spiritual, emotional, and intellectual development of the medium all affect the quality of the spirit messages. The development of quality mediumship depends on the efforts of both the medium and his or her team of helpers.

The Teaching Medium

The teacher of mediumship is in a unique position as an intermediary between the specialists in the spirit world and the medium in training. A teaching medium's personal spirit team includes teachers, who specialize in the science of interdimensional communication and understand how to unfold the mediumistic abilities of individuals in the physical world. These remarkable teachers also assist the teaching medium in connecting with the spirit teams of student mediums to assist their unfoldment process. The qualities that make a good teacher differ from those of an excellent medium. There are many mediums who instruct others in mediumship development, yet lack the skills and attributes necessary for effective teaching.

The Importance of Quality Instruction in Mediumship

Mediumship is an innate ability that everyone possesses in varying degrees. Many individuals state that they are natural mediums and subsequently do not need formal training. "I don't need training. My advanced guides teach me everything I need to know" is a remark that I have heard more than once from many self-taught or poorly trained mediums. The more training that a student of mediumship receives, the better. A self-taught medium is easily distinguished by his or her lack of discipline, amateurish presentation, and weak connection with the spirit world.

The development of mediumistic skills is similar to cultivating technical abilities in music or art. The natural skills inherent in a student are enhanced through proper education in a structured educational environment. The great master artists of the European Renaissance achieved amazing proficiency and advanced technical skill through considerable effort that included years of study and apprenticeship with more experienced masters.

Microwaveable Mediumship

Many individuals want to develop mediumship instantly with minimum study or effort. After six months or a year of training, they print business cards, launch a website, and offer their services to the world as professional mediums. However, it is impossible to purchase the development of mediumship. Mediumship training programs that promise quick results are a waste of time and money. Mediumship development is not a franchise, although it often is marketed that way.

Although mediumistic unfoldment is ongoing, it generally takes about four or five years of sitting weekly in a development circle before a strong foundation is established. It is relatively easy for an individual to receive accurate spirit messages. However, it takes considerably longer to strengthen one's attunement with the spirit world and learn proper discipline. This does not happen overnight and requires dedication, perseverance and patience by the student. A true student of mediumship never ceases to evolve and expand his or her abilities, through continual self-growth, constant practice, and regularly sitting for development.

Teaching is a Skill

The ideal teaching medium possesses considerable hands-on experience with mediumship, along with a thorough understanding of mechanics of the process.

We cannot give to others what we do not possess ourselves. A teacher can take students only as far as he or she has progressed. Not all mediums, despite knowledge and expertise, are good as teachers. There are many academic programs in education that adequately prepare individuals as teachers.

A Few Important Skills Necessary for Teaching Mediums

Enthusiasm

It is important to feel passionate about mediumship, as the intensity of such strong feelings will inspire and motivate students taking part in development classes.

Empathy

The superior teacher can understand the feelings of his or her students and the personal blocks or challenges they face in the process of development. When students sense genuine concern from a teacher, it is easier for them to progress individually and collectively in unfoldment groups.

Creativity

Effective teaching requires the constant exploration of new techniques and approaches for mediumship unfoldment. What works with one student, or in particular situations, may not achieve the same results with another student or other situation.

Deep Knowledge About Mediumship

A teaching medium knows the subject inside and out, and comprehends thoroughly the process of unfoldment along with the history of mediumship, psychical research, and ethics and professional conduct. This knowledge is obtained through intellectual study combined with years of practical hands-on experience.

Expert Communication and Interpersonal Skills

The teaching medium creates supportive and loving relationships with students through friendliness and approachability. In addition, the teaching medium possesses superior listening skills, and an ability to criticize students in an empathetic manner.

The best teachers of mediumship encourage and motivate students in their development by enthusiastically conveying their love and knowledge of mediumship. The teaching medium displays no favoritism with students, but is impartial to all.

It is important that the teaching medium is well prepared and organized for any class session, and is a role model for punctuality and reverence for the sacred act of communing with the spirit world.

Things Not to Do

I have observed many teaching mediums, over the years, arrogantly assert the superiority of their mediumship over that of their students and other mediums. In many cases, they deliberately create conflict or hold back promising students, because of jealousy and insecurity. Other teaching mediums forbid their students from attending classes and circles facilitated by other mediums. The rationale for this approach is that students should study exclusively with one teacher, lest they get confused or pick up bad habits from the methods taught by other mediums. The reason such teachers restrict their students from studying with other mediums stems largely from the desire for control and power. This mentality is completely detrimental for students, and does not assist them in the development of mediumship. I knew a prominent medium, who pastored a Spiritualist church, which she ran with an iron fist. She controlled the lives of her students, forbidding them from going to services or circles at other Spiritualist churches. She did all she could to exert power over her students. In addition, she created conflict with students, who became too proficient as mediums and drove them out of the church.

As a teacher of mediumship, I recommend that my students train with as many mediums as possible. There are many approaches to mediumship, and not all mediums are suitable as teachers for every student. Different teachers of mediumship possess different strengths and may better facilitate psychical unfoldment in some students than others. It is important for students of mediumship to learn from a variety of mediums with different abilities and approaches. Each student of mediumship possesses unique spiritual gifts that unfold in a highly individual manner. While quality instruction is essential, there is something to learn from everyone, even if it is what not to do.

Many years ago, I instructed a weekly development circle at a Spiritualist church in Massachusetts. At one point, two other qualified mediums facilitated circles on other evenings at the church Many of the students regularly attended all three circles, as well as workshops by visiting mediums at the church and other locations. All three teachers approached the process of mediumship uniquely and emphasized different aspects of the process in their classes. Some of these same students, now work as professional mediums and healers, or are involved in the Spiritualist ministry. The bottom line is that they all developed as better mediums as a result of studying mediumship with a variety of teachers.

Spirituality and Purity

The development of personal character and spirituality go hand in hand with mediumship development. The teaching medium demonstrates by example both his or her mediumistic ability and spirituality. It is important that teaching mediums, through their words and actions, aspire to and uphold the highest moral and ethical standards as possible.

Strong Link with Discarnate Teachers

It is important for teaching mediums to possess a strong ability to link with their own discarnate teachers, as well as the various helpers belonging to the spirit teams of individual students. A teaching medium is assisted by spirit teachers in the overall facilitation of any educational session, including prayers, lectures and discussions, guided meditations, practical exercises, and assessments of students.

Assessments

A byproduct of regularly sitting for development, and working as a medium, is the ability to tune into the energies of others and discern the connections they are making with the spirit world. As an individual develops as a medium, he or she will find it easier to connect with less experienced students of mediumship, and receive information from the spirit teachers about the spiritual gifts of the student that are present, the approaches best for cultivating such abilities, and any blocks affecting unfoldment.

What A Student Assessment Should Contain:

Descriptions of individual spirit team members and their functions within the team for development and mediumship work.

The names of the spirit helpers are unnecessary, but identifying information is important.

Strengths.

Present and latent abilities. Suggestions for cultivating them

Blocks.

Personal blocks, emotional, mental and physical, that impede the process of the student, and suggestions on overcoming them.

Future potential outcome in terms of unfoldment and future work as an instrument for the spirit world.

I regularly assess students in my mediumship classes as it helps gain confidence that they are making progress with their unfoldment. A student of mine in Iceland once asked me to provide assessments to the advanced students in one of her large mediumship classes. I spent several hours going around the circle, channeling information for the students from their spirit teachers about their individual abilities, and paths as mediums and healers.

Dual Relationships and Integrity

In general, it is advisable for teaching mediums to keep professional boundaries with students. Dual relationships with students, especially sexual or romantic ones, are best avoided, as the dynamics are unfavorable for the teacher's role as an authority and his or her responsibility to effectively teach. Many teachers of mediumship develop intimate relationships with their students, and sometimes even marry or enter into long-term relationships with them. A few mediums I know even abused their position to sexually assault vulnerable individuals, who approached them for mediumship or healing. Many people place mediums on a pedestal, and think that they possess extraordinary and amazing powers. In addition, a teaching medium is in a position of authority that many find attractive. It is not always easy for mediums to establish clear boundaries with their students and clients, many of whom are vulnerable and easily damaged.

Transference and Countertransference

A powerful energy exchange takes place between mediums and clients during a mediumship or healing session. This energy exchange also occurs between teaching mediums and their students during a class or circle. Transference refers to the redirection of feelings for a significant person to the mediums or healer. Countertransference is the redirection of the medium's feelings toward his or her client or student. Unfortunately, both transference and countertransference result in unnecessary emotional entanglement.

Mediumship development entails close interaction with others. The heightened sensitivity and exchange of psychic energy easily contribute to a lack of clear boundaries. The psychic energy used in mediumship is sexual energy, although a different expression of it.

The process of mediumship unfoldment involves the subtle bodies, which interpenetrate the physical body. All the subtle energy centers, or chakras, are utilized.

In addition, mediumship development affects the various physiological systems, most notably the endocrine and the central nervous.

Excessive stimulation of the psychic senses results in an accumulation of excessive sexual energy in the lower chakra region. It is important for mediums to discipline their minds and learn how to balance their subtle energies. Meditative disciplines such as hatha yoga or qi-gong are excellent in this regard.

Running Groups

It is important for teachers to never show favoritism toward particular students for any reason and always be disciplined in maintaining order. A development circle is neither a democracy nor a dictatorship.

Punctuality and reverence for what is taking place are essential. Avoid extreme rigidity and inflexibility. Friendly, down-to-earth teachers are more effective than ones who place themselves on a pedestal above their students. However, too much looseness leads to a lack of discipline and ultimately poor quality of mediumship.

How I present the subject to a group is affected by the number of participants. As a teacher, I have facilitated workshops and classes with only one individual in attendance and other programs with audiences of hundreds. A smaller group obviously makes it easier for the teacher to provide more individual attention. Five to eight participants is the ideal size for a development circle. In general, it is easier to blend and harmonize the energies of a group with fewer participants. The downside of a smaller sized group is that there is generally less interaction during practical exercises and discussions.

Larger groups mean more participation in discussions and multiple partners to interact with during experimental exercises. There are also more spirits present at a larger mediumship group, which include the helpers in each participant's spirit team. It takes much skill as a teacher to facilitate larger mediumship groups, as it is harder to achieve the same degree of harmony typically found in smaller groups.

It is the responsibility of the teacher, regardless of group size, to:

- **Maintain class discipline and properly manage the energy.**
- **Start and end each session punctually with reverence.**
- **Make sure time is used properly during each portion of the session.**
- **Properly attune to spirit teachers and respond appropriately to their influence and directives.**

It is easy to mismanage the use of class time with a larger group. A good teacher adjusts accordingly, based on the group energy, particular circumstances, and the focus of the class. Proper management of time is important. The teacher properly considers the major objectives for the session and allocates segments of the class accordingly. A meeting with the spirit world is sacred. Both the teacher and students should be punctual, and prepared physically, mentally, and spiritually for the session. A meeting with the spirit world should start and end on time. In a group, it is easy for students to go over in time, when sharing their experiences during the exercises or meditation. Some students deliberately or unintentionally monopolize conversations, while others, knowingly, go off on tangents during discussions.

What are the reasons individuals pursue the study of psychic awareness, spirit communication and spiritual healing? The more a teacher can connect with his or her students, the more effectively he or she can meet their educational needs. Many psychologically traumatized seekers take courses in psychic and mediumship development. Perhaps they are hurting emotionally because of the physical death of a loved one or the break-up of a personal relationship. In other cases, many students seek explanations for an assortment of psychic phenomena taking place around them.

It is natural for those suffering to turn to God and spirituality in times of distress. The answers revealed through the investigation of mediumship and psychic phenomena impart tremendous transformative healing for individuals. Many years ago, I noticed that about a third of the students enrolled in my mediumship development classes were mental health professionals, including psychiatric nurses and physicians, psychologists, social workers, psychotherapists and other counselors. It makes sense that many individuals study psychology, and go into the field of mental health and counseling, because they want to figure out and fix themselves. I know many practicing mediums who are also licensed as mental health professionals. Counseling is a healing endeavor that as a practice naturally awakens intuitive ability. Many counselors and mental health workers, unknowingly, operate as mediums and actively convey advice given by their guides to their clients.

The best mediums and healers are individuals who have experienced the greatest personal hurt and challenges in their lives. The most effective healers are those who have gone through the same or similar experiences as those they are working with. For example, a former alcoholic can assist others in their recovery, because he or she has gone through the same process and understands what they are going through.

Pain creates empathy, love, and understanding for others in the healer's heart. Formal education and courses are essential for the study of mediumship, but the greatest learning takes place through experiencing personal loss and hardships in life. It is important to remember that in any psychic or mediumship development class, many of the participants will be damaged, some severely, and in the process of healing. In some cases, it is best for individuals to concentrate on receiving whatever healing or therapy is necessary for their recovery, instead of attempting to develop their psychic and mediumship abilities.

Mental illness is a serious issue that impacts many individuals from all walks of life. Psychic unfoldment stimulates the unconscious mind. It is normal for individuals in life to experience negative thoughts occasionally, such as anger or depression. However, an individual suffering from severe mental illness or imbalances should not be involved in psychic or mediumship development. A teacher of mediumship needs to assess each student carefully, ideally prior to the beginning of any circle or course and not allow those seriously imbalanced from participating.

Of course, it is not always possible for teachers to vet students properly with one-off workshops or classes.

Interviewing Potential Circle Members

It is wise for teachers to interview and assess potential circle members prior to the first meeting. This is crucial, as harmony between participants is the most important factor for success with any mediumship development circle. Practical considerations include factors in the professional and personal lives of individuals that might affect their attendance, such as a job requiring overtime or young children requiring childcare.

Is the individual mature and self-disciplined?

Is he or she psychologically balanced, with no issues or fears that might impair proper participation?

Is the energy of the perspective student harmonious with the teacher and the other participants?

Is the individual capable of accepting constructive criticism and feedback from the instructor and others in the group?

Does the individual possess the level of experience in mediumship, and the skills necessary to contribute as a participant?

It is also essential to consider the motivations and goals of potential participants. Insecure individuals with large egos, who exhibit jealousy toward others, are best excluded from any group.

The desire to serve God and help others with mediumship is the purest motivation for training in mediumship. The wise teacher or circle leader, during interviews with potential sitters, pays close attention to the intuitive suggestions conveyed by his or her guides.

Difficult Students

Occasionally, a student will deliberately challenge or confront a teacher for various reasons in class in front of others or privately. It is important for teachers to know their subject thoroughly, but also humbly admit when they are wrong. Although the teacher of mediumship is more experienced, he or she is also a student learning and unfolding.

Handle challenging students with tact and care. Address their concerns and encourage their unfoldment. Encourage constructive criticism from students and always distribute course evaluation forms for students to provide feedback. I always look for ways to improve as a teacher and individual. I actively encourage suggestions from my students and always listen to their input in regard to my performance as a teacher.

Many individuals aggressively challenge the authority of the teacher to make their teacher look bad and themselves appear better. In other cases, individuals may criticize or demean other students in the group. Ask disruptive individuals, who create disharmonious conditions, to leave. Strong leadership is essential for running a productive mediumship course. At all times, the teacher is in charge and responsible for maintaining discipline and order in the group. A wise teacher removes individuals who exhibit behavior or attitudes that adversely affect the chemistry of the circle, and eliminates silly antics or unnecessary exhibitionism displayed by students.

I have experienced, over the years, amazing displays of delusion and deliberate fraud at undisciplined mediumship circles that I have attended. Although the Spiritualist movement emphasizes education, the gullibility and lack of discernment amongst its adherents are astonishing. Test the medium and the spirit world and do not believe that all displays of purported mediumship are authentic. Never throw out your intelligence and commonsense. There is a fine line between a genuine psychic impression and the imagination. Sadly, there are experienced mediums unable to discern the difference. A medium who crawls around the séance room barking like a dog is likely deluded, even though he or she genuinely believes he or she is channeling a deceased German Shepherd. A medium displaying such antics could also be a fraud.

At the same time, genuine spirit control with an unsuspecting student needs care and encouragement from the teacher. At a mediumship retreat in New Zealand that I conducted, the spirit operators unexpectedly entranced a young woman from Australia. The intensity of such an occurrence potentially frightens inexperienced students. I explained to my student, and the others in the course, why the spirits worked with her in this manner.

Refusal to follow circle guidelines, tardiness, breaking the circle, and talking at inappropriate times are issues that potentially disrupt the energies of the group. In some cases, such as with novices, dismissal from the circle may be unnecessary. Gently correct such behaviors with the unknowing party and explain how such behavior is detrimental for harmonious conditions.

A student of mine attended a mediumship development circle at a noted Spiritualist association near her residence. The participants meditated in silence, while the psychic energy in the séance room intensified. Suddenly, in the middle of the session, the president of the association broke the circle and exited the building for a cigarette break. After smoking a cigarette, she came back inside and resumed sitting in the circle. The lack of reverence and understanding exhibited in this incident appalled my student, who had studied mediumship with several qualified mediums.

A teacher occasionally may encounter a student suffering a mental breakdown while attending class. Such breakdowns often are triggered by the student's participation in various exercises or his or her reaction to the higher energies experienced during unfoldment. An individual emotionally overwhelmed in this manner should not be in a mediumship development group.

Emotional Issues

A young lesbian attended an open mediumship circle I taught at a Spiritualist church and expressed extreme reservation about sitting next to males in the group.

Personal issues such as this need to be left outside the development group as absolute trust and harmony must be felt between all participants. I invited the young woman to attend another mediumship class that I taught composed of all female students. She joined this circle and developed her abilities as a healer.

Another young woman in my development groups experienced uncontrollable panic attacks anytime she connected with the higher vibrations associated with mediumship and healing. Unfortunately, this condition adversely affected her ability to function in many aspects of her daily life. The higher spirits worked through me and identified issues from the student's childhood that affected her present condition. She eventually managed the panic attacks and achieving psychological balance in her life.

A student at my open mediumship circle utilized his psychic abilities to remotely view the underwear drawers of women in the group. He would confront his victims before class and tell them that he knew the design and color of their underwear. In addition, he disrupted class by refusing to follow circle protocol. I removed him from the class.

Exclude unnecessary ritual or superstition from circle proceedings, unless the actions create stronger vibrations and greater harmony for the psychic sessions. As a teacher, create an educational environment that is loving and supportive, and where all students, regardless of level of experience, feel encouraged to learn.

The following factors are important to take into consideration for any mediumship development course:

The size of the group

Duration of course

Objectives of course

Experience levels of participants

Physical venue

What are the educational objectives of the course? Is the focus spiritual healing, psychic art, or another aspect of mediumistic unfoldment? Are the students in the course beginners, intermediate, advanced or mixed-levels? Include exercises appropriate for the subject and level of students. Make sure that course content is appropriate for the experience level of the students. A novice is intimidated by advanced content, and more experienced students are bored by beginner material. A skilled teacher successfully works with students at any level, including mixed-level groups. Is the course held in a large or small space? A small space excludes the implementation of certain practical exercises that only work in a larger space. Plan accordingly.

Teaching Aids

Students love handouts. Many Reiki teachers give their students manuals at the completion of a course. I also provide material for my mediumship students to take home with them. Handouts encourage intellectual growth.

Music is excellent for assisting students to attain deeper levels of relaxation and altered states of consciousness. Always bring your own music for meditations or healing. Make sure that a CD player or other device is on hand for guided meditations and healing.

Visual aids make any presentation dynamic. Prepare interesting and appropriate images to project with a laptop on the wall or screen. A good talk combined with interesting visuals is dynamic.

Visually record students working with appropriate devices. Analyze the students' body language and articulation and provide constructive suggestions.

A good teacher is mentally linked with his or her teachers in the spirit world, who will advise and influence.

Teaching Different Levels

Novice

A typical novice knows little about the mechanics of mediumship or how psychic abilities work. A solid foundation in psychic awareness, meditation and the intellectual understanding of mediumship is necessary before sitting for development. The pastor of a healing sanctuary in Wales, where I served as a guest medium, explained to me that prior to sitting in a mediumship development circle, students are required to attend a three-month meditation and spiritual awareness course. I am in full agreement with this approach as it ensures better understanding and preparedness by the students.

The main objectives for novice mediums include relaxing the physical body, quieting the mind, and raising his or her vibrations. Novices need to learn to pay close attention to the contents of their minds and the feelings and sensations of their own physical bodies and their energy field around them. Basic psychic awareness exercises ideal for novices include seeing and feeling the energy fields, psychometry or object reading, ribbons, etc. Hands-on spiritual healing is also important as it helps novices develop the right motivation for serving as mediums along with enhancing their sensitivity to subtle energies and the presence of spirits.

Intermediate

Intermediate students need to learn to attain deeper levels of the altered state and enhanced awareness of their helpers and spirit team. Emphasis should be placed by teachers on receiving spirit messages through multi-layers of psychic sensing, symbolic interpretation of clairvoyant imagery, with deeper attunement and levels of control. Stand up work in a class setting should be practiced as well as more hands-on spiritual healing.

Advanced

Advanced students need to establish a closer level of attunement with spirit contacts and receive more specific and details in messages. Inspirational speaking and spirit control should be emphasized along with platform work and individual sessions.

Mixed

Many mediumship teachers find it a challenge to instruct groups composed of participants of mixed levels. A good teacher possesses the skills to engage all levels of students in both his or her lectures and practical exercises and create an educational environment in which all participants are challenged and do not feel left out.

Online Groups

Online courses or sessions are fantastic in that teaching mediums can conduct meetings with students from all over the world. A computer or device with a functioning camera and microphone is all that is required for participation in an online course. The advantage of online courses is that students can attend mediumship training programs in the comfort of their own homes without having to travel long distances or worry about accommodation. There are always potential technical difficulties assorted with working online. The class dynamic massively differs for online courses compared to in-person meetings. As a teaching medium, I found that it took a few sessions for me to adjust to teaching a course online, in terms of connecting with both my spirit teachers and participants as well as managing the proceedings in general.

Students easily can learn the mechanics of mediumship online, and they can practice tuning in and delivering messages. The problem with online courses is that the group energy is not the same as what takes place when all are physically present. The spirit operators cannot work with the chemistry of the students in the way they would in an in-person group. Online classes are limited and incomplete for proper mediumship unfoldment compared to an in-person development circle. Although the educational advantages of an online course are wonderful, I prefer teaching in-person mediumship programs over anything conducted online.

Mediumship is Holistic

Rigid rules and dogmatic approaches limit the spirit operator's capacity to unfold the spiritual gifts of student mediums. Although rules are necessary for cultivating the discipline essential for quality mediumship, they should never restrict the spirit personalities from naturally expressing themselves through their medium. Mediumistic development is holistic with all phases of mediumship interrelated. Many individuals start out with the unfoldment of clairvoyance and spiritual healing, which overtime may lead to entrancement followed by one or more physical phases.

Mediumship should never be put in a box, nor should all mediums work the same. Mediumship is not robotic. Mediums need to work in their own unique manner in a way that is comfortable, natural, and dignified, with reverence for the process. This is part of why it is advisable for student mediums, instead of becoming a carbon copy of their teacher, to study the approaches of a variety of mediums. There is not one correct way to work with the spirit world.

Many years ago, I knew a medium at the Lily Dale Assembly who displayed particular mannerisms and patterns of speech while she delivered spirit communications. This is true for all mediums. I remember observing several of her students demonstrate mediumship, who exhibited the same body language and phraseology as their teacher. While it is natural for students on an unconscious level to mimic their teacher, it is important that they ultimately develop an individual expression of mediumship.

Teacher Improvement Exercises

EXERCISE 171

Guided Meditations

Lead a guided journey meditation. Feel the spirit teacher mentally inspire your guided meditation. Allow the spirit teacher to blend with your energy as you lead the meditation. Be aware of the flow of imagery and feelings within your own head and verbalize as you direct the meditation. The words initially may be more of you, but increasingly as you allow yourself to be overshadowed by the controlling spirit, the flow of words and intonation will change with the meditation directed by the spirit teacher. The meditation will be directly beneficial for the students of the circle or class.

EXERCISE 172

Spirits in Group

While running a circle, at the end of the meditation period of sitting in the power, go around clockwise and have participants share their experiences and messages. While this is taking place, mentally connect with their energy fields and the spirits working with them, while simultaneously maintaining a link with the spirit teachers who direct your teaching.

EXERCISE 173

Spirits on Platform

Attend a public demonstration or presentation of mediumship, such as a Spiritualist service or similar meeting. Mentally attune to your spirit teacher while simultaneously connecting with individuals on the platform while they work with the spirit world. Carefully observe and feel the energy field and the spirit influences of each worker. Be aware of who is inspiring them during a public address, etc. their spirit control during entrancement and their spirit team and individual communicators while delivering spirit messages.

EXERCISE 174

Assessment of an Individual

Seated across from the student allow yourself to connect with his or her spirit teachers and team, who provide assistance with his or her mediumistic development and work. Describe the spirits as they present themselves along with their functions as part of the student's spirit team. Allow them to express the gifts of the student as well as individual blocks and suggestions for overcoming them. Often the teachers will describe the potential outcome in terms of phases of mediumship unfolded for the students' future work as an instrument for the spirit world.

EXERCISE 175

Group Assessment

This is the same as the individual assessment, but done with a group. For training, have participants seated either in a circle of horseshoe formation, although sitting in a row or rows is also fine. Proceed to quickly work with each student one after the other. Allow the spirit teachers to express a detailed assessment for each student.

List of Exercises

Acknowledgements

I am extremely grateful for the superb editing work done by my friend Dave Taub and the awesome cover design and layout by Ghislain Viau of Creative Publishing Book Design. I also thank my dear friend Juliana Beasley, a world famous photographer, for the headshot she took of me in the woods behind Etna Spiritualist Camp in Maine. I also want to thank my many students and friends for their support in getting this book out.

Resources

Mediumship Training Programs

Mediumship Mastery Training Program
www.stevehermannmedium.com

National Spiritualist Association of Churches
www.nsac.org

Cassadaga Spiritualist Camp
www.cassadaga.org

Harmony Grove Spiritualist Association
www.harmonygrovespiritual.org

Camp Chesterfield
www.campchesterfield.net

The Arthur Findlay Psychic College
www.arthurfindlaycollege.org

Resources

Recommended Mediumship Books

Hermann, Stephen, *Mediumship Mastery: The Mechanics of Receiving Spirit Communications: The Ultimate Guide*, Atendriya Press, Amherst, Massachusetts, USA, 2015.

Roberts, Ursula, *Hints On Spiritual Unfoldment*, Psychic Press Ltd. London, UK, 1987 Edition.

Roberts, Estelle, *Fifty Years A Medium*, Transworld Publishers Ltd. London, UK,(1959), 1969 Edition.

Sprague, E. W., *A Future Life Demonstrated or Twenty-Seven Years A Public Medium*, Author Published, Detroit, Michigan, USA, 1908.

Wilson, E. V., *The Truths of Spiritualism, Immortality Proved Beyond A Doubt*, Hazlitt & Reed Printers, Chicago, Illinois, USA, 1876.

Barbanell, Maurice, *This is Spiritualism*, Spiritualist Press, London, UK, 1959.

Kardec, Allan, Translated by Darriel W. Kimball with Marcia Saiz, *Heaven and Hell or Divine Justice According to Spiritism*, International Spiritist Council, Brasilia, Brazil, (1865), 2008 Edition.

Denis, Leon, Translated by Helton Mattar Monteiro, *Into the Unseen: Spiritism and Mediumship*, United States Spiritist Council, New York, New York, USA, (1923), 2017 Edition.

About the Author

Highly acclaimed for his detailed and accurate mediumship, Stephen Hermann is a world famous medium with incredible talent. A graduate of the experimental Hampshire College (Amherst, Massachusetts) for high achievers. Stephen is steeped in the history and philosophy of yoga, metaphysics and Spiritualism. Stephen holds credentials as an ordained minister, certified medium, and teacher with the National Spiritualist Association of Churches (USA), and has taught for the International Spiritualist Federation (UK).

A featured personality on television and radio worldwide, Stephen's mediumship has been documented by the Associated Press and other news media. A former research medium for the University of Virginia, he travels extensively teaching and demonstrating spirit communication and healing.

www.stevehermannmedium.com

Made in the USA
Middletown, DE
11 December 2021